D0333369

3013021625496 0

FOREVER OUTNUMBERED

FOREVER OUTNUMBERED

Simon Hooper

CORONET

First published in Great Britain in 2018 by Coronet
An Imprint of Hodder & Stoughton
An Hachette UK company

1

A CIP catalogue record for this title is available from the British Library

Hardback ISBN 9781473670013
eBook ISBN 9781473670020

Typeset in Chaparral Pro by Hewer Text UK Ltd, Edinburgh
Printed and bound in Great Britain by Clays Ltd, St Ives plc

Hodder & Stoughton policy is to use papers that are natural, renewable
and recyclable products and made from wood grown in sustainable
forests. The logging and manufacturing processes are expected to
conform to the environmental regulations of the country of origin.

Hodder & Stoughton Ltd
Carmelite House
50 Victoria Embankment
London EC4Y 0DZ

www.hodder.co.uk

To my girls - Clemmie, Anya, Marnie, Ottilie and Delilah. Without you my life would be empty, and so would this book.

Contents

Introduction

Me with my girl gang, completely outnumbered
and outgunned in every way. Who knew that all
my male-chromosome-carrying sperm would
go on strike during my procreation years? Ten
years ago I was worrying about being a father
to one child, now I'm literally knee-deep in
them – but I wouldn't change a thing.

Introduction

I'll be honest: when I first found out I was going to be a dad, I was bricking it. What made it worse was that none of my friends had embarked on the good ship fatherhood yet, so I was to be the first one pushed out to sea in a tiny boat with no sail or rudder and forced to explore the choppy featureless ocean that lay before me, otherwise known as parenting.

I was handed books by my wife that she'd highlighted sections in, but after thumbing through them, I became numb. It was like reading a textbook in a science class in school, just not as fun as there weren't any Bunsen burners to mess around with. These books were drier than a packet of crackers and soon they were collecting dust in a cupboard along with the sports kit I hung on to but no longer used and the mountains of USB cables and chargers for electronic items I'd accumulated over the years but no longer owned.

Therefore I thought it would be a good idea to make use of my free time (for those of you who are parents, you know that's a joke as there isn't any) and write a book that doesn't preach to you or explain how you should do things, but instead gives you an insight into the real life of an outnumbered parent who's just kind of made it up as he's gone along – otherwise known as 'winging it'.

For those of you that follow me on Instagram, you'll know I'm not into sugar-coating life, as frankly it doesn't do anyone any good. If anything, it leaves you feeling like the kid who was crap at sports and always got picked last – or even worse, asked to help the teacher put out cones for everyone else to run around: a bit of a failure. What I do like to do is find the humour in the mundane things that parents all over the world deal with on a day-to-day basis and hope-fully make people feel less like they're failing and OK with the fact that we don't get it right every time. After all, despite what you see around you or online, the reality is that there is no such thing as the perfect parent and even if there was, you wouldn't want to be that person as everyone else would hate you in a quiet and civilised manner – probably by talking about you over wine at a dinner party that everyone else had been invited to apart from you.

This book doesn't pretend to be a self-help guide. If it was, it would be a terrible one. It doesn't pretend to give you the answers to all your parenting queries, as frankly I'm still learning myself – after all, I'm not pretending to be a professor of child studies or a baby whisperer. Parenting is one of the steepest learning curves you'll ever climb and although it doesn't require oxygen tanks, crampons and your face freezing off, scaling Everest may sometimes seem like the easy peak to ascend in comparison. It does plateau out a bit eventually once you get into a rhythm, but from what I can tell, you never quite reach the top.

What this book is instead is a glimpse into the real life of a working parent who's had his hand in the game for a while. It's a life where we struggle with family admin on a daily basis, where shoes become the reason we can't leave the house in a timely fashion, where nappies are kicked behind doors to be forgotten and rediscovered a day later when we try to figure out what's died, and where the joy of hearing our child's first words is promptly replaced with despair when we realise they now know how to say 'No' and use it at every opportunity until we consider having our ears surgically grafted shut.

It's where our previously pristine houses, once laid out like a *Livingetc* double-page spread, get destroyed in a matter of minutes and turned into an episode of that programme where they employ industrial cleaners to dig people out of their own detritus.

It's where forgetting nappies, or milk, or that rag that our offspring suck can spell potential Armageddon and results in purchasing new ones, which will be rejected out of hand.

Simply put, it's what parenting really looks like from a dad's perspective.

Now, there's a small chance that after trawling through this, you may think, 'Why on earth do we have kids? It seems like a never-ending job that you don't get paid for.' Well, the answer is simple:

Firstly, if we didn't continue to procreate, we'd all go the way of the dinosaurs – our skeletons would probably be displayed in an alien's natural history museum with a plaque that read: 'Humans: Stupid earth species that died out because its members couldn't deal with their whinging offspring any more'.

Secondly, because having children in your life is amazing. Because being a parent is amazing (most of the time) and because I can't imagine my life without my kids in it.

Don't get me wrong – it's a daily battle that will have you questioning your own sanity sometimes. And yes, children have been genetically designed to test you in every way possible, but that's part of the challenge and without them, I certainly wouldn't be the person I am today – I'd be just another guy in the street (albeit with a lot more disposable income). Add my girls into the equation, and I'm so much more. I'm a poorly trained chef, a comedian (until they stop finding me funny and just find me embarrassing, which is starting to occur more frequently with every passing year), a DIY specialist, a puppeteer and an unlicensed doctor (I put on a mean plaster and can dish out Calpol like a professional). I'm a children's entertainer, a master Lego builder, a singer, a dancer, a reluctant make-up model, a hairdresser, the benchmark that any future boyfriends should be measured against; but most importantly I'm their daddy and I couldn't be prouder to have that job title on my CV.

So with all that said, strap yourself in and enjoy the meandering journey into my world as a heavily outnumbered father, starting from the moment I met my wife Clemmie as a fresh-faced twenty-two-year-old who had no intention of becoming a parent until I was at least thirty-two (there was way too much partying to be done to think about that!), right through to where I find myself now. I'm a thirty-five-year-old man with a rapidly greying beard, I have four daughters (Anya, ten; Marnie, seven; and identical twins Ottilie and Delilah who are two) and I'm the sole male in a house of six. I definitely didn't see that coming . . .

1

The age-old tale of boy meets girl, boy and girl find out they're pregnant, ten years later boy and girl end up with four daughters and a mortgage

This photo was taken pre-children, circa 2005. Look at us – blissfully unaware of the child-shaped bomb that was about to land on us. This was a time before decent camera phones – remember those days when you had to take a compact camera on a night out? And when 'compact' actually meant it was bigger than your own head, weighed more than an elephant and blinded everyone in the club with the flash? Good times.

The age-old tale of boy meets girl

*E*very journey to parenthood has a story behind it – after all, for the vast majority of people, it's not a case of simply meeting a partner and then suddenly having a baby right away. There's a bit more to it than that, so here's my tale of how I started out on the road to being a reluctant – initially at least – father.

When I first found out that my then girlfriend, Clemmie (now my wife), was pregnant with the first of what would eventually be our four daughters, I lost it. I had turned twenty-four and she was twenty-two – we'd been together for the grand total of eighteen months. I've had considerably longer relationships with my underpants.

I'd met Clemmie a year and a half earlier in a notorious Bristol nightclub called the Lizard Lounge – if you don't know it, then you know a place just like it: a legendary student haunt where vodka and Red Bull was served in jugs with a straw, where the music was cheesier than a trip to Cheddar Gorge, the floor felt like you were walking on fly paper and the pungent aroma of vomit and fried food immediately hit you as you got booted out at 2 a.m. and headed to the best-named kebab van in the world, 'Jason's Dona-van'.

Having spotted Clemmie on the side of the dance floor with no shoes on, I necked my remaining glucose-saturated libation and stumbled over. Even by my standards, my opening lines were a bit odd.

ME: 'Hi, can I ask why you don't have any shoes on?'
CLEMMIE: 'Because my feet hurt from these bloody shoes.'

This was my chance to shine and show my understanding of women and women's issues.

ME: 'You know what you need? You need some Scholl Party Feet insoles . . .'

Silence followed and a blank look fell across Clemmie's face. Fuck. As per usual, I'd fucked it up within the first ten seconds of speaking to a girl and she now thought I was either an orthotics salesman or that I had some kind of twisted foot fetish. Why the hell was I talking about Scholl Party Feet anyway? Was that the best I could conjure up in my semi-coherent state?

Luckily for me she saw the funny side and with the remaining £7 from my rapidly shrinking student loan, I bought us yet more energy-enriched drinks in the vain hope that it might buy me a bit more time with her before I inevitably got tapped on the shoulder by her model-like boyfriend whose looks would make me reconsider my own sexuality and politely told to piss off. After establishing that the beautiful man in the corner running his hands through his locks was in fact 'just a friend', I relaxed and before I knew it we were dancing and kissing – well, what you could just about pass off as dancing and kissing. It was more like gyrating completely out of sync both with the music and each other and licking each other's faces. (FYI, people kissing in nightclubs lose all awareness of what they look like. I guess you just get lost in the moment and don't think about it, but trust me, no one looks good.)

Perhaps she was on the rebound? Perhaps she was just really drunk? Whatever her reason, she was kissing me and I liked it.

As the lights came up and 'High Ho Silver Lining' rattled across the speakers for the fourth time, Clemmie and I exchanged numbers. Halfway through typing my all-important digits into her Samsung flip phone, I told her in semi-coherent speech that I had to go as my friends and I were leaving to go to a house party.

'Can me and my friends come?' said a hopeful Clemmie.

'Oh, this is awkward, but I'm not sure you can come actually – this is supposed to be a boys' night. Sorry. Call me!'

The next morning I woke to a hangover (something that later in life would be referred to as a 'special adult headache') that felt like it would need surgery to remove, and a text from the girl from the night before. As I read the message I couldn't help thinking about how pretty she was and what a gorgeous name she had. I practised saying Clemmie and Simon over and over in my head – it sounded right. All my happy thoughts then quickly dissipated as I actually read the mistyped content of the text:

Hi, can U send me a pic MsG of urslf as I can't remember what you luk like, thx.

Oh bloody brilliant . . . I think I'm in love with the crazy girl with the aching feet after being in her infectious, magnetic company for less than two hours and she can't remember if I've got two heads or one. It was like a crap version of Tinder, just ten years early.

I got up, stumbled to the bathroom, washed and took five or six photos to select which one to send on the low-res shit camera phone that made everything look like you were staring at the image through Vaseline. It'd been a while since I'd received the message so I needed to send something soonish – I was playing it cool, but not so cool that I'd be put in the Perspex veg drawer in the fridge with all the other cucumbers. The picture I opted for was a topless shot, since I'd just got out of the shower with my hair done. I think back to this and cringe so badly that I want to go back in time and kick my own arse. 'Why did you send that picture?' you may ask. Well, because I was twenty-three, I worked out and had boundless confidence in myself as well as my abilities. I had also recently shaved my chest. Put another way, I was an overconfident, cocksure prick.

Despite this potentially disastrous choice of photo, we agreed to go for a drink. I got dressed in the standard-issue attire of students at the time: a Trucker hat, ripped jeans, Converse trainers, bleach-tipped hair and a T-shirt with some kind of clever rude reworking of a well-known brand logo and picked Clemmie up in my beige Peugeot 205, which had been dubbed 'Spew' by my friends. We drank coffee and spoke for what seemed like minutes, but was in fact hours until it was dark outside. Eventually we left and I drove her home. Although we'd talked at each other solidly for half a day, suddenly the car fell silent; it was only later on in our relationship that I discovered why. We'd both wanted to kiss each other at the end of our first proper date, but I was nervous she wouldn't kiss me back and she didn't want to make the first move either.

I pulled up to her house and watched her go inside, cursing my inability to take action, and slunk off with my tail between my legs.

We then had no contact for two days. Two freaking days! Ice ages could have come and gone in that time! I didn't want to seem overly keen but not hearing from her was killing me slowly inside. Finally we spoke and arranged another date, and what made it even sweeter was that it was Clemmie who called me! I took her to Wagamama, we drank way too much wine and ended up in a cocktail bar where I slurred the words 'so I guess you're my girlfriend now'. That was that, done deal. Fifteen minutes later we were in a cab back to her place with the taxi driver struggling to keep his eyes on the road.

A year later, we both finished university and decided to move in together. We found a tiny one-bedroom flat in Clifton Village in Bristol that we stuffed to the rafters with our semi-broken IKEA student furniture and our now-combined CD collection (we've only recently got rid of the duplicates we had between us). The flat was damp and it had a back door that opened directly onto the fire escape of the adjoining pub, but we were happy and feeling quite grown up at the start of our combined independent adult lives.

Three months in and all was going swimmingly. I'd found a job as a recruitment consultant, which taught me two things: one, how to do cold calling and two, that I didn't like cold calling or being a recruitment consultant. Clemmie, on the other hand, was putting her degree in midwifery to good use and working at Southmead Hospital. We did the things that couples do and we were content, but that was about to change.

I'd just got home from another enthralling day of recruitment consultancy (if you don't know what you want to do as a job – as I didn't at the age of twenty-four, fresh out of university – it seems you can always get one finding jobs for other people that do know what they want to do). I walked in and Clemmie looked at me with a face that told me all was not right with the world. We sat down and as the two words 'I'm pregnant' slipped from between her lips and into my ears, everything in our future changed irreversibly. My immediate thoughts were:

- Did she actually just say she was pregnant or have I just misheard her tell me she's 'peg-legged'?
- Why is my heart trying to burst through my rib cage?
- I can see my legs, but I can't fucking feel them any more. What's that all about?

After not talking for a while and allowing my brain a moment to catch up with the events that had unfolded, I started to process the implications of the bomb that had just been dropped onto my life (at this point I really wasn't thinking about Clemmie at all; I was blinded by my own selfish thoughts about how this would affect me and my future).

I hadn't even started my career yet – was I going to be forced to go out and do a job I never wanted to do just to make ends meet? My parents – what about my parents?! This was definitely not in their plans for me at this premature age and after they'd invested in my education and upbringing, I was sure I was going to be disowned. I lay on the floor for a long time, not speaking. My legs were numb. My thoughts turned to how we could make this problem go away but then I saw Clemmie and realised she was as shit-scared as me. This wasn't in her plan either. Over the coming weeks we ummed and ahhed over what we should do and finally decided that despite all the reasons why we shouldn't be parents so young, we both could and should do this. We loved each other and it would have happened at some point anyway and though it would be hard work, this could be good for us. OK, we'd have to put some things on hold and life may not be exactly what we'd planned for the next couple of years, but we wanted to make it work.

The biggest thing for me was telling my parents. Clemmie was now ten weeks and it was starting to get to the point where she would be showing and couldn't blame it on a particularly big lunch, so one weekend, we drove over to my parents' house for Sunday roast. We sat, we talked, we drank and we talked some more, all the while knowing full well that we had an information grenade with no pin in it that I was about to lob in my parents' direction. The only problem was that I couldn't do it. The words wouldn't physically come out of me as telling them would make it very real and there was no way of taking it back. Frankly I was scared of their reaction.

Like the cowardly creature I was, I made my excuses and Clemmie and I left, but as we headed back to the damp little hole we called home, it dawned on me that I had to tell them now. I dropped Clemmie off and I returned to my parents' house with some flimsy excuse about needing to get some sports kit.

Finally I sat them both down, trembling. This wasn't like the time I told them I'd set fire to the garden when I was ten or when I was caught drinking at school, or when I opened my Christmas presents two weeks early and exchanged the gifts I didn't want for my brother's. This was big.

'Mum, Dad, I've got something to tell you . . .'

Time froze as I watched my parents' minds run through what it could be. Has he been fired? Has he lied about going to uni for the last four years and in actual fact just pissed our money against the wall? Is he going to prison for being a drug dealer?

'Clemmie is ten weeks pregnant and we're having the baby.'

The air in the room was very still. Everything had gone quiet. Very quiet indeed. I could see my mum slowly glance in my dad's direction but he was already on the move. He stood up, came over to me and to my great relief, shook my hand and gave me the most reassuring hug I've ever had in my life. 'That's brilliant news, Simon, congratulations!'

Suddenly all those fears of my parents feeling disappointment in their son for not being more careful and not living up to their expectations disappeared. I felt like this huge cruise liner of a secret was suddenly taken off my shoulders and that I was supported by those who loved me. Thirty weeks later, Anya burst onto the scene and changed the trajectory of our lives in every way you can possibly conceive of. From being unprepared soon-to-be first-time parents we were thrust into the leading roles our very own Broadway show entitled *Actually Being Parents*. We hadn't been given a script or been to rehearsals, nor did we have understudies, but like true professionals we were pushed on stage in front of the audience comprised of family and friends and winged it as best we could until we started to grasp what we were supposed to do. The show hasn't stopped since.

Marnie showed up another three years later. This time it was all different. We were established parents, and by established I mean we had a child already and through supporting each other in the hard times and celebrating the good, we'd managed to stumble our way through the sleepless nights, the weaning, the rapid evolution from lying to crawling to climbing to walking, the development of speech, the endless arguments about whose turn it was to do the nappies, the washing of shit-stained clothes, the nursery pick-up and drop-off routine, the trips to A&E for what seemed like life-threatening diseases but turned out to just be colds and the endless tidying that comes with having a child. We'd come out the other side relatively unscathed and still liking each other, so it seemed only natural to ruin the nice little life we had going for ourselves and go right back to the start of the whole process again, but this time with a toddler in the midst of it all who required more attention than a D-lister on *I'm a Celebrity . . . Get Me Out of Here!*

Since Marnie was actually planned, this time around, when I got the news that Clemmie was pregnant, I came over all Buzz Aldrin-like – i.e. over the moon.

Marnie came into the world two weeks early due to some complications that Clemmie had during pregnancy but both mother and baby were safe and sound, so as we bounded in through the door, we couldn't wait to show off the newest member of our family to an

17

expectant Anya who was waiting for us at home with Clemmie's mum.

It was at that point I learnt that bringing a baby home when you already have children can be difficult. The child that was once the shining beacon of proof that you can procreate is no longer a one-off miracle. They are now an older brother or sister which can be hard for some to swallow, especially when they didn't apply for the job or have any say in the matter.

When we brought Marnie home, Anya was initially fascinated with her. But like the shiny new toy you wanted for your birthday as a kid that you'd pestered your parents for literally months for, the novelty wore off relatively quickly and within two weeks Anya declared that we should 'take her back to the train station where we got her and send her away'. Tough luck, Anya: she's staying and you'll just have to get used to it.

Finally, to complete the story of how we got to where we are today, we had the twins, Ottilie and Delilah, in January 2016. I'm not going to lie. I took a fair amount of convincing that we should have a third child. Both Clemmie and I had come from families of three children and we both agreed that we'd want to have three children, but when we actually got around to it, I wasn't so sure any more. We were both grey-faced and tired. Our house was full of dolls, our little litter of women had left us as flat as a pint of cola that had been left out for a week and as much as I loved my girls, I just couldn't quite imagine having another one to add to the pile. Also, I just knew it would be another girl – not that that's a reason not to have a baby, of course, but if I'm honest with myself, I would have loved to have a little boy. I just knew that I'm genetically predisposed to making girls and already being outnumbered three to one, I wasn't sure I could handle any more pink in my life.

Several months of discussions followed and finally I couldn't remember why I was resisting any more. I loved having children around me and the reasons for not having another had become so vague in my addled mind that I couldn't actually remember them. So I was going to have girls surrounding me for the rest of my life, so what?! There were worse things that could happen to me and from what everyone told me, girls look after their fathers and will always side with them. I told myself that I could even put together a three-piece follow-up group to the Jackson 5 and I could be their manager – the Hooper 3 had a nice ring to it.

Two months later Clemmie was peeing on pregnancy sticks like there was a worldwide shortage of them and she had found the last stash, and lo and behold, she was pregnant. She had some initial bleeding which had us a bit worried so she went to get a check-up while she was at work at the hospital.

I spent the day at work, one eye on my computer screen moving numbers from one spreadsheet to the next, the other on my phone, willing it to buzz.

Finally it happened. Clemmie had had a scan and she had good news. She was fine and there was a healthy little person growing inside her. But there was more. Behind the healthy little person was a shadow, a shadow that might or might not be another healthy little person. Never had my emotions gone so quickly from a cruising-at-38,000-feet-high to a crashing-into-the-runway-nose-first low. How could this be? Twins?! At this stage it was too early to tell, so we had another two weeks of waiting to find out if it was indeed just a shadow effect from the scan or whether another human was lurking in the wings to make a surprise entrance from stage right. That evening when I got home we put the girls to bed and crumpled onto the sofa. Both of us were shell-shocked and neither of us knew what to say to each other. We both cried.

Those two weeks passed and once again I found myself with one eye on my computer, this time not doing any work at all, the other on my phone. Clemmie then texted me the two words that would change our whole world once again – 'It's twins' – followed by two emojis of babies' faces.

Like the passing of a solar eclipse, baby number one had moved over to reveal not the sun (or a son), but yet another daughter who had been hiding in the shadows.

Seven months later, Clemmie and I were the proud parents of four girls, all of whom look like they have 95 per cent of my genetic make-up (much to Clemmie's annoyance), and that's how we got to where we are today – me and five women in a house that is constantly filled with noise, has glitter ingrained in the carpet and more pink stuffed animals than a colour-blind taxidermy specialist, but I wouldn't change a thing because these people are my life.

In summary, I'm husband to one amazing woman and a father to four amazing girls, which is never something I saw in my future fifteen years ago, but these people have made me who I am today and I owe them everything. I did react very differently, though, each time I was told that we were going to have a baby – or in the most recent case, babies.

Daughter number one – a surprise

REACTION: Oh. My. God. Why the hell is this happening?! I'm going to sue the condom company for this.

Daughter number two – planned

REACTION: Oh. My. God. This is brilliant – I can't wait to tell everyone that Anya's going to have a little sister!

Daughters number 3 and 4 – planned and a surprise

REACTION: I bloody knew this would happen if we went for a third. It took Clemmie ages to talk me into this, and now we're completely screwed. I mean, how do you even cope with twins?

Of course I wouldn't change any of it, except for perhaps having a mute button grafted onto them at birth, but we can't have everything we want now, can we?

2

Advice to my pre-child self

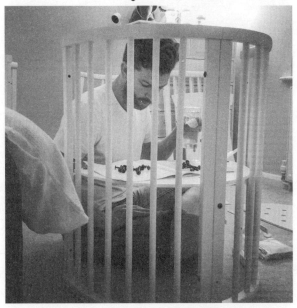

My years of erecting wobbly flat-pack furniture in my
student flat finally paid dividends when it came to
assembling a cot for the first time. It was only midway
through my second G&T that I realised I'd built the
sodding thing around me like a scaled-down Alcatraz.
Did I read the instructions properly? Did I hell. Ten
years on and I now have an Allen-key collection
that would rival an IKEA distribution centre.

Advice to my pre-child self

*O*f course before all of my girls showed up, destroying the concepts of silence and privacy in the process, I was just a guy having his first child with the woman he loved and I was scared. Even with everyone cheering us on from the sidelines, I initially struggled with the fact I was destined to become a father before my twenty-fifth birthday. I felt like a walking Molotov cocktail – one part scared shitless to equal parts excited that we were going to be parents, happy it was all going well and sad as the course of our lives had now changed irreversibly. Turns out that these are all very common feelings to experience 100 times a day, but no one told me!

As a man, pregnancy was something that I was responsible for but it wasn't actually physically happening to me, so I felt a little left out. As the weeks of pregnancy progressed and things started to get real, small pieces of 'worry shrapnel' from the baby bomb became lodged in my brain, conjuring up questions that ate away at my grey matter, which resulted in prolonged staring at the bedroom ceiling when I should have been sleeping.

Since the dawn of time, men have been perfecting the 'emotion-less state' – the ability to hide our feelings deep down inside, only for a therapist to dredge them back up in a dark twisted mess later in life and make us cry like babies. Dads-to-be are no different and the thought of confronting our feelings, let alone talking about them with other people, can be enough to send us running for the hills. I'm not saying that we're all emotionally repressed robots with tin cans for hearts, but sharing our true feelings about something when it risks revealing us to be anything other than rock solid and confident can be difficult. That's beginning to change as we learn it isn't a sign of weakness, and is actually a form of strength, but we should all get down to the mind gym and work on it a bit more.

Of course, back in 2007, I hadn't quite grasped this concept yet and was still stuck trying to be the confident young man everyone thought I was. My brain (that for some unknown reason seemed to be rooted firmly in the 1950s) kept telling me that it was the man's job to worry about the tangible things – logistics, finances, etc – and that I shouldn't burden Clemmie with any of my anxieties as she had enough to deal with. If I buried my head in the sand, surely my worries would just disappear – it had worked for men for thousands of years so surely it would work for me. I just resigned myself to developing a permanent eye twitch and using the phrase 'that's fine' a lot.

So with my concerns hidden from view, we were on our way with daughter number one. Outwardly I projected an air of pride and happiness at delivering the news that, despite excessive drinking when younger and getting kicked in the balls at the age of fourteen by a friend at a football match, my manhood worked and I'd some-how managed to get my swimmers to locate an egg and fertilise it. I smiled and said the right things to the right people, but internally I felt like the contents of a NutriBullet that had been whacked on blitz.

Should I one day discover how to unravel the mysteries of time travel, I'd go back, equipped with my ten years of parenting experience, and give my pre-child self a good talking-to. Here's how that conversation might go:

QUESTION: **Am I actually ready to be a parent?** (I've never lived down the moment I dropped my sister from the top bunk when I was six. I genuinely thought I'd killed her and insisted that my parents kill me to make up for it. I've been scared of bunk beds ever since.)

ANSWER: Right now you're not, but you will be when the time comes. Nothing can really prepare you for the real deal. It's like watching a twenty-minute snowboarding video on YouTube – you don't even finish the video and yet you expect to be able to do back-flips and immediately give up your oh-so-boring day job to live in the mountains and fly helicopters around with your other long-haired snowboarder mates. No amount of reading or videos prepares you for fatherhood either. Parenting is very much a hands-on learning experience: on-the-job training that starts when your baby comes into the world and, much like a rolling phone contract that you've forgotten you signed up to, apparently doesn't have an end date. Yes, some people are more paternal in nature, but no one is born knowing all the answers and able to handle every situation without breaking into a sweat. As long as you're prepared to do your best, to share the load and put the work in, that's all that anyone can ask of you.

I wasn't ready with our first daughter. I was twenty-four and more preoccupied with seeing my friends and watching crap on TV than getting my head around the fact we were having a baby or the impact that might have on our lives. In fact I think Anya was the first baby I'd held since holding my sister when she was born, and that was twenty years previous. Consequently, in all our photos from the day I became a dad for the first time, I looked like a rabbit caught in the headlights.

The point I'm trying to make in a roundabout way is that as long as you're mentally ready, the rest will come with practice, so don't be too hard on yourself. The best way I know of getting your brain to prepare and to recognise things are going to change is by talking about them honestly and openly. As someone once said, 'A problem aired is a problem shared', so if you don't feel ready, talk to Clemmie or someone you know who's been through it before.

QUESTION: **How much is this bundle of joy going to cost?** I had all the finances working like a well-oiled machine: direct debits, standing orders – all as predictable as an atomic clock month in, month out, with money left over to have a bit of fun with. I was anxious that having a baby was going to cost a lot and mess this up. Child ISAs, nappies, buggies, a fully equipped nursery – this baby wasn't even bigger than a tangerine yet and already it was mentally costing me a fortune.

ANSWER: Well, to be honest, this is really a 'How long is a piece of string?' kind of deal. Yes, you're going to be buying stuff that you wouldn't have had before, but it doesn't mean you have to spend the GDP of a small European nation in order for your offspring to be comfortable.

When we had our first daughter, we were young and hadn't really started our careers, so money was tighter than an extra-small wetsuit on a guy who's pushing 300 lb. We lived in our overdraft so we had to get creative.

When it comes to buying things, Clemmie and I have very defined roles. She's the creative director who will look for things that are aesthetically pleasing, I, on the other hand, play the role of financial manager and rein in the budget so that we don't have to end up eating cold beans for four months. Let's act out a little scene . . .

Clemmie wants to buy something – it could be anything really, but for the sake of argument, we'll say it's a new kitchen table. She'll go to the expensive design magazines and pick out the table she wants. Clemmie will make the case for this table being the only one we can possibly have. During this sales pitch, I'll hold my breath and grimace as we approach the reveal of the financial damage this beautiful slab of wood and metal is going to inflict. I'll choke on my tea as the price is disclosed, and then spend the next two weeks on the internet trying to find something exactly the same, just without the branding, for a fraction of the price. This is exactly what happened when we were buying stuff in preparation for our first little one. Anya grew out of the early months baby clothes in the space of two months and I was concerned because, being the first of our friends to enter into the world of family life, we weren't able to borrow anything. However, as luck would have it, both Clemmie and my parents are hoarders/sentimental old things, so we managed to get hand-me-down clothing that both Clemmie and I had worn when we were babies. Then we just topped that up with bulk-buy babygros. It was then that I learnt that babies truly are the bamboo of the human world – I swear if you strain your ears, you can actually hear them stretch – and within two months 25 per cent of the clothing we'd bought hadn't been worn: Anya had grown out of it before we'd even had a chance to put her in it. We tried to squeeze her into a few of these items but she ended up looking like a baby in a mankini.

Our subsequent girls have had the pleasure of wearing second-hand clothing that has been lying dormant in the loft along with furniture that should have gone to the tip and most of my personal belongings pre-2007. I'm just glad we had four girls – if a boy had rocked up, especially in place of the twins, he would have been screwed for clothing.

Much like Mariah Carey, babies seem to come with a lot of para-phernalia, half of which seems to me to be surplus to requirements. We've gone through this process three times now and with each re-entry into the baby years we've whittled down the big-ticket items to the ones we really need. First up there's the all-terrain, all-purpose child transportation vehicles, also known as buggies. The price of these things can be punch-you-in-the-gut, poke-you-in-the-eye-and-steal-your-wallet expensive – they can lead you to consider taking out a second mortgage or selling a lung to afford them. I don't know when the child transportation market went absolutely insane, but let's just say that you could go on a really nice holiday for the price of some of these all-singing, all-dancing, iPad-wearing, 360-degree-sound-system-including, coffee-cup-holding, storage-compartment-having contraptions. To my mind, it's like putting 20-inch alloys on your little hatchback car, installing a massive subwoofer in the boot and painting it fluorescent lime green – it's just not necessary and has the potential to make you look like a bit of a dick when people ask you how much you paid. Whichever buggy you opt for, when your child reaches toddler stage, they will no doubt try to wiggle out of it or give themselves a mega-wedgie, leading you to stop and manhandle them back into position every 7 feet, meaning that getting down the street can end up taking hours as your little one's head glides along 4 inches above the pavement as they arch their body over the side.

Then there's the car seat. Safety isn't something that you want to compromise for the sake of a bit of money. Imagine going bungee jumping for £100 on a proper rig versus going with a guy who's standing next to a bridge selling jumps for a fiver using his home-made bungee cord made from old elastic bands and chewing gum. Not worth the risk, is it?

Last but not least, unless you're planning on making your fresh new child sleep on the floor among your discarded pants and the spaghetti of wires that protrude from under your bed, you'll probably need a cot.

QUESTION: **What other jobs am I going to be expected to pick up now my other half is out of action?**

ANSWER: Well, there's a multitude of things, but the main one I ended up with was cleaning.

I'm not sure this happens to all women, but there is a period that suddenly arrives unannounced towards the end of the pregnancy, officially termed the 'nesting phase'. This basically entails women needing to make the house so tidy and spotless that even someone with chronic OCD would walk in and say it was too clean. A multitude of cleaning fluids, creams and sprays started building up in the cupboard under the sink until we got to the point where we had more bottles in our house than there were on the shelves of the local supermarket. Clemmie was actually getting high off the smell of them (well, not actually high – she wasn't smoking Cif or intravenously injecting Mr Muscle. She just liked the smell A LOT). I was even forced to go and find the floor-cleaning fluid they used at the hospital she worked in, as the smell of it was all she wanted. The day I turned up with a 2.5-litre drum of Flash professional floor cleaner was literally the happiest I'd seen her in weeks.

The difficulty was that by the time Clemmie was thirty-six weeks pregnant, she was basically lugging around a full-size baby, so cleaning wasn't that easy. This is where I, the more messy of the two of us, had to step up my game. No, I didn't do it to her standards, yes, I used the wrong product for the wrong job, and yes, my cleaning got constantly criticised while comments like 'Well, if you're not going to do it properly first time, I might as well do it myself' echoed in my ears, but I kept reminding myself that walking out on a pregnant woman is largely frowned upon and it was the hormones talking. Probably.

Here are some other jobs I found I was responsible for:

- Putting shoes on for a person who could no longer see their feet.
- Providing back-rubs on tap.
- Holding hair back when Clemmie succumbed to morning sickness.

QUESTION: **Does this mean booking a spot in the mortuary for my sex life?** A purely selfish thought here, but remember we're talking to a twenty-four-year-old me, so it's totally allowed.

ANSWER: Sex is an important part of most relationships but the need, willingness or energy to have sex can drain away during pregnancy. That said, due to the rush of hormones flowing around their bodies like a river rapids ride at the theme park, some women are literally like a dog on heat; they can't get enough of you to the point where you're actually making excuses not to do it – 'Sorry, sweetheart, I've got this documentary I recorded on multiple universes that I really want to watch.' Other women will shut up shop for the duration of the pregnancy – it's different for different people.

Before we dive into details, let's get one thing out of the way straight off: no, the baby is not going to grab on to your manhood, and even if you have been gifted/cursed with a 16-inch trouser python, you are not going to hurt the baby by jabbing it in the eye during sex. Even then there is something called a cervix, which you'd have to overcome. It simply ain't gonna happen.

My experience was that for the first couple of months, we didn't have sex. It wasn't Clemmie not wanting to or me completely losing my libido, I think we were just both a bit nervous. It was our first baby and we didn't want to do anything that might dislodge the little chickpea from its warm new home. After about sixteen weeks, Clemmie obviously took a swim in a hormone bath because suddenly she was all over me like a rash that no ointment could cure – I couldn't beat her off with a stick so we had sex. My problem was that I found it hard to overcome the knowledge that it wasn't just the two of us in bed any more, it was now a *ménage à trois* of sorts. I was constantly thinking about the baby. What's it doing in there? I was very conscious that there was a bump where there hadn't been one before and I didn't want to be on top in case I somehow slipped and crushed her – ridiculous I know, but this was what was buzzing around my head at the time.

Of course, when my performance was below par due to all the worries coursing around in my head and I wasn't able to complete the task in hand (you know what I mean), Clemmie would ask if it was because she wasn't attractive to me any more because of the changes in her body, which would be followed by silent tears rolling down her cheeks. This made me feel particularly shit – tending to a crying woman after trying and failing to make sweet, sweet love with her is not ideal. In fact, it feels pretty rubbish. Of course I still fancied her and found her attractive but something had changed, which led her to think that along with all the hormonal changes to her pregnant body had come a free dose of man repellent.

34

As the due date approached I remember people telling me all sorts of old wives' tales, tips and tricks to get labour going. Turns out that one of the most effective ways of giving the whole birth process a kick-start is sex, the very act that got you here in the first place. To Clemmie this wasn't particularly appealing as she was mega-uncomfortable by this point, but this sex was purely functional. I even considered saying that I was doing her a favour to help get the baby out, but in the end I saw sense as I didn't fancy walking into the hospital with a black eye and a bloody nose.

QUESTION: **Should we find out if we're having a boy or a girl?**

ANSWER: At the twenty-week scan, the question of whether or not to find out the sex of your in-utero child will raise its head. There are pros and cons to each choice: making my peace with the fact that it wasn't the sex I was secretly hoping for, being able to decorate the way we wanted, making the decision over names easier and getting my parents to stop asking what we thought we were having all the time were reasons I was in favour of finding out. But another part of me felt there weren't enough surprises left in life, and who needs to worry about paint colours anyway? A nice neutral room is more my style.

So having considered all of this, the first time around we decided that we didn't want to find out. In a world where you can access any information you're looking for within minutes just by typing things into a search engine, this has to be one of the only genuine surprises you might have in your life. Ultimately, though, the big decision about whether to find out or not didn't matter in my case – my list of pros and cons was surplus to requirements.

During the scan, I was peering at this amorphous blob on the screen, nodding along as the sonographer pointed out bits of the baby that I pretended to see. I could barely make out the arms and legs, let alone the sexual organs. Clemmie, on the other hand, saw the screen, and being a kick-ass midwife, immediately saw that we were having a girl. Bless her, she waited a whole two hours before blurting out that she knew what it was and asked me whether I wanted to know too. I tried to stick to my guns and keep it as a surprise. I categorically told her that I didn't want to know and hell would freeze over before I changed my mind. I held out for about four days before the fact that she knew and I didn't started to kill me slowly from the inside.

Once we both knew, we decided not to tell anyone else, mainly as I was running a back-alley gambling racket in the form of a sweep-stake on the sex, weight and arrival date of our firstborn and I wanted to make some money. That's not awful, is it? Doesn't matter as my mother won in the end.

I'm not going to lie, I did have a mini grieving period of a day or two after discovering that my boy, Optimus Ronaldo, would have to wait, but I got over it. Besides, that name would never have got through the vetting process. Little did I know that I'd go on to have three more girls. Damn you, you lazy-ass male-making sperm – what the hell were you all doing? You've had so many chances and you've blown it every time! Maybe it was a bank holiday every time we conceived and they were all pissed at a barbecue or something. Lazy. Just plain lazy.

QUESTION: **Giving birth seems a bit full on and from every-thing I've seen and heard, men seem to be a bit of a spare part in the whole process – essentially there to be yelled at. What am I supposed to do?**

ANSWER: Birth can be full on but I learnt that the thing Clemmie needed most during the labour wasn't the playlist of hand-picked orca songs, or the pre-made snacks, or the painkillers, or the lavender relaxation spray that cost an eye-watering £40 for 10 ml. It was me. I needed to be there to support and comfort her and be involved.

So I've addressed the thoughts *I* had first time around, but it's important to acknowledge that there are usually two people in the baby-making partnership. Men's brains aren't the only ones that are working harder than a hamster in a wheel that's training for an ultra-marathon. Women's minds are no doubt burning the midnight oil with similar questions and many others besides: What's going to happen to my body? How's work going to take this? Am I really ready to be a parent? Will we get all the DIY around the house done before an additional family member turns up? What kind of birth do I want? Is the man-child I'm with able to support me through pregnancy and labour, let alone look after our future child?

If I could give my pre-child self one piece of advice it would be to make sure Clemmie and I talked to each other more about all the questions buzzing around in our heads. I guess we were both scared of the unknown and that actually vocalising our concerns would make them real and something that we'd have to deal with, but as I said earlier, a problem aired is a problem shared. Clemmie and I both had the same worries about how our lives would change, how we'd cope financially, how it would affect our relationship and whether we were up to the task of looking after another life without adult supervision (although we were classed as adults in the eyes of the law, we definitely didn't feel like it). So until Google pulls its finger out and invents a chip for our brains to enable mind-reading (and maybe direct access to the internet so we can all procrastinate even more than we do today), talking things through is the best solution to put your mind at rest and reduce the chances of a stress-related aneurysm days before your child is born. And no, before you ask, we did not name Anya after an aneurysm, they just happen to sound very similar!

3

From man-child to man with child

I'd eaten a 12-inch sub fifteen minutes before
this moment and stank the whole place out.
I considered telling my wife I had painful
stomach cramps from eating too quickly, but
quite fancied staying alive, so I didn't.

From man-child to man with child

None of our children have been on time. Three of them were born early and one was late. As time has passed, they are all now in the habit of being late, for everything, which means as a result *I'm* late for everything. I hate this, but short of putting them to bed fully dressed for the next day, I'm resigned to the fact that now we are just those people you can rely on to arrive at least thirty minutes after the time we were expected to be somewhere.

When Clemmie was pregnant with Anya, I discovered that the due date you're provided with does not, in fact, represent a precisely scheduled event that will happen exactly when you expect it to, like the 2.35 at Aintree, and my logic-based brain found this hard to deal with. I'm a man that likes lists and plans. I also like sticking to those lists and plans and take even greater satisfaction in being able to tick things off once they are done. However, much to my frustration, the female body has its own natural rhythm so when it came to the birth, I had to be ready when Clemmie's body was, which is why it was important to be prepared well in advance.

Having now witnessed four births (yes, the twins count as separate ones even though they were only fifteen minutes apart – I saw what Clemmie went through and I dare anyone to tell a twin mother that it only counts as one birth: just make sure you're wearing body armour when you do it), I've come to realise this experience can be both amazing and harrowing in equal measure. It's magical to be involved in the process of welcoming your newest family member into the world, to hear their first noises and see them experience life outside the warm protective bubble they've been in for the last nine months. You'll probably be one of the first things that your child gazes upon after being born. Think about that. It's awesome.

The flip side of this, though, is that it's no fun seeing the person you love in pain. What made it worse was my inability to do anything about it. Sure, I could have pinned a medical staff member up against the wall and quietly whispered in aggressive undertones, 'Just give her all the drugs now!' like they do in the movies, but I'd have been promptly escorted from the hospital and in the process got myself a nice little criminal record to hang above the loo once I was out of jail. Plus in all likelihood I'd have missed the whole reason I was there in the first place – the birth of my child – so I decided it was best not to take this route.

For guys, birth also has the potential to make us feel a bit like a spoon at a private dinner dance for knives and forks – i.e. out of place and surplus to requirements, which is why I found it important to define a role for myself so I could be helpful along the way instead of just being a spare part.

Many of the jobs that I've been responsible for in the days before

42

and during the birth are, coincidentally, pretty much exactly the same jobs I had when it came to planning our wedding: pack the bags, arrange the location, organise the catering, get the music sorted, know the plans for the day, say the right things at the right times, celebrate . . . Along with these jobs are a few other key tasks, which I present to you here, grouped according to the different stages of the birth process:

PRE BIRTH

Pack the bags

This is going to sound a bit weird but for the twins' birth, both Clemmie and I decided that I should be in charge of the hospital bag. 'Why on earth did she let him be in charge of that?' I hear all the women say. Yes, it's true that men have made a career out of complaining about women's bags. When I'm put in charge of packing for a holiday, my mind is on weight restrictions and avoiding having to hand over our hard-earned money to a budget airline because of indecisive and inefficient packing. I don't and probably never will fully understand the need to bring eight pairs of shoes for a week's holiday, or why every floaty dress my wife owns has to come with us. Handbags are another object of desire I don't understand. Why do women need to carry so much stuff around with them? And what's with the obsession over owning a designer bag with a price tag that could feed your family for half a year? You can buy one that looks almost exactly the same and that's made from the same leather for a fraction of the price! I know I'm going off-piste here, so

I should get back to hospital bags, but it's something that I can't wrap my head around.

I wasn't responsible for the hospital bag for our first two births. My role was not dissimilar to being Madonna's assistant: I'd pick up bags, move them from one location to another and set them down within reaching distance while having orders barked in my general direction. On multiple occasions I was told to get a specific item from the bag, aka the magic tardis, while Clemmie was in the middle of contractions. Patience isn't something that women are famous for having a lot of during labour – and to be fair neither should they have, as they are busy pushing a baby out of their body. So, in a fluster and under pressure to not screw things up by taking more than ten seconds to perform a simple task, I'd scuttle over to the bag and turn the whole thing upside down. The looks I got from Clemmie after she'd seen all her stuff strewn across the floor almost made *me* go into labour. The problem was that I hadn't packed the bag and as a result I didn't know where anything was. I briefly considered asking her to come and show me where she'd hidden her headphones, or if she was sure she'd packed properly and hadn't, in fact, left things on the bed at home, but I could tell that would go down badly and didn't want to make the already overworked midwives more stressed by having to clean up my corpse, so I left it.

So when it came to the birth of the twins, I was intimately involved in the packing of the bag. The bag and I were one. I knew everything about what was going on in that bag and there weren't any secrets between us. I put time and effort into getting everything squared away as I really didn't want to be on the receiving end of another passive-aggressive tongue-lashing from a woman with a dilated cervix. I even created a spreadsheet of the items and colour-coded them to ensure that I knew which items should go in which compartment. Time well spent in my view.

Location, location, location

With Anya and Marnie, Clemmie was desperate for a water birth at home. I personally wasn't sold on the idea of having a massive tub of water in the living room, held back by only a single-skin plastic membrane – it sounded like a home insurance nightmare waiting to happen that would end with my precious electronics getting drenched and me being forced to repaint the lower 4 inches of the downstairs walls once the mini tsunami receded – but I was assured that this had never happened. Being an uneducated half-wit who hadn't read much of the birth book that had been waved under my nose, I thought it also seemed like a sure-fire way to drown our newborn child seconds after she had been introduced into the world – unless she'd been taking in-utero tiny tots swimming lessons.

Of course that's not the case at all, as sometimes babies don't even know they've been born since their lungs haven't taken their first gulp of air, which can also mean there's barely any crying or screaming.

With Marnie, the thing I did genuinely worry about was the noise – not from the baby, but from my wife. Clemmie has never been what you'd call a quiet person during labour or ever, despite her best efforts to keep things at an acceptable level, so what would the neighbours make of 130 decibels of shouting? I can almost imagine their conversation now:

'I think he's finally done it – he's killed her. I knew she could be a handful to deal with but he's actually done it. Should we call the police or shall we have dinner first?'

In the end, thinking this through was a complete waste of time with Marnie's birth as Clemmie had a complication that meant she had to go into hospital and be induced. It's possibly the oddest feeling ever to get a bus, pillows and bags under each arm, with someone who is pregnant but not yet in labour, knowing that you're going to have a baby at some point that day.

With the arrival of the twins, it was different again. We knew Clemmie would have to give birth in hospital and that we'd be seeing the twins before the full forty weeks was up as they'd basically run out of space, so at thirty-six weeks we drove to the hospital to be induced. We did still have one issue to deal with though: what should we do with the older girls? We had a couple of options available:

- Option 1: Make like it was the Second World War and send them off to the countryside to see their grandparents.
- Option 2: Get them involved. Would we be one of those families you see on the internet that let their three-year-old be involved in the birth? Er, no. I really didn't think seeing your mother screaming in pain was appropriate for a young child to see.
- Option 3: Get Clemmie's mum to come and stay for a couple of nights.

Of course option 3 was really the only viable one.

Organise the catering

As the number of children we had increased, so too did the amount of food and entertainment I brought to the birth. First time-round I was frankly ill-prepared. Some squashed cheese, ham and tomato sandwiches wrapped in an insufficient amount of cling film which led to soggy bread and a pool of tomato pips in the bottom of the bag. I was left feeling really hungry, so I rectified this by doing something that I really wouldn't recommend to anyone – but we'll get to that in a moment . . .

For the second birth, I brought a full picnic with me in a hamper. I ate 90 per cent of this as I discovered that women in labour really don't fancy having a sit-down lunch as they have 'other things on their mind'. Also, be prepared to get looks like daggers if you make too much noise when you decide to eat. I ate a banana – what I would consider to be a relatively quiet fruit, perfectly designed as an on-the-go snack: it's soft and comes in its own wrapper for goodness' sake, and yet I still got told that the sound of my chewing was making Clemmie feel sick. Can't a man eat a banana these days without getting ripped apart? Apparently not. But that's not as bad as what another guy did while we were in hospital with our second. He brought what must have been a leftover curry that he and his partner had probably ordered the night before in the hopes it would get the birth process moving. It stank out the whole area – no one wanted to be *his* friend that day.

For births three and four, I brought the hamper again, but also made time to go to Subway for a foot-long sub. We'll cover this later too, but I will say in my defence that I only went there initially for

Clemmie. It just turned out there were some rather tasty fringe benefits to being a good birth partner/husband.

The one thing I have never done is buy food in the hospital. Much like in cinemas – where, as you munch bucketloads of dry popcorn, they pump the place with enough hot air to make the building lift off like a balloon, and you get such a dry mouth you have no choice but to splash out on drinks that cost more than the cinema ticket itself – hospitals have you as a captive market. They know you're there for a while and are unlikely to go too far, so they jack the prices up. I suppose we have to fund the NHS somehow, I just didn't think it would be through my belly.

Just call me DJ Dad

Remember the days before Spotify and decent Wi-Fi? I seriously wonder how we managed to survive back in those primitive times. I mean we actually had to get up and insert physical circular discs into a sound system to get music out of them – our kids don't know how good they have it. When it came to preparing for Clemmie's first labour, I had what I thought was one relatively simple job to do: burn a CD with songs from my massive back catalogue of tunes from my university days in the early 2000s – you know the ones, right? Compiling this CD should have been a piece of cake, yet somehow I didn't get the tone quite right. After a half-hour-long blissed-out Ibiza chill session, the music really ramped up with some random hard house and the Prodigy spilling out of the speakers – it seemed I'd forgotten the purpose of the CD halfway through making it and had basically made a mix of pre-going-out music, the kind you played to get you pumped – not what Clemmie was looking to listen to between contractions.

Since those dark days, technology has moved on. Steve Jobs did me a favour and invented the iPod and Clemmie decided to take control of the playlists. In fact she took to wearing headphones for the subsequent births, which meant I was left in silence while she drifted off to whatever her random collection of songs consisted of (I wasn't privy to her audio accompaniment thanks to the noise-cancelling headphones she had fastened to her head like a vice, and I didn't dare ask to have a listen as I've been taught it's best to let sleeping dogs lie for fear of getting your fingers removed by gnashing teeth). It did put a distance between us as she was in a different place to me mentally, but it seemed to work.

Back to school

At the very least, dads should get educated as to what's actually going on when it comes to pregnancy and childbirth. Obviously I knew enough about human anatomy and the sexual reproductive process to get someone pregnant, but that doesn't mean I knew everything. Like a contestant on *The Apprentice*, I had to learn enough to sound like I knew what I was talking about, to understand what was going on and to be informed enough to ask questions. The difference between me and an *Apprentice* contestant was that I wasn't going to then go and use my newfound knowledge to sell poorly conceived products to the general public. I was going to have a baby.

When we were having Anya I knew exactly the same amount

about childbirth as I do about the principles of thermodynamics – i.e. not a lot. The delivery room was full of hushed conversations between the medical staff that left me feeling like I was on holiday in a foreign country when the people at the table opposite are talking about you in a language you don't speak. You know they're talking about you but you're not quite sure if they're being nice or if they want to tell you to piss off, which is a bit disconcerting.

There were lots of medical terms I didn't understand, so instead of nodding along as if I was in a meeting where I wasn't paying attention, I decided to ask questions throughout. I probably annoyed the hell out of the midwives, but I needed to understand what was happening so that I could put my mind at rest. And in this situation, there really is no such thing as a stupid question. Hang on, I take that back. Asking, 'Can I go to the pub to catch the end of the football?' is definitely a stupid question, so don't ask that.

Had I had the knowledge I'd gleaned by the time we had the twins, I would have had the ability to make informed decisions and not rely on Clemmie to make them all. Maybe it was because she's a midwife and I assumed she'd make the right calls, or maybe I was burying my head in the sand as most emotionally repressed British people do, but whatever it was, I should have studied more and been more supportive. I'm told that I did well, but I can't help feeling that had I been at school, my report would have said something along the lines of 'Simon could and should have paid more attention. He has the potential to do well, but prefers to be the class clown and covers up his lack of knowledge with humour, which he uses at inappropriate times', promptly followed by a C grade for effort.

By the time we got around to having Ottilie and Delilah, however, I was a walking encyclopaedia of birth knowledge – not because I wanted to show off, but because I wanted to have an opinion on things and have my say.

DURING BIRTH

Killing time like a pro

Labour can be a quick process, especially if it's your second, third or fourth time at this particular rodeo, but for most people who are doing it first time around it can take a while. Birth never seems to go exactly as you plan and much like when you go to a gig, there's a lot of milling around before the main event kicks off.

With Anya, we rushed to the hospital. It was early afternoon and quite frankly I got bored quite quickly. Clemmie, being a midwife at the hospital we were in, was surrounded by her friends and colleagues, so after being there for two hours during which literally nothing happened other than a lady turning on some taps to fill a birthing pool, I took the opportunity to go and have a breather. After asking if Clemmie wanted any food as I was 'just nipping out', I got in the car, leaving my labouring wife in the capable hands of the midwives she knew and loved. Once there, I took a call from my mum in the car park and when I'd hung up, I drove straight past the nearby shops that I'd been intending to stop at, and drove on to my parents' house. The brief phone chat with my mum had resulted in her inviting me for lunch and I'd said yes. To be clear, at this point I hadn't told anyone that Clemmie was in labour, including my parents, so as we sat down for a good hour's lunch they were completely oblivious to the fact that Clemmie may well be giving birth to their first grandchild. I thanked them for lunch and promptly left to go back to the hospital, figuring that if Clemmie had needed me, the midwives would have called me.

I strolled back in, two hours after popping out for sandwiches and with the remains of a roast dinner around my face, looking contented and relaxed.

'Where the hell have you been?!' said a mildly uncomfortable Clemmie.

'Just to get some food – oh, and my parents say hi—'

'Your parents? When the hell did you see them? And where's my sandwich?'

'I just had lunch with them. Don't worry – I didn't tell them you were in labour or anything.'

The silence from both Clemmie and the midwives was deafening and suddenly it dawned on me that my decision to go and have a slap-up home-cooked meal probably couldn't have been made at a worse time. Mind you, my mum does do the best roast potatoes and if they'd tasted them, then they might have been slightly more sympathetic.

CrossFit pregnancy instructor

Contractions sometimes seem to have a mind of their own. One moment they're tightening away as regular as clockwork, the next they disappear like a biscuit that's been dunked in hot tea for too long.

While we were waiting for contractions to become stronger and more regular with the twins' birth, it was suggested to me that I should get Clemmie up and active. Visions of having to run down to Sports Direct to buy some kettlebells in order to do a complete CrossFit workout flashed before my eyes but then I came to my senses. What they meant was we should start walking around and find a decent set of stairs to pace up and down, so gravity could do its thing and get the baby down into the right position. When we finally located the fire escape, we discovered a traffic jam of pregnant women being frog-marched up and down the hallway by husbands and partners who were providing quiet words of encouragement to women who frankly would rather be lying on a bed somewhere. We did our pacing and step work and retired to the labour room. The exercise did the trick and before we knew it, Clemmie was contracting all over the place, only – much to everyone's frustration – for the contractions to fall away again.

In one of these lulls I was sent on a very important mission. Clemmie had a craving for ice throughout all of her pregnancies; I'm not sure if it was the coldness or the feeling of crunching it in her teeth, but whatever it was, it meant that there was always a full ice tray in the freezer at home and under no circumstances was I allowed to use any of it for my gin and tonics. But now we were not at home and I had to go and find some, and ice, I found out after a lengthy investigation, is a rare commodity in a hospital.

Then I was hit by a brainwave – hold on, I'm sure the high street has a number of fast-food places, they'll have ice! So off I set: down the stairs, out the doors, past all the people smoking in hospital gowns and down to the nearest Subway. In hindsight I should have just gone straight up to the counter and demanded ice as my labouring wife across the road was going to divorce me if I didn't return with it within ten minutes, but being British, I queued up like a good law-abiding customer for my cubes of frozen water. It took ages as it was lunchtime and the place was full of indecisive office workers who were obviously milking their lunch hour for everything it was worth. In the end I returned with two massive gulp-sized cups of ice and the remains of a 12-inch sub, which I'd bought for myself as a reward, promptly stinking the room out. It's a shame that Clemmie's lasting memory of the twins' birth is the aroma of meatballs and cheese exuding from my pores, but it's not my fault that she had a heightened sense of smell, is it? A man's got to eat, right?

Transition – from helpful to helpless in the blink of an eye

I've always thought it must be strange for Clemmie to go to hospital to give birth. She works with the people who are about to assist in bringing our child into the world. I'm not sure how I'd feel about my office colleagues seeing me butt naked, but then again, I doubt in the moment she cared that much, so I guess I shouldn't. They're professionals, after all.

Transition is the point at which you begin to actually push the baby out, and I remember clearly Clemmie reaching this stage at each birth because every time it happened, it scared the living shit out of me. I'm not kidding, I had to check my pants for skid marks.

As it's the last leg of the birth process you can see the light at the end of the tunnel (no pun intended) but it's also the hardest part to go through – for the observer as well as the labouring woman (albeit for different reasons). I found myself feeling as useful as a stapler with no staples. The noises coming from my tired and aching wife had changed from low grumblings into something that was reminiscent of the noises you'd hear in a farmyard – only I'm not talking about nursery rhyme-style chickens clucking or pigs oinking – it was more like a cow with depression that had tripped over onto a box of razor blades and broken all its ankles in the process: deep, primitive sounds that you're unlikely to hear anywhere outside of the delivery room.

The woman who had lugged our baby around for nine months was in acute pain and all I could really do was reassure her that I was there, that this was part of the process and that our baby was really close to arriving. It doesn't sound like much, I know, but that's the best I could muster and I know it made a difference as Clemmie regularly reminds me of how much it meant to her.

When Clemmie went through this with Anya, I really wasn't ready for how quickly the change would happen. It went from a Sunday drive in the countryside, stopping off for cakes and to browse overpriced antiques that we had no intention of buying, to doing a flying lap around a Formula 1 track at high speed in the time it takes to say 'What the hell's happened?!'.

All was going well. Clemmie was sucking away on the gas and air and everything seemed calm and tranquil – and then I made an error of judgement. I started to pour water over her back using a jug, which she seemed to like – in fact she was almost drifting off and there was a moment of serenity. Perhaps I was relaxed, too; perhaps I was being lulled into a false sense of security that this birth thing was simple and straightforward. Then I dropped a clanger. Before I could stop myself, the words 'this is just like pouring gravy over a big fat turkey' rolled out of my mouth.

I don't even know why I said it.

The midwives turned to stare at me like owls that had just heard a field mouse somewhere nearby; their eyes told me they were poised to sink their claws into my flesh yet they managed to keep grins plastered across their faces. Clemmie rose up like a killer whale from the water and drenched me, SeaWorld style. I probably deserved it. Another lesson learnt: don't ruin the mood of the room by being a dick and making wisecracks at inopportune moments. I still struggle to remember this lesson to this day.

With Marnie, Clemmie went into this phase of birth precisely at the moment when all the midwives had left the room and I became very aware that we were alone. I felt like a work experience kid who'd been left in charge of running Heathrow Airport for the day while everyone else sodded off to the bar – I knew I needed to do something, but had no clue as to what that was. Although I'm married to a midwife and I know a fair amount of detail about how the female body works and the mechanics of the birth process, and although I had seen Clemmie go through transition before, I genuinely thought something had gone horribly wrong and visions of bringing up my children alone in a caravan in my parents' garden, since I wouldn't be able to afford the mortgage on my own, zipped through my mind. No way was that happening. My parents wouldn't allow me to put a caravan on their lawn anyway, so with alarm bells going off in my head, I pulled the emergency cord and within fifteen seconds, four midwives burst in through the door ready to deal with whatever had happened. Once they'd established that it was only that she was close to giving birth, everything calmed down – the midwives laughed and Clemmie told me off for pulling the cord, but how the hell was I to know that was the wrong thing to do?! I felt a bit stupid for doing it but with hindsight, I'd do it again as I was on my own with my wife and didn't know what else to do. I didn't want to leave her side to go and find someone. Besides, at that point, I was like a salmon in an eagle's talons; Clemmie's nails were dug so hard and deep into my hand that she'd drawn blood and there was no way I could have got away without losing a limb. Mentioning that she was inflicting a fair amount of pain on me didn't seem like the right option at that point either.

With the twins, I was more prepared. I knew what was coming and could see the tell-tale signs. And yet, having been through this four times, I still haven't found the magical combination of words that helps to make the process easier in any way. I guess I'll keep trying – hang on, that implies we're having more, which we are definitely not (he says as he books himself for a vasectomy). The best advice I can give is to be close by, be as calm as possible and quietly reassure each other.

Oh – one last thing: I'm not going to write a whole paragraph on the subject, but a common concern of men, and even more of labouring women, is pooing during childbirth. (For what it's worth, I'm obviously talking about ladies pooing in labour here; if you're a man and you feel like you need to go to the toilet then you're allowed to go and find one.) I don't know what all the fuss is about, frankly, but here's what I do know: the movement of your little bundle of joy as he or she potholes down the birth canal can create a bit of pressure on the bowels. For some people, this may mean that a little bit of poo comes out. For others, it doesn't. It largely depends on the size of the takeaway you've had the night before.

In the end, though, it's a normal bodily function and if you're at the stage of having kids together, it's more than likely that you've walked in on each other while on the toilet, no doubt reading a magazine, playing Candy Crush on your phone or just staring blankly at the wall, so it's really not a big deal and definitely not something that either of you should worry about. If it does happen I doubt very much either of you will care or even notice as it's a little-known fact that midwives, besides being incredible people that help bring life into the world, are also excellent arse-wipers. Oh, look at that, I did write a whole paragraph about it.

POST BIRTH

I'm not a robot, I just don't cry.

Don't get me wrong, I'm not devoid of all human emotion, but I'm not a crier. When it comes to things happening in my life, I seem to have developed some kind of internal dam that holds back the production of tears and means I'm incapable of crying for joy or otherwise. This is probably some kind of twisted coping mechanism that's hardwired into my soul and no doubt a psychiatrist would tell me it's extremely unhealthy, but it works for me. So when it came to the births of all four of my daughters, my overriding emotion was relief that Clemmie was OK, and joy that my child – or children – was here safe and sound. But if I could go back and change anything, I'd try and cry a bit. Clemmie was, and I think still is to this day, genuinely annoyed that I didn't shed a tear at any of the births, and brings it up regularly – especially at dinner parties, which is just a riot for me.

The problem is I can't just turn it on like a garden sprinkler. I cry at *Forrest Gump* because I'm a sucker for a feel-good film and I cry at *The Shawshank Redemption* because of what Andy Dufresne went through and the strength of his friendship with Red, but that's pretty much it. Oh, and when the kids pull my body hair too hard. Other than that, my emotions stay in check.

So my advice to future dads (and this is tongue-in-cheek stuff, as there is no way you'll be thinking about this advice the moment your little one is born) is if you can squeeze some tears out it may be beneficial to you in the future – your other half's friends will love hearing about how you're a real modern-day man. If the worst comes to the worst, just go to the bathroom and splash a little water on your face and rub your eyes a lot so you too can avoid playing the lead role in the story of how you didn't cry at the birth of your child. A story that will get wheeled out on a fairly regular basis as a way of demonstrating what a heartless beast you are.

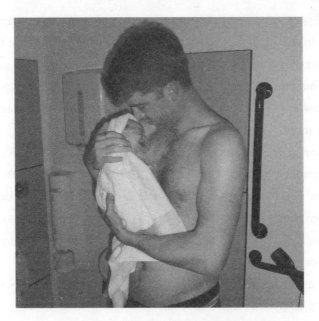

No, I don't have a fetish for revealing my
body to medical professionals. This is the all-
important first skin-to-skin contact which
I've done with each one of my daughters.

How to feel like a parent in under a second

Remember that moment in *The Lion King* when Simba is held up to
the world by some weird monkey fella on top of a windswept rocky
outcrop in a gesture that health and safety must have been having a
heart attack over? Well, this is an opportunity to re-enact that very
moment but hopefully without the safari animals around. After
nine months of talking to another person's swollen midriff, squint-
ing at scans of things that look half human, half squirrel and feeling

a small person try and re-enact a scene from *Alien* in your partner's stomach, you finally get to see and hold your child for the first time.

I'll never forget the first time I held each one of my four girls – it's a moment that stays with you. It's the moment that you're pinned with your invisible dad badge, which will be attached to you forever more.

I wasn't sure I believed in love at first sight. Lust, sure. But love? The moment I held my first daughter changed my opinion on this. Perhaps it was the hormones in the room, or the smell of her newborn skin, but as I held her next to my bare chest, I knew that it was love at first sight and it's been the same with every subsequent daughter that's come along.

You are no longer a young man, you are now classified as a parent and you now have the awesome responsibility of looking after another human being. That little person in your arms is looking to you to guide them through life. You'll be their role model as they grow, you'll be their shoulder to cry on when they're down and you'll be the person they celebrate with when they're up.

So as you gaze down at your new family member for the first time, give some thought to the journey both you and your partner have been on to get to this point and what the future holds for you all. It's quite something. Christ, I'm actually crying while writing this – turns out I'm not an emotionless robot after all!

4

Family life

I'm not very good at going to hospital when I'm
ill. It's not a hang-up about hospitals themselves,
it's just that every time I've been to one in
the last ten years, I seem to have come home
with more people than I went there with.

Family life

After Anya was born, I was kicked out of the hospital and sent home. It wasn't because I'd snuck a four-pack of beer into the room (although I'm sure that didn't help to show me in my best light), but because dads weren't allowed to stay overnight then. I'm not sure what they thought would happen if I stayed – I wasn't planning on stripping naked and running around the wards while taking selfies with sleeping people – but as a result, I spent my first night as a parent on my own.

Cast your mind back to the feeling you got as a kid on Christmas Day when you opened your present to find it was the thing you'd circled in the Argos catalogue in red biro and talked about for months. It's a good feeling, right? But then imagine that present was then put in a cupboard out of reach. The arrival of Anya, followed by being told I had to go home, felt something like that.

I'd been surrounded by people only to then be thrust into the quiet isolation of my own empty home, which left me feeling, well, a bit empty.

I'd only been in the presence of my daughter for a handful of hours, yet I was addicted to her. Her smell. Her tiny hands. Her squashed nose that I blame my parents for. I missed her, which sounds totally ridiculous when you think about it as only the day before, she hadn't been in my life, at least not as a person who wasn't contained within someone else's body. Then it slowly dawned on me that this might well be the last time I had a night on my own for a while, so I decided to celebrate. For my eighteenth birthday my parents had bought me three bottles of port from the year I was born (I hear 1982 was a good year). The idea was to open one when I got married, one when we had our first baby, and the last one was to give to one of my children. Well, I'd messed up the order slightly as we'd had the baby before the wedding, but sod it, I wanted to celebrate. As I peered into the mirror in the living room, I opened one of the dusty bottles, poured myself a glass to toast the start of my new life as a dad and smiled to myself. The smile was promptly replaced by a contorted retch as I spat the port out into the sink. The prized vintage bottle tasted like the smell of feet after they'd run a marathon without socks on in trainers that a dog had adopted as its chew toys. I brushed my teeth, turned out the light and went to bed, trying not to think about my new future too much and failing dismally as the smile returned to my face. Tomorrow was a big day.

The next morning, after some relatively messed-up anxiety dreams about dropping expensive breakable objects (my unconscious mind is so unsubtle), I got a call from Clemmie to say she and Anya were going to be discharged. I had the house tidy and everything was prepared for our baby to come home and start family life with us. The only job left was fitting the car seat, which somehow I'd managed to completely forget to purchase and had only bought that morning. Despite relatively clear instructions printed in twelve languages, I spent a long time wrestling this plastic and polystyrene monstrosity – which seemed to weigh more than I did after an all-you-can-eat blow-out barbecue – into position, moving seats back and forth, crawling into the car and whacking my head more than once. I finally figured out the mechanism to fit it using the seat belts, at which point I realised that my car had ISOFIX and what had taken twenty-five minutes could have been done in about ten seconds. The battle was over and I could head to the hospital at top speed to collect my family.

When we left the hospital, we wandered over to the car and slotted this tiny pink being into the car seat. It seemed to completely engulf her. We set off and although the drive from the hospital to the house was only 3 miles and I'd done it many times before, this time it was different. I was very aware there was a new life in the car with us that I was now responsible for and as a result my driving changed. Suddenly my hands were in the perfect ten to two position. I checked my mirrors every few seconds and changed gears so smoothly that a cat in silk pyjamas playing a saxophone would have had to congratulate me on my smoothness. I genuinely don't think the speedo passed 15 mph and I let more cars pull out in front of me at turnings and roundabouts than I ever have since.

Fast-forward eight years, and our family had swelled. We were now the proud owners of two daughters, with two more on the way, and things had changed. I had been allowed to stay the night at the hospital on what had been advertised to me as a pull-out bed. In reality, it was a chair that was covered in wipe-clean red leatherette fabric that you could remove the cushions from and sleep on on the floor. The house we'd be returning to was now also home to two girls who were anxiously waiting to become big sisters, and the concept of a silent night on my own was a distant pipe dream.

The car had been parked in the hospital car park overnight, so I strolled down to play the slot machine that no one ever wins and injected yet more money into the parking meter. I then went to retrieve the car seats, all the while harbouring a secret that no one else knew was knocking around in my head: 'I've got twins up there, and you don't know.' I felt very smug about this fact and I couldn't stop a grin spreading across my face as a gentle mist of rain fell from the heavens. Then as I walked back from the car with a car seat, it dawned on me. Oh Christ, we've got twins! And I've only got one car seat. Bollocks. I knew I was supposed to buy another one, but as per usual, life had got in the way and I'd become distracted before completing one of the most basic tasks I had on my list of dad jobs – make sure you can get everyone home safely.

The pride was still there, but it had retreated a little to be replaced by a touch of fear that this was all becoming very real.

I found my way back up to the ward through the rabbit warren of corridors by following rather confusing coloured stripes on the floor, like a tourist trying to figure out a tube map. Then Clemmie and I got into the lift down from the delivery suite, staring at each other in the mirrored doors, me with Ottie in the car seat and Clemmie with Delilah clutched against her chest, as it slowly clunked its way down to the ground floor. In relative silence, we walked over to the car, which was no longer big enough to fit all the family in at one time (I'd refused to admit to myself that we'd need a bigger one and had kept putting it off).

After wedging Ottie into position and securing the seat in place, I opened the door for Clemmie to sit in the back. Of course, as I did so, a mini waterfall comprised of forgotten toys and old crisp packets that the big girls had conveniently left there spilt out onto the pavement.

The big girls had been at home with Clemmie's mum but they were fully aware that two new sisters would be gatecrashing their cosy little set-up within the next twenty-four hours and would potentially change everything – and, at least in their minds, not in a positive way. That said, they did their best to hide their contempt for their newest siblings and outwardly seemed excited about their role in making them feel welcome.

What the hell do I do now?

With Anya, we arrived home and gingerly got out of the car so as not to wake up the precious new cargo. This was mainly because we wanted her to sleep, but also because if she started crying, we would immediately be thrown into the chaos and confusion that so many new parents experience. I carried Anya in the car seat and plonked her down, slap bang in the middle of the living-room floor.

Clemmie and I looked at each other and both said, 'So what the hell do we do now?'

We'd been so used to having people around us at the hospital telling us what to do that we were now acutely aware that we were on our own and no one had handed us any instructions. We did what most people do: made a cup of tea and left Anya to sleep because no one wanted to be the first one to wake her up.

The temptation to hold and play with your baby like a doll is undeniable, and for a long time Anya just lay in my arms, drifting in and out of consciousness to the rhythm of my chest movements as I took deep inhalations of her head. There is nothing quite like the smell of a newborn baby – if I had ovaries, I'm sure they would be twitching away at the aroma. The first day passed and the world around us seemed to take a deep breath and settle as the craziness of the last forty-eight hours drifted away. We were now on our own. Well, at least until the visitors turned up.

Put the kettle on – here come the visitors . . .

Once we'd left hospital the news quickly spread that we were back home with our new arrival – or arrivals, in the twins' case – so we needed to prepare ourselves for the onslaught of visitors.

VISITORS WE EXPECTED

First time around, I was a complete novice when it came to crowd control. I was a trainee bouncer who'd lost the guest list and just let everyone in to make my life easier, flooding the place with bodies and flouting all health and safety regulations. How was I to know that having so many people around was going to be so knackering and that they would outstay their welcome? Of course, over time I've learnt what to do, so perhaps you can use my experience as a shortcut to getting it right first time.

Much like on the release of a new iPhone, initially the crowds were deep at our door, all wanting to get their hands on this shiny new gizmo.

Within two days the house ended up looking like a florist had dumped all their old stock in our living room as the smell of many types of flowers pervaded the house. Of course, Clemmie loved the flowers, but getting to the bathroom involved taking a machete and a day's supply of water should we not be able to find our way back through the foliage.

We were also knee-deep in babygros with cleverly worded slogans splashed across them and toys that fell into two distinct categories:

1. Beautifully whittled wooden toys, no doubt responsibly sourced from mature, sustainably farmed pine forests in Scandinavia by skilled craftsmen in the age-old traditional way. Usually these were bought by other mums and dads, grandparents and those that just simply liked the aesthetics of them. In reality half of these ended up on a shelf in the bedroom as they were deemed too nice to let the kids get their grubby mitts on them, which is actually pretty twisted when you think about it. Toys in plain sight in a child's room that are just out of reach and that they aren't allowed to play with? That's like putting a starving person in front of a three-course meal but not allowing them to gorge themselves. And what if *Toy Story* is real? These guys would be social outcasts, having not been allowed to integrate into toy society. They'd simply be known as the shelf

toys, who thought they were too good to mix with the rabble below and would slowly but surely give everyone else an inferiority complex.

2. Battery-operated flashing plastic toys that made the type of noises you would expect to be played to someone under interrogation. These were the kind of toys that we didn't want around as they drove us insane, but toy designers know their market – these flashing pieces of hard plastic depicting the children's TV character of the moment act in the same way a can of cola does to wasps on a hot day. Kids are drawn to them and although initially I was quietly cursing the people who bought them, especially when their noises and tunes were still going round my head when I was trying to sleep, I had to thank them as they did a good job distracting the little ones and buying us time to get on with things.

Some people actually didn't bring a gift and instead asked if we wanted or needed anything. My reply was always home-cooked food that we could freeze as we didn't have the time or energy to cook things ourselves. Our freezer was stuffed with lasagne and shepherd's pie and in fact I'm pretty sure that under the ice, there's one still in there somewhere that's the same age as the twins. Perhaps we'll eat it on their eighteenth birthday. Then again, perhaps not, unless we want the party to be centred around people vomiting.

The other thing that made me think, 'Ahh, that's so thoughtful,' was when people brought gifts for the big girls. With all the attention on the two newest Hooper additions, it would have been easy for Anya and Marnie to feel left out as many older siblings do when a new version of them turns up and starts to steal all the limelight.

However, some of our friends and family put real thought and effort into getting them something too, which made them feel more a part of it all and less like a couple of Nokia 3210s that had been tossed to the back of the kitchen drawer and forgotten about after an upgrade. It was also great to see people talking to them about how nursery or school was going when I didn't have time to be with them during the craziness of the visitor phase, as it went a long way to reducing the amount of parent guilt that was pressing heavily on my shoulders.

VISITORS WE DIDN'T EXPECT

People just dropping round can be wonderful as it's nice to get a surprise and it shows that people care. However, it can also be a total pain in the arse, especially in those first couple of weeks. You suddenly find yourself having to tidy up to convince people you've got your shit together, and dole out the nice biscuits that you were saving for yourselves as all the previous well-wishers have polished off the digestives and rich tea biscuits you bought for them.

For us, it wasn't just about unexpected visits from dear friends, there were also some even bigger surprises. It wasn't just a case of me not following the 'Don't speak to strangers' rule that I'd spent years drumming into my kids, I went one further and let someone in that I didn't even recognise. Clemmie had been at home with the twins for a couple of days and I was still on paternity leave so was knocking about the house, trying to make it sound like I was being useful, but actually not doing a huge amount other than making endless cups of tea. Having heard the doorbell ring, I opened the door to find a nice lady who had brought some smoothies round for

Clemmie. I didn't quite catch her name but being polite, I invited her in nonetheless, assuming she knew Clemmie (after all, she knew where we lived and Clemmie has so many friends I can never remember them all). I sent the lady up to the bedroom to say 'hi' to Clemmie, who was busy being a mobile restaurant – i.e. tandem feeding the twins. It was only when the lady left some ten minutes later that I heard Clemmie yelling my name. I was being summoned upstairs.

'Who the hell was that?!'

'Wasn't she one of your friends?'

'No! I've never met her before in my life and you sent her up while I had my tits out.'

On reflection, I really should have asked the random woman at my door a bit more about herself. It wouldn't have taken a lot to determine if this person should be invited in to see my wife's engorged breasts. 'So how do you know Clemmie?' would have sufficed. Oh well, you live and learn.

VISITORS WHO DIDN'T REALLY VISIT AT ALL

The visitors I really appreciated were the ones that didn't actually knock on the door or want to come in. A couple of times I got a message on my phone that simply read, 'We've left something for you outside your door – let us know when you're ready to see people as we'd love to come over and help you for a bit.' Outside the front door was a basic shop that some of our friends had done for us, with a few treats thrown in – magazines, chocolate, a bottle of wine and home-cooked lasagne, accompanied by a note.

It was probably the most thoughtful thing that anyone had done for us – perhaps it's because they were parents themselves and knew the kind of gift that would really hit the spot. Whatever the reason, it was well received.

So having been through three rounds of managing visitors, what pearls of wisdom can I share with you?

- If your partner is in bed, for God's sake, make her stay in bed. Visitors can come to her, unless she really wants to get up to avoid boredom. Labour was no walk in the park and Clemmie needed to rest, so visitors making the trip up to the bedroom was the least they could do. Meanwhile cleaning the house, making cake, partaking in idle chit-chat and serving tea to guests became my domain.
- Try and limit the time that people stay if possible. Visitors can be like the dregs of a house party: you know the ones I'm talking about – the music has stopped, you're clearing up and daylight is peeking through the window, yet there are still three or four people milling around, trying to chase the fun. Get the message, people, your time's up and we have stuff to do now! I'm not saying that to deal with all the visitors and well-wishers you need to develop some overly complicated ticketing system like the one at the supermarket deli counter, although I can see how that might play out:

'OK, number 57 – that's you, Auntie Sarah – pay attention or you'll have to take another ticket and start at the back of the queue. Right, you've got thirty minutes, keep your hands where I can see them and place all hot drinks down there on the side table. If you have a present, give it to me for vetting first and I'll place it somewhere where it'll get mixed up with all the others. You can expect a relatively non-descript generic "Thank You" card in a couple of weeks in which we'll make every effort to not actually mention the gift you gave us because we don't know which one is yours. In all honesty, it's your fault as you should have written your name on the wrapping paper.'

Leaving the house for the first time

After three days of being at home with Anya, and as the number of knocks on the door dwindled, we started to develop a common affliction that parents suffer from – cabin fever. We'd been staring at the same walls for seventy-two hours with only a couple of trips to the local shop to replace all the stuff that had been used by our guests – milk, tea, biscuits, bread, toilet roll – and to stock up on large amounts of Galaxy chocolate for Clemmie.

Then on day four we both decided we needed to get out and go for a walk around the block.

After an initial wrestle with the buggy and a struggle to establish how the footbrake worked, we set off looking like a couple straight from the pages of the Mothercare catalogue – our new parenting equipment gleamed in the sunlight and a bag was packed with enough baby products to survive a week in the wilderness, should we somehow make a wrong turn at the shops and find ourselves in the Australian outback.

Pride turned to concern. I became acutely aware that everything in the world was a potential death trap – and I mean everything. The old lady making a beeline for us from the other side of the street to come and have a look in the buggy? God knows what diseases she's breathing all over the place, and that coffee cup she's holding – what if she trips and pours the entire contents into the pram, leaving my baby with a permanent disfigurement? Or, worse, what if the contents are actually neat whisky and she's a mad alcoholic who wants to grab my newborn child and sell her on the black market so that she can afford yet more booze? It's amazing how protective you can become of something you've only had for four days.

Cars are driving way too quickly down the street. The signs say 20 mph, people, yet you must be doing at least 70 as you flash by in a blur of metallic blue and bass-heavy tunes that rattle the windows of the shops lining the road. Slow down! Don't you know I have the world's most precious and beautiful creation snoozing in this ridiculously expensive all-terrain super-utility buggy?

People shopping on the high street all seem suspicious to me now. Why the long coat in 22-degree heat? Who's that person talking to on the phone in hushed tones and why is that woman taking so long to look at pastry products in the window of that shop – she's no doubt using the reflection from the glass to watch where we're heading. Put all this together and it's obvious to me that there's some kind of child-snatching ring operating in my area that I've never noticed before.

And what's with all the birds today? Are those pigeons, or are they in fact a flock of eagles (eagles come in flocks, right?) that are hell-bent on swooping down in attack formation and carrying off my pride and joy while I watch in disbelief, forcing me to resign myself to the fact that my daughter will now be brought up by birds and live in a nest somewhere, never to be found again.

OK, I'm exaggerating, but you get the picture. I immediately had a greater sense of what was going on around me, hyper-aware that the tiny little being in front of me was my responsibility out in the big, wide, scary world.

We took baby steps with our outings to start with: little trips to the shops, then trips to the park, and finally out for lunch to a local restaurant or pub. And this is an important step forward in your lives, as it can be all too easy to stay in the comfort of your own home.

Of course, trips that should only have taken a total of ten minutes door-to-door became elongated as strangers stopped to talk. It seemed that as soon as we had a baby, I transformed from an unapproachable mid-twenties male to a respectable member of society, and it was now OK to come and talk to me.

The nocturnal adventures of family life

One of the biggest changes that we went through when we went from being a couple to being parents was the realisation that the nights were no longer for lock-ins at the local pub, eating kebabs, watching awful movies or sleeping. They became an extension of the day, just with less light. Having been several times through the parenting cycle of getting no sleep, getting some sleep and finally back to a full night's sleep again, I can tell you that there are some hard lessons to learn when it comes to what happens when the lights go out at night . . .

As a parent, you will become partially nocturnal for at least the first year of your child's life

No one enjoys not getting enough sleep, as it can make you as much fun to be around as a bear who's woken from hibernation to find he's been hit with a huge energy bill as he forgot to turn off the heating before he took his three-month snooze. Pre-children, the only legitimate reasons for sleep deprivation were:

- Going out to overpriced nightclubs to buy diluted drinks, eating questionable kebabs on the way home and falling asleep in the back of taxis that you didn't have enough money to pay for.
- Being paranoid that you haven't locked the front door and hearing a creaking noise downstairs that you're almost certain is someone stealing your beloved TV. Either that or it's the heating system cooling down.
- Sex (the very thing that leads to the demise of a pre-child life).

Despite not being the one who's breastfeeding, you will be up as much as the person with the boobs

I'm not sure how this happened and I certainly don't remember agreeing to it, but Clemmie was finding it hard to sleep with the baby next to her in the crib, so the crib was swiftly transported to its new location: my side of the bed. Oh joy. The theory was that as a guy, I could sleep through the noises without my nipples starting to tingle and leak milk everywhere. However, with the move, I discovered I now had a new job. Previously my brain would reduce my energy consumption when asleep and shut down all non-vital body parts including my ears, allowing me to sleep soundly through the night feeds. I would wake in the morning and proclaim, 'I can't believe she slept through, that's amazing!' only to find out that this had not been the case. Clemmie would stare at me with a grey, gaunt face, a changed nappy on the floor and a sleeping baby in her arms, softly muttering the words, 'Are you fucking kidding me . . .' However, with the change of crib position I found myself in the role of a UPS delivery man, responsible for putting the light on and passing the baby over to the human dairy farm – otherwise known as my snoring wife – in order to relieve some of the pressure in her swollen mammary glands. I personally don't think I added anything to this process and could have easily been cut out, but Clemmie assures me that the change was essential.

There is no good way of making up bottles in the night without getting out of bed

After Clemmie packed in tandem feeding the twins and moved on to bottles, I suddenly found that we were sleeping in separate rooms, each with one twin, and I was now jointly responsible for feeding. The gravy train of unbroken sleep had been derailed and gone up in a ball of flames with no survivors.

Personally I found that the most painful part of the whole night feed wasn't the feeding itself, but having to go downstairs to make up the bottle, which woke everyone else up and made it impossible to get back to the land of nod in a decent time. There had to be a way around this; all I needed to do was apply my logical brain to the problem and come up with a solution. After much time spent thinking about it while on the loo (it's the only place I get to think these days), I hit upon a brilliant plan.

Solution 1: I'd sleep with a ready-made bottle between my thighs at night, ready to issue the much-needed milk at a moment's notice. I was officially a genius. I'd created a shortcut to the perfect bottle temperature which didn't involve getting out of bed and required minimal effort. It worked for several weeks until one night the bottle lid came undone. In the middle of the night I woke to a completely soaked crotch. Oh Christ, had I become a horny fourteen-year-old kid again and had a wet dream? No, I'd just doused my boxer shorts with 6 oz of formula milk, which was sticky and smelt rank.

OK, back to the drawing board. Still not wanting to get out of bed because, well, who does, I had to revise my initial plan so that my 'little accident' didn't happen again.

Solution 2: With a few tweaks, I moved on to night feed 2.0. This involved taking a bottle of pre-measured formula powder to bed, along with a flask of boiling water and a bottle of cold water. When Delilah made it known she wanted milk, I'd make the bottle up by pouring in hot water a third of the way and then topping it off with cold water. Bingo. I had made my very own baby-milk cocktail bar beside my bed and it worked a charm. That was until I knocked over the boiling water one night and was left with a proper mess that involved a trip downstairs not only to make up another bottle, but also to locate the carpet cleaner, which was not what I wanted to be doing at 2.30 a.m.

Solution 3: Finally I found something that worked. We bought a bottle machine that makes up bottles at the perfect temperature in a minute. This was a real game-changer and genuinely saved me from being a complete sleep-deprived wreck. For the next three months, it sat in the spare room between my single bed and Delilah's cot, ready to jump into action at the touch of a button.

If you fall asleep with a baby in the bed, you will wake up in a cold sweat convinced you've suffocated them

No one tells you this, but babies have the ability to breathe in a similar fashion to that of an experienced free-diver – so shallowly that they appear to not be breathing at all. (Babies would genuinely be really good extras in scenes set in a morgue – you know, the bit in a drama where you stare so intently at the chest of the actor who's lying on the slab to see if you can catch them breathing, and in the process totally ignore any of the dialogue that's being said.) This really fucked me up. On several occasions, I've been convinced that one of my children is no longer alive – it's one of those moments when your heart stops, drops out through your arse and runs away to hide under the stairs. Visions of being unable to forgive myself and wondering how to live with the grief and guilt filled my head. I was going to have to explain to my wife what had happened, she would forever hold it against me, which would eventually lead to divorce and my moving to a bedsit somewhere, putting on huge amounts of weight and finally having to be hoisted out of my own house to be loaded onto a flatbed lorry to transport me to hospital for life-saving surgery. Then, of course, after a little prod and a bit of blowing on the face, my precious daughter would snort in a big gulp of air and the visions of my alternative future would dissipate, and with them so too would the chances of me going back to sleep.

Yes, this was completely against the manufacturer's guidelines, but when your wife has been out for the first time in a year and needs child-free 'special sleep' thanks to all the cocktails, it's important to have easy access for those night feeds.

But when they get older it gets easier, right?

I don't want you to finish this chapter thinking that once they start sleeping through, it's all plain sailing, as that's not the case. Sleep regression is a real thing. Just when we thought we had it nailed, at about the nine-month mark, each of our babies felt that we were having it way too easy and for no apparent reason, decided to start waking up again in the night. The eye-bags that had started to recede came back in full force as we embarked on another round of nocturnal baby bouncing. This regression didn't last too long, but it helped to remind us how good we'd had it when they slept through, and just who was in charge of our sleep patterns.

Luckily, we've now got to the stage where from 9 p.m. onwards, all four of the girls are asleep and we can be 95 per cent sure that we won't be woken again until the morning, but we're still subjected to infrequent night-time intrusions, usually resulting from either a nightmare or someone about to violently vomit, so as a final parting gift I thought it was important to leave you with a little story.

Anya had never been physically sick in the nine years I'd known and loved her. Then nine months ago she popped her puking cherry in style, and of course it happened in the middle of the night when Clemmie was working a night shift at the hospital.

I could hear noises directly above our bedroom at about 2.30 a.m. and initially thought nothing of it, but as the noises grew louder I realised it wasn't the usual tossing and turning in bed, but someone walking around. Then came the blood-curdling call that parents never want to hear in the dead of night – 'MUMMMMY!

DADDDDDYYYY!' I bolted out of bed, ran up the stairs and swung open the door. As I did so, the door acted like a wave machine and sent a tidal surge of vomit back into the room. As the tide receded and came to rest, it washed gently over my toes. Poor Anya was hunched on the floor crying. In her confused state and with no light to guide her, the poor girl hadn't been able to orientate herself and find the door to get to the bathroom, resulting in a real-life *Exorcist* moment of projectile vomiting against the bedroom door.

After escorting Anya to the toilet and holding her hair back, with Clemmie at work it fell to me to get down on my hands and knees to clear up the sea of sick that had covered everything in a 180-degree radius of where Anya had been standing. It was on the door, her bed, the wall, her books, her dressing gown, the collection of soft toys at the end of her bed and of course my feet (there's nothing quite like the sensation you get from cleaning someone else's sick out from between your own toes). This was when I learnt several very important lessons:

- You will always need more kitchen roll than you think to clear up sick.
- Always turn the light on before you enter a room so you can see what you're about to potentially step in.
- Don't feed people food from plastic tubs in the fridge when you have no idea how long they've been there.

After picking up chunks of another person's partially digested food, I've decided that it's really not something that I want to make a career out of, but I doubt very much that it'll be the last time. I've still got the teen years to come where they start experimenting with alcohol, and if they're anything like me at fifteen, I fully expect to be kneeling beside them, rubbing their backs and passing them water while they pray to the porcelain gods and swear never to steal alcohol from the kitchen cupboard again.

Looking back at all of this, I am genuinely shocked that the human race hasn't just died out in a sleep-deprived mess on the floor. Despite all the trials that newborns bring with them, so many of us jump back onto the parenting rollercoaster for another ride. Oh, how quickly we forget the dark times, but as soon as we go for the second, third – or, like us, fourth – it all comes screaming back to us. It just goes to prove that although sleep deprivation is a UN-recognised form of torture, it's something you can live with and still come out the other side of – with a twisted version of Stockholm syndrome that leaves you wanting more into the bargain.

5

Welcome to your new social lives

Getting down the street can be a slow process when you have babies. Before children, I was just another unapproachable guy you thought might mug you, but with children in tow, I'm now an upstanding member of society and get politely interrogated by complete strangers about my personal life. Yes, they're all mine! I'm not in the kiddy-snatching business.

Welcome to your new social lives

*I*f our lives, both domestic and social, were small industrial towns, the girls would be jointly appointed mayor and council, since they are, fundamentally, in charge. It's just the natural way of things when every waking hour, apart from the 180 minutes between getting your children to sleep and following them to bed yourself, is spent focused on their needs.

It's therefore no surprise that Clemmie and I, who both had relatively busy social lives before we had kids, see less and less of the people we were friends with before we blindly embarked on our meandering journey into parenthood. Instead we find ourselves spending time with an increasing number of the people that we've been introduced to through having our girls: friends from postnatal classes, the kids' friends' parents, teachers, sports coaches, and other parenting bloggers we've met through Instagram. The sorts of people you will most likely find yourself spending time with from now on include, but are not limited to, the following:

Other parents

Believe it or not, unless you live on a small island off the coast of Scotland of which you're the only inhabitants, you are not the only ones to have had a baby recently in your area. You may well have met other parents-to-be through classes you attended while pregnant, by walking in the park and chatting to the nice-looking couple who have the same buggy and baby bag as you, or through friends who have introduced you to other friends who have just had a baby. This is great as you immediately have something in common to bond over. But this meeting of new people is the start of a shift in your social circle that will no doubt change shape more and more over the months and years that follow. Old friends (unattached bachelors living in east London who party every night and pretend they're still twenty-one) will make a dutiful visit once in a blue moon but you'll slowly realise that you can't go out whenever you feel like it any more and the life your friends lead is suddenly not so appealing either. Although vodka and Coke mixes well in the club as the night rolls on, hangovers and looking after babies the next day don't.

Of course you're still friends, but the fact is that your lives have started to splinter off in different directions and until they have kids, it's unlikely your paths will cross as frequently as they did before.

Competitive parents

As your child develops and becomes a functioning little person, if not exactly a contributing member of society, you'll start to want to crow about their achievements. Don't worry – it's natural. But I've got to warn you, you're not the only one that has children and your friends will be showing off too.

You can find yourself in a conversation with someone, covering all the idle chit-chat from the weather and current affairs to who's now sleeping with who on your favourite TV soap, yet as soon as you start to venture into discussing your kids, the conversation essentially becomes selfish. You surreptitiously ask questions that will steer the conversation towards an area in which your child has recently achieved something. You'll politely listen to the other person tell their story, and nod along like a boardroom full of executives who really couldn't care less until your chance comes.

For example:

'How's little Casper getting on with sport – have you enrolled him in any clubs at all?'

The person asking this question has recently joined their daughter up to a local gymnastics club. OK, it's the tots' roll-around session, but they are really proud that the instructor/coach/person in charge of twelve three-year-olds has said that their little girl is particularly flexible and strong. Starting this conversation off has given the parent the perfect opportunity to talk about this, while also making them seem like a nice inquisitive person. Genius.

Most people's favourite topic is themselves. Most sentences start with 'I' and I'm not saying that's a bad thing, it's just in our nature to pull from personal experience as that's what we've lived and can therefore talk about fluently. When we become parents, instead of 'I', we start to broaden out and talk about the achievements or experiences of those closest to us, i.e. our kids.

The kids' friends' parents

Getting the girls over to friends' houses for an afternoon or, better yet, a sleepover, should be a time for celebration – after all, it buys us valuable time to focus on the twins, or time to get the house straight (yes, it will be turned upside down when they return, but for a couple of hours it will look more like a nice home and less like a stable used to contain disruptive animals).

The challenge with going to friends' houses isn't the drop-off: Anya and Marnie couldn't be happier to be leaving the confines of their own home so as we approach their mate's front door, they run ahead and the door's opened by a tired-looking parent who I imagine was in the process of clearing up homemade slime, or is trying their best not to look like they've just had a blazing row with their partner about not disciplining their kids to the same standard. My daughters briefly acknowledge the existence of the parent with a quick 'Hi' and then shoot straight into the house and out of sight, leaving us parents to carry out the standard 'at the door' conversation, which is especially difficult if you don't know them that well.

'Hi, love, how are you doing?'

(Note that if this is a relatively new friend, the parent may avoid saying your name as although you've exchanged pleasantries in the school playground, they can't quite remember what to call you – expect lots of 'love', 'sweetie', 'fella', 'dude' or just skirting around sentences to sidestep the need for names at all.)

'Fine, thanks. Just a bit tired. Sorry we're late, we were having issues this morning.'

'I know the feeling. Do you want to come in for a quick drink?'

(This is probably a genuine offer, but you've clocked that they're not really dressed yet, so decide it's better not to. Besides, you want to maximise the amount of child-free time you have at home, so why cut into that by sipping tea in someone else's house when you could be doing it on your own sofa?)

'No, I'm good, I've got to shoot. We've got loads to do today, but thanks for the offer' – said while looking down at my wrist, which doesn't even have a watch attached to it.

'OK, no problem. What time do you want to pick her up?'

The answer I want to give is, 'In a couple of weeks', but etiquette doesn't allow for that. So my actual response is, 'Around 6-ish, is that OK?'

'Sure, no problem, but she might as well stay for tea in that case as we eat around that time.'

Quelle surprise! six p.m. was not a random time I picked out of the air. I know most people's kids eat around that time and I was secretly hoping they'd offer to feed my child as it's one less mouth to feed at home.

'That's really kind, thanks. Right, gotta run – you've got my number if you need to get in touch. See you later.'

Note that I avoided saying their name too. I'm pretty sure it was Katie, but why run the risk of looking like a dick who doesn't pay attention or remember names? No one wants that embarrassment standing in someone else's doorway at nine thirty on a Sunday morning.

I shout into the house towards no one in particular, 'Right, I'm going – be good, please, and I'll pick you up later. Please have your stuff together.'

The pick-up is more of an issue, since invariably my child will have decided that rather than go back to their own boring house, which is full of their own boring crap, they want to stay.

For the next fifteen minutes the other parent and I wander around the house, looking for my daughter who has decided to hide. I guess she's thinking that if I don't find her, I'll just leave and she can then see out the rest of her days with an entirely different family, living with her best friend in a perfect utopia where they play all day and no one tells them to do anything.

As I thinly disguise my rising stress levels by forcing a laugh into my voice and making comments like 'Oh, these kids!' to the other parent who is performing the same charade, I finally hear a giggle coming from a cupboard on the landing. There, behind the water tank, is my daughter. She's in a completely different set of clothes to the one she arrived in, barefoot and with her face covered in make-up in a similar style to that of a drag act that was running late for a burlesque show and had got prepared in a room with poor lighting and no mirrors. Another ten minutes will pass before she finally realises that the stand-off isn't going to end well for her.

The car journey home is silent apart from the occasional muttering from the back seat of '[insert friend's name]'s parents would never make them leave'. My mental response is, 'Well, maybe you should go and live with them then', but I'm pretty sure that's what she wants me to say. Manipulated by a child. Again.

Dad mates – a type of friendship I never knew existed

When you're a first-time parent, you enter into a world of baby groups, mothers' meetings and postnatal classes. It's like speed dating for new parents, where you get to compare notes on how you're doing in comparison to other people in your local area, while also meeting people who might actually be worth hanging out with. Mums are great at this. I'm not sure if it's because they are naturally more sociable creatures, or because they need to speak to people other than the small ball of flesh they are responsible for at home otherwise their heads will explode. Either way, ladies lead the way when it comes to making new friends. Of course that then means we dads are brought along to make polite conversation with the other mums' partners.

My first experience of meeting other dads was when we'd just moved to London for my job. Anya was five weeks old and Clemmie and I had moved into a basement flat in Herne Hill. The flat had as much natural light as a well-sealed cardboard box, and in the winter the drains would overflow after heavy rainfall, meaning our little place would smell like a sewage works after a national drive to flush all toilets at the same time on the same day.

I'm not sure if this is an inbuilt trait in all women, but my wife loves to play match-maker. Clemmie came back from a mum meeting one day with a glint in her eye which I knew meant I was about to be forced to do something that I probably didn't want to. In their infinite wisdom, the hive mind of the mums had made the decision that all their socially reclusive husbands, who liked nothing more than working on creating deep arse imprints on the sofa after being at work all day, should be forcibly removed and made to meet up with each other. Initially the idea was floated to me as follows:

'I'm seeing my friend Sarah tomorrow from the mum group – you should go and have a beer with her husband Tom and do some dad bonding. He likes cycling too. I think there are a few other dads going.' My knee-jerk response of 'That so sounds like something I don't either want, or have time, to go to' was met with a look that told me if I didn't take her up on her suggestion then I might be subjected to an amateur testicle removal, and just like that, my calendar suddenly opened up.

Despite my initial reservations, meeting other guys who looked as tired as I did and who were going through the same life alterations as me was worthwhile. I have to admit that I found it useful to discuss the old life I'd left behind, how my wife was driving me up the wall, and compare notes on how our houses now smelt like baby poo.

I walked the short distance to the Duke of Wellington and opened the doors to find a table of six shattered-looking guys, complete with a full set of matching luggage under their eyes, none of whom was sure if they wanted to be there or not. I worried I'd have nothing in common with these men who were all a good few years older than me, and having convinced myself that my quota of friends was full and anyone else would be surplus to requirements, I decided I would be polite, neck a pint or two and do as Clemmie had asked, but then probably not see them again and go about my life being self-contained and self-reliant. What followed in the next fifteen minutes could only be described as speed dating for dads. We introduced ourselves by stating who our partners were, then we all chatted politely while avoiding going on about ourselves too much and instead asking how the other person was getting on, as well as covering all the other basics you do on a date: what job you do, where you live, etc. As the evening drew on and the empty glasses filled the table like transparent skittles waiting to be knocked over by a gesticulating arm, I realised something: these guys may have had a few more creases across their foreheads than me and a few more grey hairs, but they were going through exactly the same stuff as I was. They weren't acting old or too serious, in fact they were just like my mates – the difference being that they understood when I said the last time I'd slept for more than two hours straight was three months ago and that my living room was now a dangerous obstacle course of baby clutter. These men sitting with me under-stood, because they were living it too.

I wandered home a little the worse for wear and Clemmie was still up feeding Anya.

'Did you have a nice time?' she asked without looking up.

'You know what – I actually did.'

Some of these guys are still in my life now and I can count them as true friends, but when you're four kids deep, the idea of going to the baby groups and having to go through the whole parenting speed-dating scene again is too much to handle. It's not that we didn't want to meet new people, it's just that this time, being parents already meant that we didn't want to talk about all the stuff that the newbies did. We'd been there, done it and bought all the T-shirts. We're now in a different stage on the parenting roller-coaster so the common ground isn't there with new parents. Also we just don't have the time to socialise as any spare time we have (and I use that term very loosely) is spent doing family stuff. The only thing I do feel bad about is that the twins don't have any friends to speak of, which is definitely something that the older girls gained from us socialising more, but then again they've got each other. Besides, who wants us for a playdate? The other kid would be totally outnumbered and forgotten within minutes of setting foot in our house. We've probably done everyone else a favour!

Strangers who want to talk to you because you have children

As a guy I'm not likely to go up to a stranger carrying a baby and strike up a conversation. If I did, I'm sure the first thing the person would be thinking is, 'What the hell does this weirdo want and why is he asking me these questions? Is he trying to sell me something or is he about to give me a monologue about how Christ can save my soul? Perhaps he's one of those charity workers that I crossed the street to avoid earlier. Be polite so he doesn't hurt us and walk away.'

Women, however, seem to be totally OK about striking up a conversation with me when I'm out with the girls. I'm not against it in any way, shape or form as I know the sight of four blonde-haired girls with a single man has the attractive properties of a supercooled electromagnet, but they do sometimes catch me off guard.

I don't know if being on my own makes me more approachable, but it seems that people who want to strike up a conversation have the same inbuilt timing as predatory cats: they strike when their prey is at its weakest. For me, this is usually when I'm trying to corral the older girls on scooters back towards me and away from the road, while I wrestle one twin who's performed a Houdini and broken free of her constraints back into the buggy, and retrace my steps to find the other one's dummy which was dropped *somewhere* between the house and where we currently are.

Over the last ten years there have been many of these scenarios and I have held many conversations with complete strangers that cover every part of the parenting spectrum you can imagine. Here's my run-down of the top five standard lines that I've encountered.

1. **'Dad's out on his own – where's Mum? Are you giving her a break?'**

   These are just some of the patronising words that dads get thrown at them on a fairly frequent basis. It's like there's an assumption that dads are somehow either incapable of looking after babies without the supervision of wives/girlfriends, or struggling in some way that mothers don't. I may look like a lumbering octopus with my arms all over the place and beads of stress-sweat rolling down my forehead, but I've got this relatively under control. Even if I didn't, I certainly wouldn't admit I'm struggling to a stranger unless I needed real assistance, because that would help me in precisely zero ways apart from making me feel like a big fat failure. So here are some go-to responses that I've created to flummox my interrogators:

'She's actually left me.'

'She said she didn't really want to be a mum any more so she's moved to Ibiza to be a yoga instructor. I believe she's now dating an aromatherapist called Lesley.'

'She's behind you' (then run away when they turn around).

Why do you want to know? Are you a stalker? Or a burglar who's essentially checking if my house is empty so you can go and take my collection of cuff-links that I haven't worn for at least three years or my sports kit that's tucked away in a box from when I actually used to play sport? Or is this in fact an elaborate phishing scam in which after five minutes you'll be walking away knowing all my personal details including my card number and PIN?

2. **'Well done you for getting out and about!'**

Do I look like a geriatric? Do you see me with a Zimmer frame trundling down the street? Do I look like someone with acute agoraphobia? The answer to all of these is 'No', unless you've caught me on a bad face day and mistaken me for a ninety-year-old man – and even then, I'm not going to be dressed in head-to-toe beige, so you should be able to tell the difference.

3. **'Ahhhh, he's lovely. What's his name?'**
People will often make assumptions about the sex of my baby without any thought or observation of the tell-tale signs that suggest whether it's a boy or a girl (i.e. the fact that it's all dressed in pink and has a bow on its head which is clinging to the small wisp of hair you managed to locate on what is other-wise a bare desert of inactive follicles).

To me, making an assumption that a child is a certain gender is almost as bad as making eye contact with a large woman while on public transport, assuming she's pregnant and then offering her your seat – only to discover that she's just large.

Surely the rule of thumb should be that unless you're 100 per cent sure, just don't mention it.

4. **'Are they all yours?'**
No, I've just been to the local park and scooped up a collection of random children whose parents are now panicked out of their minds.

5. **'That's a lot of girls. Are you going to try for a boy next?'**
Are you insane?! I have four children and that's enough for me. Also, why is there this assumption that because I have all girls, I'm somehow not fulfilled or I'm dissatisfied with what I have already. My girls are my life.

The twinning inquisition

If you have twins, it's even worse. Standard one-liners that are in no way meant to help or provide support include the following:

1. **'You've got your hands full there!'**
   This one especially pisses me off as it's not even a conversation-starter; the speaker is simply making a statement that your life looks like fucking hard work in comparison to theirs as they stroll off with a wry smile across their face at the completely unoriginal and witless remark they've made. They don't even give me time to reply, 'Well, actually it's fine. We don't know any different and if anything my household is probably more efficient than yours and my elder children more helpful as we all need to work together as a team. Go stick that in your pipe and smoke it!' Of course, what I actually do is smile, push a small muffled laugh out from between my gritted teeth and move on.

2. **'I don't know how you cope.'**
   There's an easy remedy for that. I don't know you from Jack, but why don't you come round to my house at 6.30 a.m. tomorrow? My wife and I are pretty tired so we could do with a break. We'll be back by 8.30 p.m. to see how you 'coped'.

3. **'I'd struggle to tell them apart.'**
   To be fair, I still struggle to tell the twins apart and I play up to it a bit. Women seem to be able to pick up on the differences

between twins a lot quicker than men. Perhaps I'm face blind, or perhaps I'm just not paying attention as I'm more focused on keeping them alive and happy collectively, rather than as individuals. Whatever it is, for the first twenty months of Ottilie and Delilah's lives, I simply referred to them as 'the twins', or 'this one' and 'that one' – that might sound like a joke, but I'm deadly serious. I'm hoping that by the time they go to school I'll be able to tell the difference but I'm not going to be putting money on it.

Nursery workers

As working parents, we have sent all of our daughters to a nursery of some kind in order for us to go and further our careers and earn money, of which a vast proportion then goes towards childcare. It's a vicious cycle in which we put our kids in childcare so we can work and work so we can put our kids in childcare.

These wonder women (and sometimes men) see our kids more than we do and do an amazing job of raising our children while working in what is essentially a sauna that has a strong residual smell of nappy offal. Nursery staff are worth their weight in diamond-encrusted gold. I do, however, have one niggling bugbear.

For a man, there is nothing more disconcerting than being called 'Dad', or worse still, 'Daddy', by another adult when they are talking directly to you. I don't know why, but it makes me extremely uncomfortable, as though I'm some kind of sugar daddy with a nineteen-year-old Russian girl on my arm. I know dozens of parents come through their doors on a daily basis so I'll forgive them for not remembering my name, but I still find it unnerving.

Then there is the parting gift at pick-up time. After an initial debrief of our daughters' achievements throughout the day, namely playing with sand and creating a series of aggressive crayon squiggles that are supposed to resemble me and a house, the ritual of the present-giving commences. If you have children who are potty-training, then you'll know the sort of 'gift' I'm talking about. It is of course a sad little plastic bag that has a pair of shitty knickers in it for you to take home with you. With any luck I'll actually remember it's in my pocket when I get home, but there have been multiple times when I've rediscovered it in the office the following day. There's nothing worse than feeling inside a coat pocket as you sit down at your desk to discover a moist plastic bag. You sit there wondering what the hell it is as you delicately run your fingers over it, trying to identify it without removing it, until it dawns on you: you've been carrying around your daughter's excrement.

Children's TV presenters/characters

OK, I don't know them personally, but these over-happy, highly caffeinated individuals have become well-known figures in my household. I see them 100 times more frequently than my actual friends, and their tunes and catchphrases echo round the house from dusk to dawn.

Over the years we've seen presenters come and go, but the one constant we've had to endure is Justin, otherwise known as Mr Tumble – or one of the other many names he's used for tax purposes. (Just so we're clear, on the advice of my legal team, I would like to stipulate that this is a joke. I am in no way inferring that Justin has, or ever intends to use, his multiple identities for tax evasion purposes.)

Justin is the kind of person you want to punch in the face, but you know that he'd still be nice to you afterwards and probably smile as you were knocking his teeth down his throat, simply infuriating you more. He's a multi-talented children's entertainer who dresses up as different characters and affects funny accents. He has cornered this market like no one else before and CBeebies is milking him for all he's worth – I swear he's on four different programmes back to back during the day and must be raking it in. Come to think of it, why wasn't he on the BBC's top earners list? He must have a very creative accountant and offshore accounts all over the world. (A joke again.) I have no idea why I have such a visceral reaction to him as I'm sure he's a lovely person, but he evokes some primeval hostility in my soul that makes me want to gouge out my own eyes with a really old spoon. Perhaps it's because he's just so nice that my brain can't accept him, but it's more likely to be the fact that Justin has been part of our lives for almost ten years now and I've simply grown to hate him.

Then there's Peppa Pig. If you haven't come across Peppa Pig, I can only assume that you've been living in a nuclear bunker with no access to the outside world for the past decade. But don't worry – if your children have anything to do with it, you'll have the misfortune of meeting the whole gang soon enough. For those that don't know, Peppa is a rather annoying madam who seems to think that the world owes her a huge favour all the time. She constantly belittles her little brother George (no doubt teeing him up for some kind of inferiority complex later in life), frequently leaving him in floods of tears. She also has a particularly unhealthy infatuation with jumping in waist-high muddy puddles, drenching her clothes in God knows what and in the process, tripling her parents' workload when it comes to washing. Her parents, Mummy and Daddy Pig, have the kind of patience that indicates to me that they are heavily medicated most of the time and probably shouldn't be allowed to operate heavy machinery or drive. Peppa's father has really let himself go physically, but seems content with his midlife spread. He holds down an office job that no one in his family understands and likes nothing better than forgetting he's an adult and playing with his kids. Peppa's mummy is a stay-at-home parent and makes it known that she thinks her husband isn't capable of doing half the things he says he is, since she puts him down in front of the children at most opportunities that present themselves.

It's scary how close *Peppa Pig* is to real life for me.

Then there is *In the Night Garden* and I don't even know where to start with this one. As far as I can tell, this programme follows the aftermath of a failed genetic-modification black ops project to create an army of superhuman weapons that went hideously wrong. These mutant outcasts have been sent to live in a far-off land to live out the rest of their days in captivity, aimlessly wandering around an enclosed woodland code-named 'The Night Garden'. From what I can deduce, Igglepiggle is the result of testing the endurance of the human body. After extended periods of reduced exposure to daylight and being subjected to sub-zero conditions, his skin has turned blue. His body must be close to shutting down as he is permanently tired and looking to nap. Upsy Daisy was the scientists' failed attempt at making a real-life Medusa, able to turn enemies to stone with a single glance. After a lobotomy and several painful operations to graft nine snake-like creatures to her cranium, the sad result is a simple being who can only say her name over and over and over again. In the depths of the woods, you'll also find a shy creature known as Makka Pakka. After prolonged exposure to radiation, Makka Pakka (who was originally 6 foot 2 and built like a brick shithouse) mutated. Now standing at just over 2 foot, he has been left with the body of a potato, a head shaped like a rugby ball and legs that are essentially stumps that stop above the knee. Unable to walk, Makka Pakka uses a wheeled Zimmer frame to get around and spends his time trying to please the larger creatures he shares his enclosure with by washing their faces. Reclusive by nature, Makka Pakka lives in a cave at the end of a dried-up riverbed with his stone collection, and would be the first one to perish in a flash flood. Finally there are the Tombliboos – the outcome of a genetic cloning experiment that was a precursor to Dolly the Sheep. These three beings are actually over fifty years old, but due to a side effect of their genetic coding haven't advanced physically beyond the age of three. Together, they live in a large semi-spherical dome covered in fake grass.

I haven't a clue what the point of this programme is. The only lesson I can take from it is, don't venture too far into the woods alone as you never know what you'll come across.

Now we come to YouTube stars. My older girls don't watch normal TV any more. In a world where they have access to every kind of content they could ever want at the click of a button, the idea of waiting for a programme to come on is on a par with cooking things over an open fire in a cave while wrapped in the skin of a sabre-toothed tiger – it's prehistoric. They just can't wrap their Wi-Fi-addled brains around the fact that as a child my evenings used to be structured around the TV schedule and that often I would have to wait a whole week to see the next episode of a series I was engrossed in. My viewing routine consisted of *Neighbours* at 5.35 p.m., *The Fresh Prince of Bel-Air* at 6 p.m. and *Hollyoaks* at 6.30 p.m. if I was lucky. Instead the girls watch YouTube. Now I have to be careful not to look like a hypocrite here as I'm known for being on social media, but these YouTube kids are something else, and they've managed to hook Anya and Marnie to the point that withdrawal might break them. Like most people over the age of thirty, I use YouTube to listen to music while I'm at work, to look up 'how to' videos about plastering and electrical wiring, and to watch random documentaries on space travel. The girls, however, use it as an online portal to a world where anything is possible. It's also a key procrastination tool. It has a lot to answer for in our house:

- YouTube is the reason that my British children walk around affecting American accents and putting an inquisitive and highly annoying upwards inflection at the end of their statements. This often leads me to make annoying comments like, 'Sorry, are you asking a question or making a statement? I can't tell because the way you've said those words makes me think you're asking me something.'

- YouTube is the reason I have to ask my girls to help multiple times, like a parrot with Tourette's, before I get any response to indicate whether they are, in fact, still alive.

- YouTube is the reason that my house is a cottage industry for slime manufacture.

- YouTube is the reason Marnie is obsessed with gummy sweets and is on the road to having dentures before she hits her teens.

- YouTube is the reason my girls can't open something without turning it into a live unboxing video.

- YouTube is the reason Anya now reviews everything as if she's talking to millions of followers commenting on her daily life.

So there you have it: a quick run-through of the folk that we commonly cross paths with in the ever-changing and evolving network of people that has sprung up from having our daughters in our lives. This will continue to morph as the years go by, leaving our social circle to dwindle as our daughters' own friendship groups expand. I just hope that they're able to have some real physical friends instead of them all being virtual, as I'm pretty sure that's the direction the world is heading in. Social skills are dying out as the kids all sit behind keyboards and tap away while slowly forgetting the art of being able to hold a polite conversation that doesn't involve the use of emojis, slang or abbreviations (which I'm constantly having to research on Google to decipher what the hell they are talking about). Maybe in the future there will be detox facilities like the Priory, but instead of focusing on drugs or alcohol, they will be weaning square-eyed youngsters off screens. I may already have lost the older ones, who knows; and both Clemmie's and my social calendar is looking more and more like a blank chessboard, but I think there's still time to save the twins.

6

A day in my life

I used to think when I was twenty-three that I
worked hard. I used to think I knew what being
tired was after a night on the smash. I used to think
that I was doing my best. As a parent, I now know
that you can cram a whole lot more into a day. The
phrase 'I'll sleep when I'm dead' comes to mind . . .

A day in my life

*I*f you haven't realised by now, when you've got kids, having a routine and sticking to it like a wasp on jam is very important, especially if you ever plan on having any kind of social life again outside of your own family. Every parenting book you read will likely talk about routines: what's good, what's bad, and provide conflicting information about what the 'right' routine is. I'm not going to preach to you about how you should do things; frankly each family is different, with different circumstances, and dictating a strict regime without knowing the ins and outs of how your lives work would be pointless.

If you're after a structured way of getting children into some sort of routine, there are plenty on the internet, but you may also find that you'll discover a natural rhythm that works for you and your life without even really looking for one.

Our routine is a difficult one to define, especially since the twins' arrival, since that added a whole new set of ingredients to our already complex family-sized cocktail that no one but us would fancy necking. We would have really benefited from having an assistant to organise our lives, but in the absence of that particular luxury, we learnt our roles and we play them out on a daily basis.

The routine that follows will give you an insight into my life with five women. It's what I live every weekday of my life, it's chaotic to outsiders looking in, but there is some kind of structure that underpins it all (though admittedly you would only spot it if you squinted *really* hard, much like one of those magic eye pictures that were all the rage back in 1993).

6.00 A.M. I wake up by being kneed in the back as soon as the baby noises float across the still, stale air in the bedroom. After a short time, I realise that my wife's touch wasn't a sign of affection, but a muted nudge to get me to go and make the bottles. I stumble downstairs, eyes still sealed shut, make the bottles and plod back up, passing Marnie travelling in the opposite direction with her duvet. She's on her way to the sofa to get her morning fix of children's TV. We've tried every which way to curb this habit, but we have lost the battle as we lost the will to keep fighting. She's ground us down and learnt that persistence will usually get you what you want. We used to hide the remotes in random places and unplug the TV at the mains, but she is obviously cleverer than I gave her credit for: every morning, within five minutes of her being downstairs, we'd hear some high-pitched American voice bellowing from the speakers at a volume that was unacceptable during the day, let alone before the sun has risen. This was a signal that she'd been successful in her

TV-remote recovery mission and found the all-powerful rectangular black box hidden deep in the biscuit tin.

I sigh and bring in a mug of tea to Clemmie – who is also inspecting the insides of her eyelids – before slowly opening the door to the twins' room. Giving myself some time to acclimatise to the pungent odour of their recently filled nappies, which hangs like an invisible fog in the air (everyone loves a morning poo, right?), I scoop them up and transport them to the other room in the same way you'd carry two kegs of beer. Finally, I plonk them down on the bed, ready to insert the bottles before too much noise is allowed to escape from their mouths. They promptly guzzle their milk as if they were in a drinking competition between two sailors and slide off the bed to crawl around the floor and pick up things that they probably shouldn't.

7.00 A.M. By this time most of us are up and the house is alive with the dull noise of low-energy people doing things slowly – apart from the twins, who act like they're attached to an invisible but very real intravenous adrenaline drip. Marnie is still watching TV, despite having been asked to stop four times; each time the request is met with literally no response of any sort, until I shout, at which point she tears up and I feel like a complete shit. The TV's off though, so every cloud does have a silver lining.

7.30 A.M. Breakfast time. Anya will invariably still be in bed so Marnie will take full advantage and finish off the cereal, which will result in an altercation later on. I'll round up the twins who are at opposite ends of the house, pulling electrical cords and generally getting a head start on destroying our home one room at a time. I'll put the girls in their high chairs and make them a nutritious bowl of Weetabix with a dash of honey, place the bibs around their necks, which will be wrestled off within seconds, put them back in their seats as they are now standing on the table shouting at some flowers, and place the food in front of them. This will go one of two ways. It will either get rejected out of hand or wolfed down within seconds, quickly followed by one of the few words they've managed to grasp – 'More'. It's like I'm living with a modern-day female Oliver Twist and her identical twin.

7.45 A.M. Anya comes down to breakfast to discover that not only is there no cereal, but the milk has been finished as well. I point out that if she wants to have cereal she needs to be down earlier, which is met with a face that tells me that while she listened to my point, she is going to completely ignore it and just eat whatever she fancies from the fridge. We come to an agreement that she can have a crumpet with Nutella on it and peace is restored.

8.00 A.M. Having got the twins down from the table, I go to the bathroom for a fake poo. I'm actually drinking tea and looking at my phone but my trousers and pants are round my ankles to add to the realism of this charade, just in case anyone should come in and confront me. All's going well until the door opens and I'm met by three of my children. Two of them want to get their teeth brushed; the third one just followed to see what all the commotion was about.

Oh joy. I'm told that I'm disgusting and they all leave. At no point do I remember inviting any of them in to have a conversation with me. I make a mental note to get the lock on the door fixed but we all know that will never get done.

8.15 A.M. The breakfast table is an absolute bomb site: there are Cheerios everywhere and puddles of milk cover the table to create what looks like a topographical picture of the earth from space. Clemmie makes her way downstairs and I'm yelled at for not cleaning it up. I try to explain I was in the toilet and can't be in two places at once, but it falls on deaf ears. I spend the next three minutes on my hands and knees clearing up, quietly cursing everyone in my family and the fact that we have children who wouldn't know what work was if it slapped them in the face with a three-day-old fish. Then I blame myself for not making them do chores.

8.20 A.M. I chase Anya and Marnie around to get socks, shoes and hairbands. I was told this was done about twenty minutes ago, but on closer inspection, absolutely diddly-squat has happened. If there was a world championships for procrastination, my children would win (although I'm sure that it would take years to actually get to the final and determine a winner). They're all running around doing something, looking as busy as an office worker who's trying to get a big report out the door before he goes on holiday for a week, yet they achieve the sum total of zero plus nothing. Either they have the attention span of a forgetful goldfish, or they just don't care. Whichever it is, it's annoying.

8.23 A.M. I get started on the socks and shoes as no one else is doing it.

8.25 A.M. The girls go and change their socks and shoes as they aren't the right ones, while I cry silently into my hands.

8.30 A.M. I get a letter from school thrust under my nose that's been sitting in a school bag for God knows how long. Apparently I need to pay for a school trip and sign a couple of things that I know absolutely nothing about. I reread the letter – the trip was last week. Oops.

8.31 A.M. I'm not sure how this has happened but I am now the only one in the house that is capable of doing high ponytails (the hairstyle of the moment at school) without it hurting, so Anya and Marnie line up and get me to do their hair. I get to the finishing point only to discover that no one has a hairband. They seem to have all disappeared along with half of my socks and my plan to leave on time for once.

8.33 A.M. We're finally out the door. Clemmie is staying at home with the twins. It's at this point I realise I have actually barely seen Clemmie all morning, apart from when we were in bed. She has an impressive ability to focus only on getting herself ready, while not actually drawing attention to this fact. Now I think about it, she was in the bedroom for a good twenty minutes drying her hair, choosing outfits and God knows what else, only to then come downstairs and complain about the mess! I make a mental note to talk to her about the balance of the workload in the mornings, which I'll then either forget to do or wimp out of by the time I get home. No doubt she'd point out that she cleared up last night, got the school clothes cleaned and ironed, and signed for Anya's school trip last week, which I knew nothing about. This would be a valid point.

8.45 A.M. In the car, I discuss what's happening at school with the girls. Anya and Marnie then fight over the radio station until they find a song they both like and sing along until one of them gets a line wrong and the other pounces on their mistake. I look at the clock and take a deep breath. Internally I start to question why it is that there are so many bad drivers on the road these days, especially when I'm in a hurry to get somewhere. This is not a tourist hotspot where people need to drive slowly to take in the beautiful vista, this is grey suburban south London, dammit! You can do more than 12 mph, people.

8.55 A.M. We arrive at school and perform what is known in our family as 'the bin drop'. There was a time when we'd take the girls in and help them get settled, but with Clemmie at home with the twins, the girls now at an age where they don't want us to come in with them to their classrooms, and me needing to get to work, we've fallen into a routine of dropping them as close to the school gates as we can while avoiding the glare of the teacher on duty and driving away slowly to make sure we can see they made it in safely. When they were at nursery I'd walk in, push them through the door, say my goodbyes and leave as quickly as Usain Bolt out of the blocks so as not to have to deal with my children clinging to my legs while I tried to manoeuvre myself towards the door. It's never nice to hear your child crying for you while you walk away but frankly, I knew they'd be fine within minutes of my departure and I had to get to work! Oh, how times change as they get older. Now they can't get rid of me quickly enough, and they don't want to be seen anywhere near boring old Dad in case I spontaneously break into a dance at the front of the class or tell a particularly cringeworthy joke.

9.30 A.M. Having crammed myself onto a train that smells of coffee breath and armpits thinly overlaid by a heady cocktail of perfumes and colognes, I get to work only to find I have a missed call from Clemmie and three unread text messages. Opening them reveals the following:

> Message 1: 'Get baby milk on your way home, please.'
> Message 2: 'Oh and nappies.'
> Message 3: 'And some chocolate. You can choose.'

How lucky I am to be able to choose the chocolate. What a privilege that's been bestowed on me. Of course, this is a loaded offer, I'll no doubt buy the wrong one but I can't begin to think about this right now.

10.30 A.M. I get a call from Clemmie who is wrestling with the twins to get them down for a morning nap. She's been to a baby sensory class this morning in which the girls crawled off in opposite directions, paying zero attention to what was going on in the class and made Clemmie look like a newly qualified nanny who'd been lumbered with twin lunatics on the first day of her new job. I point out that I'm in the office and can't really do anything to help, which goes down like a cold sick-filled sandwich.

12.30 P.M. I go to the local supermarket to queue up with the same bland people to buy the same bland lunch that I've had every day for the last five years. I consider changing the drink to inject some excitement into my day, but then quickly reconsider and stick to the set menu of sandwiches, fruit and fruit juice. Good old Sainsbury's meal deal, you never fail to make lunch soulless – but for £3, I can't really complain. After all, it's my choice to subject myself to this flavourless lunch routine, but I tell myself that every pound saved here can go towards something that I want in the future. This is nonsense, of course – I'll only spend it on something that we need instead, like nappies.

I get a call from Clemmie, claiming there is nothing to eat in the house and that she is existing solely on tea and biscuits.

3.00 P.M. I get another call from Clemmie who is walking around the park and commenting on other mums doing the same thing. With the chit-chat out of the way, the real reason for her call is revealed – she's checking that I've got the bits she asked for and is adding on 'food for dinner', since going into shops with a double buggy and crying twins is less than desirable. I walk back into the meeting I was in looking sheepish; I told them it was an important call, when in reality that couldn't have been further from the truth.

5.15 P.M. I receive a text to ensure I've left the office to pick up Anya and Marnie from after-school club, which in reality is just kids running around the school with the occasional cheese sandwich thrown in for good measure. In actual fact, I'd forgotten that I was on pick-up duty so I quickly finish off the email I've been composing for the last hour, unplug my headphones and stash the laptop in my locker, avoiding eye contact with colleagues who must get sick of me leaving before them every day of the week. Don't worry, folks – as soon as you have children, you'll also have an excuse to leave early, but until that day, suck it up and get on with your spreadsheets.

5.20 P.M. I reply with a text saying I'm on my way, but in actual fact I'm still at my desk finishing off work as the email didn't send. I've figured out the very latest time I can leave in order to get to school, but it relies completely on the trains running to schedule and there being no kind of delay. It also involves a brisk jog to the school in a full suit as no one wants their kid to be the last one there, especially on a regular basis; if they are, you start to worry that the staff and other parents think you're the worst person in the world.

5.58 P.M. I get to the school and hare round to pick up Anya and Marnie, who are unhelpfully housed in halls at opposite ends of the school. I arrive to be informed that I am being awarded a £5 penalty for getting there after 5.50 p.m. Of course Anya is the last one there in a room with half the lights turned off and all the members of staff with their coats on. At least it's not like the nursery days and I'm not taking home a small plastic bag with some shitty pants in along with my children.

6.15 P.M. I get home and before even getting the chance to take my shoes off, I'm immediately given a baby by a sweaty wife who's trying to cook dinner while simultaneously cleaning up and entertaining two small people who have been floating around her ankles. We have a two-minute conversation about the items I've bought and why they are the wrong ones.

6.45 P.M. Still in my clothes from work, I go to run a bath, which is a great dad job. I get to sit down next to the tub, swishing my hand about making bubbles. If you do this right, you can eke the job out for a good five minutes. I've learnt not to push it too far though. I dunk the twins in the bath while Clemmie makes up the bottles, then I brush their teeth while singing 'Five Little Ducks Went Swimming One Day' on repeat until the words no longer have any meaning. I eventually walk away from the bathroom with my clothes spattered with water, while the girls' clothes lie abandoned on the floor, kicked into a corner along with a half-wrapped nappy which may be retrieved later on in the evening. Or it might be left there forgotten until someone else stumbles across it the next day.

7.00 P.M. Having bathed the girls, we dry them off and battle to get nappies loosely fastened around their waists, in the knowledge that there is a 50 per cent chance of at least one of them being off by the time we get them up again in the morning. We wrestle them into their night clothes and attempt to read *That's Not My Unicorn*, which involves the girls grabbing the book and turning the pages in the opposite direction, basically ensuring I never get to the end of the book to discover what the person's unicorn actually looks like. We pull the cord on the music-playing balloon thing that hangs in the corner of their room and slowly back out like you would if you were trying to get out of a lion's cage at the zoo, ensuring that all creaking floorboards are missed and that the closing of the door doesn't trigger some kind of violent reaction. Upon closing the door, I hold my breath until I know the chance of a reaction has passed and slowly walk away with a sense of achievement at getting 50 per cent of our girls down.

7.15 P.M. I go downstairs to make some tea. I always take a sip way too soon and scald the roof of my mouth, only to be called upstairs to deal with an argument that has broken out between Marnie and Anya. I won't see the tea again until much later. After scaling the stairs for at least the tenth time in only thirty minutes, I'm met with two girls warring over possession of some slime. Clemmie has given up and kindly passed over responsibility to me to negotiate a truce, while she clears up the bath toys and the gallons of water that cover the bathroom floor. It really is like being at a SeaWorld show, but instead of sad killer whales soaking you, it's two kids who between them have the power of an industrial wave machine.

7.30 P.M. I manoeuvre the girls towards the shower and ask them to put their clothes on their chairs ready for tomorrow. While they're in the shower, I go round and remove screwed-up knickers from trousers and put them in the laundry basket. I place tomorrow's clothes on their chairs, realising my asking them to do it was a waste of energy. I knock on the shower, informing them that they are using all the hot water and that showering should take five minutes max.

8.00 P.M. The girls are out of the shower and doing a dance or gymnastics routine in Anya's bedroom. Calmly I inform them it's time to start getting into bed, at which point I'm presented with a ticket for a show that starts in ten seconds' time. I'm a sucker for this kind of thing so I sit down in my usual VIP box seat (in the corner on a bean-bag) and settle in to four minutes of clapping along to a performance of moves that I've seen 10,000 times before, just in a slightly different order.

8.15 P.M. Clemmie comes upstairs and puts Marnie in bed and I say good night to Anya who's got a book open on her bed, ready to dive in. Clemmie and I retreat, having told them they have fifteen minutes to read.

8.16 P.M. I go back into Anya's room to catch her with her mobile phone, which she's secretly removed from the drawer we put it in and hidden down the side of her bed. This is met with calls of 'But it's not fair!' to which I immediately respond: 'Aren't parents just the worst?' and leave feeling victorious in this particular round of parent vs child.

8.30 P.M. I go downstairs to rediscover my now-cold tea which has developed a skin over the top of it so thick that you can touch it and it doesn't give. I whack it in the microwave for forty-five seconds and start to make dinner as it's my turn, while simultaneously posting on Instagram.

8.45 P.M. I receive an email from Amazon that informs me I've bought three books, all by Jacqueline Wilson. It's Anya on her Kindle – which is linked to my Amazon account, so she now buys books like there's a world shortage. Decide not to fight this particular battle as she's actually reading and not watching rubbish videos about how to make slime on YouTube. I resign myself to having to think of it as just another direct debit that will slide out of my account along with the rest of them.

8.55 P.M. I finish off dinner and go to place the rice in the microwave to discover the fecking tea that's destined never to be drunk. It's cold again and the rim of the mug has become discoloured. I replace the tea with the rice and serve dinner to Clemmie who is writing while simultaneously watching BabyTV. It's been playing in the background without her realising. We're so used to having it as a soundtrack to our lives that often we forget to change the channel once the kids are in bed.

9.20 P.M. Clemmie and I argue about who's going to load the dishwasher and clean up after dinner. Then we both spend a romantic evening sitting on the sofa looking at our phones and responding to Instagram comments. Finally we'll actually talk about what's

happening over the next three days. My ability to take this information in is limited by this time of the day, so we'll end up having the
exact same conversation tomorrow evening, where the same thing
will happen again.

9.30 P.M. We ignore the noises from the monitor for as long as
possible until we have to acknowledge the fact that someone has to
go upstairs to settle the twins. With the ace of having already made
dinner this evening in my back pocket, I sit back as Clemmie trudges
off, but not before issuing me with strict instructions not to change
the channel (as if I'd dare).

9.35 P.M. I become aware of the creaking stairs as a child descends
them in a way that says they want to be noticed. Anya can't sleep.
What I'm supposed to do about this is unclear to me. What is clear,
however, is that she won't go back up without an escort/bodyguard
as she's scared. Despite me pointing out that both the twins and
Marnie are sound asleep upstairs already and that she managed to
walk down here just fine on her own without being attacked by
burglars, negotiations go the only way they were ever going to –
with me frog-marching a child up the stairs.

10.30 P.M. Clemmie goes to bed leaving me a list of what needs to
be cleared up. This signifies the start of 'me time' as I'm now the
only one up in the house, so I can actually get the stuff done that I
want to do. I'll get to Clemmie's list later but I realise I was only half
listening when she issued her instructions. I'm pretty sure it

involved spraying down the hob and putting the dishwasher on, but I can't be sure.

10.35 P.M. I start writing this book, but not before rediscovering the undrunk tea, which has now basically changed state from a liquid to a solid. Consider drinking it, and then think better of it and boil the kettle.

10.45 P.M. I finally drink a hot cup of tea and search the fridge for something to snack on as my stomach is telling me that dinner wasn't enough to keep my creative juices flowing.

11.00 P.M. The dream feed is a term you may well have heard of but have little idea of what it actually is. Before you ask, no, it's not when you dream about eating a particularly huge meal and then wake up feeling full (although I'd imagine that would be handy for those on a diet – note to self, must look into this as a business idea). A dream feed is when you feed a baby while they are not fully awake and are still drowsy in an effort to get them to sleep a bit longer through the night. Obviously if they are truly knocked out they aren't going to drink anything, but if they are half asleep, they have a natural response to suck when a bottle or nipple is inserted into their mouth. To be 100 per cent clear, I have never put my nipple in the twins' mouths. No one wants that, especially me.

11.15 P.M. I go downstairs again and continue to write. I get distracted by an email from school informing me that I need to pay for steel drum lessons, after-school club, an upcoming school trip and lunches for next term. I tap in my card details in the online payment section of the school website, reeling at the total cost. I'd earmarked that money to buy new bike components, but I suppose making sure my kids actually eat is more important.

1.30 A.M. I come to bed to be told that I'm making too much noise and that I should get changed and brush my teeth downstairs as Clemmie has work in the morning. So do I, but this isn't the right time for an argument about who deserves sleep the most.

2.30 A.M. I start to hear muffled noises that sound like foxes having enthusiastic sex outside, but is in fact a baby crying in the next room. Now starts the game of who can pretend to be asleep and not react to the noise the longest. The sound of a baby crying is a bit like a dog whistle; in the same sort of way that only a canine can hear the high-pitched noise, mothers are naturally more attuned to the sound of a crying baby, whereas dads are notorious for being able to sleep through the racket. That said, I do often wake up, but I wait for Clemmie to rouse me from my fake sleep and ask me if that's a baby crying. 'How would I know, you just woke me up!' I exclaim, even though really I have been awake for the last three minutes while doing my best corpse impression. Despite 'taking turns' to go and settle the twins, I find that it's my turn more often than not – strange how that happens. Mind you, if you asked Clemmie, she'd no doubt say the same thing.

6 A.M. The sun pokes in through the gap in the curtains I was told to sort out the night before but didn't, and the dawn chorus of children piling into the room fills my ears like a runaway freight train coming towards me, carrying an orchestra playing at full volume. That's right, folks – I exist on four hours of sleep. This is my life. Before you know it we're back at the starting point of the routine. Oh joy!

So what have I learnt from all of this?

Some of the parenting experts offer minute-by-minute breakdowns of how a day should look to a family, and aid you in implementing a military-style routine that is so precisely detailed that you'd find yourself equipped to invade a neighbouring nation. Personally, however, I feel that as long as you've got the sleep part nailed and you've got three square meals in somewhere in your day, then the rest will fall into place.

Having gone through a series of ever-morphing routines with both singleton babies and twins, I have learnt the following things:

- Spend time getting a sense of the basic structure you need to look after your little pig(s) effectively. Once the foundations are set, the big bad wolf can come along and blow himself into a hyperventilation-induced dizzy spell and the structure shouldn't move. It might shake a little bit, but as long as you have the right pillars in place you'll get through it.

- Sharing parenting responsibilities down the middle as much as you can means that it's a lot less likely that one of you will burn out and be reduced to a walking zombie. I'm not saying that you have to have set jobs, but sharing the workload will definitely make parent life a whole lot easier to deal with.

- When you find a rhythm that works for you and your family, then go with it. It's tempting to compare your routine with what others do, or say they do. Parents seem to enjoy dropping little comments into conversations like, 'Oh, [insert your baby's name] isn't sleeping through yet? Our little [insert their little darling's name] is getting eleven hours a night and a good three hours in the afternoon.' They're not showing off, they're just proud of their accomplishment, but every child is different.

- Don't sleep with a bottle of hot milk between your legs. That's just stupid.

7

Solo parenting – I dad it my way

I don't know if you can get eyes surgically implanted into the back of your skull, but if they need a guinea pig, I'd be up for it. Keeping track of what my offspring are doing while outnumbered and solo is as difficult as building a working computer out of custard. Herding cats that are high on speed would be easier.

Solo parenting - I dad it my way

Now I can only draw on my own experience in this area, but from what I've both heard and seen, I think I'm probably a good representation of most of the male species out there who have procreated. For many partners, 'what dads do when they're left in charge of children without proper adult supervision' is one of those age-old scientific mysteries that is yet to be solved, like what's actually in a black hole? Why don't duck quacks echo? And who ate the last of the cereal and put the empty box back in the cupboard to piss everyone off? Unless you're willing to invest in a complete home surveillance set-up and turn your house into a CCTV-monitored *Big Brother*-style house, you're unlikely to ever find out. Until now, that is.

I thought it would be a good idea to lift the lid on what men do when the more responsible parent needs to leave the house to avoid both cabin fever and a mini breakdown, leaving us guys in command.

But before I dive in and reveal all – and in the process resign myself to spending the rest of my life receiving bags of hate mail from other fathers, who want to lynch me after revealing our secrets – let's air some of the assumptions that women make about what happens in their homes when they aren't there:

- Dads only feed children food that comes from a plastic bag in the freezer.
- Dads spend the day doing exactly what they want, letting the kids turn the house into a war zone.
- Dads don't clean up when there's a mess.
- Dads avoid doing any of the jobs on the list that was left for them, either out of sheer laziness or simply to annoy their partners.
- Dads don't closely supervise children, they observe them from a distance, which results in mess and mayhem.
- Dads rarely enforce the rules of the house when alone.
- Dads don't like to leave the house.
- Dads don't know how to use the washing machine.
- Dads don't make beds.
- Dads don't bath children unless they are caked in dirt from head to toe.
- Dads cook terrible meals for themselves when they are left alone.

Some of these may be accurate, some less so. Let's see how the reality matches up with the perception and we'll do a stock-check at the end.

Learning experiences

I'm a firm believer in facing a challenge head on and I can say in all honesty that taking charge of my brood single-handedly when I'm so heavily outnumbered is just that – a challenge. That said, it's not like I'm babysitting for someone else's little ones – these are my girls, so I see it as just part and parcel of parenting, pulling my weight and giving my wife the breathing space she needs to avoid a nuclear-scale meltdown (I really don't fancy donning a hazmat suit and clearing up the aftermath of that).

Secretly I've grown to love solo days, weekends and weeks, as the strict regime of Clemmie's OCD-level cleanliness makes way (albeit temporarily) for a new father-led revolution, in which the rules are relaxed and the house can settle. I know that Clemmie trusts me to look after the kids, but maintaining the house is a completely different matter altogether. Unfortunately (and I'm not sure why this stuff only happens on my watch), I've had a number of what we'll call 'learning experiences' when left with the children that haven't reflected on me particularly well. Here are some recent examples:

- The time I was cooking in the kitchen one evening with one of my daughters (I won't name names here) safely secured in the bouncer watching TV. My nose was suddenly hit with a familiar smell. Had I been cooking with crap? Not to my knowledge. Upon further investigation, I discovered my beautiful daughter had escaped the clutches of the bouncer, removed her nappy and was rolling around on the floor *eating* her own poo. As the saying goes, she looked as happy as a pig in shit. Clemmie was not.

LEARNING POINT: don't assume that restraining a child with straps means they'll stay where you put them. They are all escapologists in training and seemingly have vertebrae made from jelly, enabling them to wiggle out of the tightest of harnesses.

• The time I was downstairs and had forgotten to pull across the stair gate. Noticing it was quiet, which is usually a good indication that something bad is happening, I ran up the stairs to find both the twins at Clemmie's dressing table. They had removed all the expensive lipsticks from their protective ornate sheaths and snapped them in two. On closer inspection I discovered that they were in the process of creating a masterpiece of expressionist artwork using all of Clemmie's favourite and most expensive lip colours on the 18-mm-pile carpet we'd had laid several months earlier. Just so you know, lipstick doesn't come off carpets and if you try to wipe it, it just smudges, resulting in something that is reminiscent of a murder scene minus the chalk body outline. It's still there today.

LEARNING POINT: children gravitate towards things they know they are not supposed to touch. I also learnt that my wife really should put all cosmetics at ceiling height in a lock box that only she knows the combination to.

- The time I left Marnie to do some painting while I emptied the shed, only to find that the paper I'd left out and Sellotaped to the table for her to paint was still immaculate, yet the walls had been vandalised by a young Banksy in the making.

LEARNING POINT: children love to paint and make the world a more colourful place. They need an artistic outlet and who am I to stifle that creativity by forcing them to stay inside the A3 white rectangle provided? I just need to make sure I have the cleaning products at the ready before the paint sets next time.

- The time I did a science experiment with Anya and Marnie while Clemmie was out for the afternoon with the twins. Clemmie doesn't like us to make a mess, but with her away we took our chances and decided to make a vinegar and bicarbonate of soda rocket using the instructions from the 'indoor science experiments for kids' book we'd found. Having not been overly impressed by the pathetic 'pop' that lifted the bottle only a few centimetres from the kitchen table, I did what any self-respecting man would do – quadrupled the quantities and gave it the kind of violent shake that can only be replicated by those industrial paint mixers you see in DIY superstores. The bottle shot to the ceiling and sprayed its contents everywhere in the kitchen – and I mean everywhere. Instead of owning up and telling Clemmie straight away, I repainted the whole room and ceiling in under two hours before Clemmie could see the damage, but I was caught out by the smell of the paint fumes when she returned and made to confess my sins.

LEARNING POINT: not all paints are odourless. I really must remember to write to Dulux about that!

- The time I decided to sand the kitchen table back to bare wood while Clemmie was away for a weekend. I thought that I could do it in the house with an industrial belt sander and still clear up the mess by the time she got home. I was wrong. In hindsight I really should have done it outside. I also should have attached the dust-collection bag. Oh well, you live and learn (or not in my case). The kids had it in their hair and up their noses for days.

LEARNING POINT: if you do have to do woodwork, do it in a well-ventilated area. Or make sure that your wife is away for longer than two days to allow yourself a sufficient amount of clean-up time.

This list of my 'mishaps' could go on forever, but I won't bore you with all of them or you'll be reading this book for the next five years. However, looking at this handful of examples does make me sympathise with Clemmie when she says that having me around 'is just like having a fifth child in the house'. No wonder she's rarely excited about coming home when she has been away for more than a day. It's not because she hasn't missed us – of course she has: she can't wait to see us. It's the five minutes after she gets in through the door and starts to assess the state of the house that she hates.

Three common approaches to solo parenting

In my experience there seem to be three types of approach that most dads adopt:

1. **The 'balls out' approach**

   If you're going to do something, do it all out. This means taking everything you could possibly need, loading it into a buggy and actually leaving the house to go and do something.

   And why the name? Well, this might be the approach that would be adopted by the kind of guy that happily walks around a public changing room naked with no towel – he's confident (perhaps a little overconfident), takes everything in his stride and doesn't care what people think. This kind of attitude is handy when your kid is having a seismic-scale meltdown in the supermarket after – unbeknown to you – losing their favourite toy in the chilled foods aisle five minutes earlier. You haven't realised and can't understand why the little person has turned red and is screaming with so much force that it's now actually become a silent scream that is occasionally interrupted by massive intakes of air and short, sharp, ear-piercing shrieks.

2. **The 'fox out of the hole' approach**

   This essentially means taking a cautious approach to things.

   You want to leave the house because, frankly, you and your baby are bored of staring at the same four walls and watching the same shitty programme on BabyTV (you know, the one that has that annoying theme tune that's so ingrained in your brain that you find yourself humming it when you're in the shower, or in an important work meeting). That said, you also don't want to take them out for a full day of culture to the local museum because a) they won't appreciate it – babies don't look at artwork and try to understand the emotional torment the artist had to endure in order to create this masterpiece. They're more likely to be entertained by the rice cake in their hand, or the other baby in the buggy a couple of metres away that's been dragged to the same museum – and b) it's a ball-ache to actually get there. See the chapter on getting from A to B for more information on this but here's a brief synopsis:

- If you use public transport, you're reliant on someone else's timetable. When you have a child of any age, leaving the house at a time you actually need or plan to is a near impossibility. When you do finally get on the bus or train, having manhandled the buggy past people, running over toes and apologising several hundred times to total strangers, you end up feeling like a set of temporary traffic lights – an annoyance to everyone that slows things down and generally gets in the way. By the time you get where you're going, your little one will most likely be asleep, rendering the whole trip a complete waste of time.
- If you take your car, you can at least work to your own timetable, and enjoy the added benefit of legitimately using the parent-and-child car parking spaces without feeling like a total fraud. Plus all the noise and mess is contained in a space

that you own. Even so, you'll probably still walk away from your day out thinking, 'Was that really worth the effort?' Don't get me wrong, it's important to get out and do things, but the effort vs enjoyment ratio is an important one that parents need to consider when deciding on where to go. Taking all this into consideration and making sure the enjoyment ratio far outweighs the effort usually results in a quick walk down the road to a local shop to pick up some essentials.

The 'fox out of the hole' approach is probably one for someone with less confidence than the 'balls out' dad, but enough experience to be 'allowed' to look after the baby without the need for a WhatsApp message from their partner every fifteen minutes requesting proof that their baby is still alive and well.

3. **The 'let's not push it' approach**

This is potentially the most common approach and the most favoured, especially the first couple of times dads are left in charge without 'adult' supervision. Cover the basics: get cosy at home, stick to the list, keep them alive and try not to trash the house in the process.

To be honest, we all default to this option. Being a parent is shattering and leaves you with as much energy as a six-year-old Duracell battery you found at the back of 'the drawer of crap' in the kitchen – the one with all the takeaway menus, old keys and USB cables for things that are either broken or that you flogged on eBay years ago.

Over the years, as you would expect, I've found myself on my own with my girls many times and have combined the approaches mentioned to develop a kind of solo parenting hybrid methodology. Yet as the number of small people has increased, my ability to track them all at once has diminished dramatically. It's led me to consider surgery that should be offered to all parents free on the NHS: to have eyes inserted into the back of my skull. I'm still on the lookout for a doctor who's up to the task of giving me the 360-degree vision I desperately need in order to see everything at all times.

That time I looked after all four girls on my own for a week and won. OK, I was only actually solo parenting for five days and had my parents' help for two, but who's counting?

Clemmie was going away to the Caribbean for a week. At first she was hesitant to go, as the thought of being away from us for what was the longest time she had been apart from the girls and me filled her with dread, but I reassured her that I could handle it and I wanted her to go. After all, it's not every day that you get opportunities to go away to far-flung places without your children and enjoy yourself, and I was pretty sure I owed her for all the business trips I'd been on over the years, so it only seemed fair. The only thing I hadn't taken into consideration was that the trip was due to happen over the half-term holiday, which meant that with school shut for the week, I'd be looking after all four of the girls for the whole time and I needed to take a week off work (this wasn't exactly a chore, however, as I'd rather spend a week solidly with my girls than sit at a desk making PowerPoint presentations that no one will ever read).

The day that Clemmie was due to leave arrived, so with her bags packed and ready next to the front door, we sat down to talk through the following:

- The twins' routine.
- The calendar of events that was in the diary during the time she would be away that I hadn't paid any attention to.
- The list of jobs that needed to be done to make the house run as smoothly as a recently serviced priceless Swiss timepiece.

I nodded along, taking in roughly 70 per cent of what was being said, before the taxi pulled up outside (knowing full well that the 30 per cent I'd missed was the part that would get me in trouble). With barely enough time for the list to float down to the table, in a flurry of kisses, Clemmie jumped into the waiting taxi. As I closed the door, I swear I could hear the words 'Go, go, go!' being yelled at the driver amid the sound of squealing tyres, but I didn't have time to look again as the twins were already on their way up the stairs. We were now on our own.

Solo Dadding Diary: Day 1

MORNING: The house was in pristine condition and I had every intention of keeping it that way for as long as I physically could, purely so that I had less to do at the end of the day. It was one of those rare days in April when the sun actually proved it was still up there and able to produce heat, so I decided to strategically move everyone and everything outside. The girls set to work erecting tents and much like migrating birds, all of their belongings travelled from the cool climes of the inside of the house to the warmth of the garden. As literally armfuls of colouring books, electronics, bedding and food rushed past me like floodwater, I said (in such an unconvincing tone that even I didn't believe it), 'Remember, whatever you bring out, you have to take back in at the end of the day.'

The a.m. hours passed largely without incident, apart from the explosive shits that the twins did simultaneously that required a clothing change. Having not planned to leave the house on day one, I dressed them in the same way I do when I'm not expecting to see anyone outside of my immediate family – using the clothes at the top of the pile in the drawers with no thought given to coordination or style. They looked like they'd been dressed from the bags left outside a charity shop, but they didn't care and neither did I.

AFTERNOON: For lunch, seeing as we were all al fresco, I opted for a picnic plate, which is a standard family favourite that comes out when we parents can't be arsed to cook or when the fridge is looking more bare than our savings account. The process of making up a picnic plate is simple: open the fridge, poke around for a bit, stroke your chin, then chuck a load of random pieces of food on a plate and hey presto, a nutritious meal made in under thirty seconds. My go-to ingredients are usually chopped raw veg, a Babybel cheese which will end up half eaten with the red wax screwed up into a ball and squished into the carpet, some fizzy hummus that is a week out of date (but is fine to serve as long as the kids don't notice), some pitta bread that I'll likely leave in the toaster for thirty seconds too long, rendering it like cardboard, some ham, and a handful of olives which may or may not get eaten. Dessert is a yoghurt. The spoons that I gave the girls to shovel the fermented milk into their bodies with were returned to me completely untouched. Anya and Marnie poured it directly into their mouths and the twins did a Winnie the Pooh and stuffed their whole hands into the pots, making pink slimy fists which they then waved in the general direction of their mouths, before wiping them on every-thing else in a 1-metre radius of wherever they were sitting.

I put the twins down for a nap early as I couldn't entertain them any longer, which left Anya, Marnie and me to watch a film and eat popcorn like it was going out of fashion. The cushions all ended up on the floor thanks to a mid-film pillow fight and gymnastics session.

The twins were up again at 2 p.m., having only slept for one hour (I have now learnt why it's important to put them down at the right time as if you put them down early, they don't sleep for very long). Not wanting to pull myself away from the god-awful *Tinker Bell* film I'd been forced to watch but had somehow now found myself caught up in, I left them an extra five minutes hoping they'd go back to sleep; shockingly, they didn't. Instead they filled their nappies to the brim and as I flung open the door, the smell of arse-produce was hard to bear. Had I put them down like that or had they pooed while they slept? Also, how do you poo while you sleep? Don't you have control of your sphincter when you're in the land of nod? How annoying must it be to go to sleep clean and then wake up with a turd pressed between your buttocks?

As I carried the twins downstairs, Anya and Marnie rushed in the opposite direction to spend the afternoon avoiding responsibilities by playing in their rooms. This was the only time I saw the girls in the afternoon apart from when they came down to quietly steal snacks for some kind of party they were having. The twins and I never did receive an invite.

EVENING: I bathed the twins and got soaked as we got carried away with the farmyard animal impressions. The towels are still in a heap on the floor in the bathroom and I know there is a nappy knocking around under the bath, which I'll retrieve later on. Clothes are starting to build up on the stairs but we can still walk round them so it's no big issue.

Anya and Marnie didn't want to have a shower but I made them – Clemmie would be so proud. I am, however, still losing the argument over the girls' inability to remove their inside-out knickers from their trousers. Threats of pocket-money reduction have fallen on deaf ears – the search for that elusive item they care about not having continues . . .

As predicted, this evening I spent a good hour bringing everything back inside under cover of darkness, but without Clemmie to supervise. The semi-damp items didn't quite make it back to their homes and instead ended up in two heaps: one on the kitchen table, which will no doubt leave a mark, and the other by the back door, which may or may not still be there when Clemmie comes home in six days' time.

The plates were still on the side from lunch but they weren't going anywhere in a hurry unless a kind burglar stopped by to do a spot of midnight washing-up, so I went to bed safe in the knowledge that they'd be right there waiting for me tomorrow.

Day 1 accomplishments:

The children are alive.

The house looks acceptable (to me anyway).

The twins are still in their routine, sort of.

Anya and Marnie haven't inflicted any lasting damage on each other.

Solo Dadding Diary: Day 2

MORNING: Having crashed out on the sofa, I woke up at 1.14 a.m. with Netflix still blaring out from the TV. I carted myself upstairs and was overjoyed at being woken five hours later by Marnie staring at me from a distance of just 3 inches from my face, demanding to know where I'd hidden the TV remote. I got out of bed, tripping over the cushions that I'd discarded on the floor the night before, and silently cursed all soft furnishing everywhere. I immediately kicked them all into the corner of the room where they'd stay for the rest of the week. As I left the room, I glanced back to see that half the bed still looked like it was untouched. Then it dawned on me: I had become so used to sleeping on the 12-inch strip on the edge of the bed that even when I had access to the entire space, I didn't know what do with it all.

I went into the twins' room, which is directly above the living room. Marnie had already started up her YouTube journey for the day and kicked proceedings off with Little Mix. Of course the music was muffled as it came up through the floor, so it sounded like a bass test facility in which the whole of the band was being slowly drowned.

As I walked round the house, I started to notice that perhaps I hadn't been quite as tidy as I'd originally thought. Clothes lay strewn around as if everyone had decided to go streaking all at the same time, the table hadn't been wiped down so the food from the day before had turned from a nutritious meal into an industrial-strength adhesive that had welded itself to the surface, and there were small plastic toys dotted around the floor like mini land mines, ready to inflict pain on unsuspecting barefooted passers-by when they least expected it.

AFTERNOON: Since I hadn't put the dishwasher on in two days, the pile of plates was reminiscent of the Leaning Tower of Pisa. We also had no clean bowls for the twins to eat out of and we were down to plastic cutlery for all of us. There is something not quite right about eating a hearty lasagne with a neon plastic spoon. Then again we only had two dishwasher tablets left so I needed to use them sparingly and cram as much as I possibly could into the cavernous metal cube to be efficient. Clemmie always tells me that if you put too much in at once it won't clean everything but that sounds like nonsense to me. We'll see . . .

EVENING: I've lost the list that Clemmie wrote for me, but I can't call or text her and ask her to dictate it out again as that would indicate I'm failing.

Day 2 accomplishments:

The dishwasher is on and the pile of plates removed from the counter.

The dinner table got cleaned (and was almost immediately made messy again).

Solo Dadding Diary: Day 3

MORNING: Confident that I was now in command of the controlled mayhem around me, and having successfully banished the cushions to the floor of the bedroom earlier in the week, I felt it was time to introduce some of my own personal touches to the interior design of our home (something that I rarely get to do usually).

All flowers were binned. It's not that I don't like flowers, but as soon as you put them in a vase they are resigned to slowly dying in front of your eyes. So instead of going through the long goodbye, I became the Dignitas of the foliage world and ended their lives by popping them directly in the bin, which is only where they would have ended up anyway.

With no one to reprimand me, I laid out my key grooming tools that are usually banished to the dark confines of the cupboard; my toothbrush charger, the electric shaver, my deodorant, my after-shave and moisturisers now take pride of place next to the sink. (Note to self: remember to put these away before Clemmie comes home.)

I removed my shoes from the cupboard under the stairs and put them on the shoe rack where they belong.

AFTERNOON: After lunch I realised that the washing was still in the sodding machine, wet from two days ago because I forgot to get it out and hang it up. It was at this point I learnt that wet clothes smell. As a last-ditch attempt to rectify the situation I crammed everything in the tumble dryer and hit the 'make everything so dry it shouldn't be put near a naked flame' button and hoped for the best.

NOTE: not all clothing can go in a tumble dryer, and what's more important is that 50 per cent of those items that can't go in the hot drum of wonder are Clemmie's clothes. I mean, why buy cashmere clothing if it can't go in the washing machine on a normal cycle, or in the tumbler dryer, without ending up looking like doll's clothing? Surely that's just making more work for yourself than is necessary?

Not everything can be tumble-dried. Delicates
need to go on the line. This includes children.

As I changed the twins this afternoon I noticed two more things:

1. I hadn't taken the blackout blinds down in their room for three days now.

2. A pile of dirty nappies had started to accumulate on the window sill. Wow, Clemmie was right, I really was incapable of putting dirty nappies in the bin, despite it being all of 12 inches away from the changing table. What was up with that? Was it laziness or did I need to see a therapist to unlock some dark psychological secrets that I'd buried over the years? Nah, probably just laziness.

After thirty minutes of arguing and wrestling shoes onto feet, we went out to the shops, followed by a quick trip to the park. We got stopped several times by strangers, who wanted to ask me questions about where my wife was and to tell me I looked tired. Not exactly the pep talk I was looking for.

On the way home I realised that we'd lost one of Ottie's shoes. We retraced our steps, but it had vanished like a fart in the wind. My initial reaction should have been 'Oh, poor Ottie, she'll have a cold foot now' but in actual fact was more along the lines of 'Oh crap! I'm going to be killed for losing that when Clemmie gets home.'

Note to self: order shoes from Amazon ASAP so she never finds out.

EVENING: The girls didn't want to have a bath so they didn't have one. I still managed to find some inside-out knickers stuck in trousers wedged behind the bedroom door though. I thought it was just boys that were supposed to be gross?

I Skyped Clemmie who was on a cruise ship in the Caribbean drinking a cocktail. Before calling I cleared a space on the sofa and made sure that the camera was only angled at the 2 metres of clean space in the living room. I ensured that I didn't moan about anything so that she wouldn't feel bad or stressed. My collection of dad points is going to be epic by the time she comes home.

Day 3 accomplishments:

I introduced a masculine touch to the décor of our home.

We left the house.

Solo Dadding Diary: Day 4

It has now been four days since I last spoke to an adult who isn't our postman.

I don't know if Anya and Marnie are even in the house any more as I haven't seen them for a long time. The only indication that they are alive is the trail of cereal leading up the stairs to their bedrooms and the occasional muffled noises of an amateur boxing match taking place somewhere in the house.

The pile of random oddities on the stairs has now become a real health and safety hazard yet we're all managing to step around them successfully.

The twins got into Clemmie's make-up drawers and went to town on the lipsticks again. Vanish carpet cleaner wasn't touching it – if anything, it made the bright red spot into a wider, angry red smear. I put a rug over it – out of sight, out of mind.

I finally rounded the kids up to go for a walk around the lake near our house. We bought hot chocolates and ate doughnuts and everyone was nice to each other for three minutes before having to head home again, at which point I regret bringing two steel-framed bicycles with us. They must have been made from leftover scaffolding poles as they weighed more than the entire solar system. The girls refused to push them, so I pushed the buggy and carried both bikes on my shoulders as all four girls skipped along in front of me. By the time we got home I was drenched in sweat, had lost about three stone and had suffered a mild heart attack.

EVENING: I realised I'd lost track of what the twins had worn and what was clean and left for me to put away, as it was all in one big pile in the corner of their room.

Solo Dadding Diary: Day 5, I think.
I'm starting to lose count . . .

MORNING: My parents took pity on me and I decided to pack everyone up in the car and drive three hours to the West Country.

I had no idea if I had everything we needed but there were shops near my parents' house so if I'd forgotten essential items I could buy them down there. We just needed to leave this place ASAP.

The journey was broken up by three stops. The first stop was to close the boot properly as the warning light was blinking away and I didn't notice until we were about to join the motorway. The second was a toilet break, which involved all five of us cramming into a service station toilet cubicle as the girls didn't want to be left alone. There is nothing worse than having to watch each other go to the loo in such close proximity – especially when it's your turn. Eye contact was avoided at all points. As we left, I spent £25 on snack food to keep everyone quiet and we hit the road again.

The final stop was to pull over just 10 miles away from Mum and Dad's house for Marnie to vomit into a bag while Anya retched in the back seat at the sight and smell.

By the time we got to my parents', the inside of the car looked like an angry bear had got into a picnic basket and ripped it apart.

Solo Dadding Diary: Day 6

MORNING: Today was a cheat day as I had my parents. And they have a massive trampoline, which means I didn't see the older two girls for the entire morning. The twins 'helped' to cook by playing with the Fisher-Price kitchen that my sister had when she was young. It must be twenty-five years old now but it's the gift that keeps on giving. Anya and Marnie walked to the shop to get the papers while my mum looked after the twins and my dad took advantage of my being home by getting me to help dig out a particularly stubborn tree stump.

AFTERNOON: I learnt how to do a backflip at the age of thirty-four. I was so pleased with my accomplishment that I spent the entire afternoon waiting patiently for the girls to do their jumping and pretending to be interested so that I could then boot them off and have a go. The kids ran around basically naked and completely carefree in the back garden, while my parents drank an endless succession of cups of tea and got the girls to help pick veg. The girls' sugar intake has skyrocketed since being here as they are dealt out continual 'treats' by the glucose-pushing drug dealers otherwise known as their doting grandparents. The comedown and withdrawal will be such fun to deal with as we drive away tomorrow.

EVENING: Having run around the garden like lunatics all day, the kids had tired themselves out. The twins passed out before having a bath, and although Anya and Marnie managed to stay up to cook marshmallows on a fire in the garden (which they burnt to a crisp and promptly dunked in the bird bath to extinguish), they too had waved the white flag by 8.30 p.m., leaving my parents and me to reminisce about times gone by and talk about – you guessed it – the girls.

Solo Dadding Diary: Day 7

MORNING: Having put the bags back in the car, we said our good-byes to two tired-looking grandparents who would no doubt enjoy the sound of silence again as soon as we'd departed, and slump into a chair thanking their lucky stars we only see them every other month or so. It must be so nice to see us, knowing that we'll be leaving again at some point soon.

The drive home was relatively uneventful apart from the explosive poo that made itself known literally as we passed a service station. For the next 40 miles we all complained about the smell while poor Ottie sat in her own filth.

AFTERNOON: The start of the clean-up operation. The big girls were each given a task, while the twins strolled around the house completely oblivious to the hive of activity around them and decided to take small bites out of every single one of the raw vegetables in the veg rack. Anya and Marnie downed tools within five minutes of starting work, protesting that they were hungry and they hadn't made the mess so didn't feel they should clear it up.

EVENING: Clemmie came home!!!! She was so tired she didn't notice all the things that I'd put back in all the wrong places, but there would be time enough for that tomorrow. The most important thing was that she was back, she'd brought presents, and I'd managed to keep all the girls in roughly the same condition they were in when she left. My week of soloing was complete and I collapsed into the open arms of my wife and my bed by 9pm.

So let's see how I did against those assumptions at the start of the chapter:

- Dads only feed children food that comes from a plastic bag in the freezer.
  This is not completely true. Yes, 50 per cent of their food was originally stored at -20°C and yes, they did eat a lot of the colour yellow, but I made them eat fruit for dessert so that has to count for something.
- Dads spend the day doing exactly what they want, letting the kids turn the house into a war zone.
  This assumption has been blown out of the water. I only spent 15 per cent of my time doing what I wanted, and most of the rest of the time was spent breaking up fights and taking sharp implements out of the hands of toddlers.

- Dads don't clean up when there's a mess.

  Wrong – we just clean up to a different standard. I can clean until my knuckles have disappeared and my wife will still pick holes in everything I've done. She also has the ability to see things that I don't. A great example of this is the pile of stuff that accumulates on the stairs that needs to be taken up to the kids' rooms. I walk past this and honestly just don't see it.

  I also don't believe that clearing up during the day is necessary. What's the point if all your hard work is simply going to be undone in the space of five minutes when the kids get home from school? Do yourself a favour and clean up when the kids are in bed. Then you only do it once and no little people are around to destroy it for at least ten hours. I also get the added pleasure of completing all their half-done puzzles, only to find that two crucial pieces are missing, rendering the entire thing completely useless and an utter waste of time.

- Dads avoid doing any of the jobs on the list that was left for them, either out of sheer laziness or simply to annoy their partners.

  Once again not true. I did as much of the list as I could before it went walkabout. And it's not my fault if that list gets misplaced or chewed by a child to the point where the words just become a combination of smudges and black marks around the twins' mouths.

- Dads don't closely supervise children, they observe them from a distance, which results in mess and mayhem.

- I'd say this has some truth to it but it's not completely accurate. I don't want to be looming over them all the time, as part of being a child is exploring and being independent. It's true, though, that I have a tendency to get caught up in doing something and leaving them unsupervised for what feels like seconds but can be anything up to ten minutes, which usually leads to something getting broken or them inflicting damage on each other – or worse, my stuff.

- Dads rarely enforce the rules of the house when alone.
  Guilty as charged. When my wife and I parent together we need to present a united front when it comes to rules, but while the cat's away, the mice will play and I'm the king mouse – the fat one with all the cheese. My priority when I'm in charge is to have as much fun as possible; unfortunately this approach is usually accompanied by industrial-scale mess but seeing as I don't mind mess, that's OK by me. They'll have enough rules and regulations to deal with when they're older, so while they're kids, let them get on with the business of being children. I acknowledge that this makes it difficult to bring the rules back in when Clemmie returns, but I want to be seen as 'fun-time dad' so I take every opportunity that comes my way to be that guy!

- Dads don't like to leave the house.
  There are two points to make when it comes to the amount we leave the house: With ten years' experience, I can confidently take all my girls out on my own as I know what I'm doing, but truth be told, it's never what you'd call a pleasure. So, when we do go out, it's usually because we have run out of food, the girls need to go to the playground to burn off some energy or

because there is something in the diary that we have to do. If I had my way we'd be inside 100 per cent of the time when I'm parenting alone, but there is a danger we'd all end up killing each other.

- Dads don't know how to use the washing machine.
  I will never know which liquid I'm supposed to put into which drawer, but then again who does? It doesn't mean I can't do a load of washing. I will admit to being terrible at checking if any clothes are left in the machine when I'm emptying it, though, which has helped me learn that wet clothes that stay in the drum for more than three days don't smell clean any more.

- Dads don't make beds.
  Up until a year ago I would have said that this was true, but now I'm a master bed-maker. I still can't get my head around the need for all those cushions, which are only ever just discarded on the floor when it's bedtime, but I guess that's just one of the many lady secrets I'll never understand.

- Dads don't bath children unless they are caked in dirt from head to toe.
  Wrong (kind of). Most of the time, I'm on it when it comes to bath time as it's my responsibility to make sure that the food and general debris that has collected around my children's faces/hair/backs of their ears during the day actually comes off their bodies so that they don't start incubating a new species of parasite. That said, if it's late they can skip it – it won't kill them. Come to think of it, I let them skip it for three days on the trot once. That's not great, is it?

- Dads cook terrible meals for themselves when they are left alone.

  The idea of cooking a meal for oneself that takes forty-five minutes to prepare and two minutes to eat isn't appealing to me in any way, shape or form. In fact, it's depressing. So yes, I eat badly. I make sure I hide the two days' worth of pizza boxes and Chinese takeaway containers in someone else's bin. I just thank my lucky stars Clemmie does come back home, as I fear I'd be in the queue for a gastric band and a heart transplant if she weren't around.

Looking after the gang on my own has given me a newfound respect for parents that do this day in, day out on their own, or while their partners are out at work. If you're a stay-at-home parent, make sure that you wear that title as a badge of honour – apart from being a professional sewage-pipe cleaner or perhaps a shark wrestler, you have one of the hardest, yet most rewarding jobs going.

8

Home sweet home

I have no idea why, but irrespective of how big your house is, everyone seems to congregate in one place like a shit game of Sardines that no one wanted to play. If I were claustrophobic, I'd be permanently hyperventilating as I have no space any more.

Home sweet home

*H*ouses – they're just a collection of bricks, mortar, electrical wiring and copper pipes that we then spend our lifetimes filling with objects and aesthetically pleasing furniture that will look dated in five years but on trend again in thirty. However, when you fill them with people, they become so much more. They become a home. They are a place where the vast majority of us make our family memories, good and bad, and each room has a story to tell. So with that in mind, I'd like to take you on an *MTV Cribs*-style tour of our home. Just don't expect to find the obligatory bottle of Cristal in the fridge and immaculate rooms that have quite obviously been professionally cleaned hours before the film crew arrived. I want to give you an honest picture of how we live.

I should make a point here, though, before I kick off the walk-through of the house we call home:

I do live here too, you just wouldn't know it.

Over the years, I've noticed a disturbing trend that's happened so slowly that I didn't even notice it until recently. If I trace the origins of this evolutionary style change back to its source, I'm pretty sure it started when Clemmie and I first moved in together after university. The change I'm referring to is, of course, the eradication of any sign that a man resides in the house. It's like I'm a dirty black mark on the family history, like the uncle who once ran a Ponzi scheme from his bedroom back in the 1970s and is now never talked about and was removed from the family tree. If you were to walk into my house, the only indication to the casual onlooker that I live there is my single pair of size 10.5 shoes on the rack next to the front door, and my Barbour jacket that's buried under all the other brightly coloured coats in the hallway. Everything else I own has, over time, been consigned to a place out of the direct line of sight. Heaven forbid that anyone should suffer the indignity of viewing items that aren't perfectly in keeping with the décor of the house. My belongings have usually been silently removed to one of the five following places:

1. The shed – items that are left out for a period of more than two days will usually end up here. It's turned into a dumping ground for any of my belongings that are remotely bike-related or tool-like, and the sheer number of these means I can never find them again.
2. The loft – things like back issues of *Cycling Weekly* magazine, books I had on the bookshelves and my DVD collection eventually all emigrate to the prism-shaped space that's bursting at the seams with all the other precious goods that reside in a limbo-like state – not good enough to be out on display, but not shit enough to throw away and banish from our lives altogether.

Despite telling them the loft is both haunted
and a death trap, in an effort to maximise
'me' time, the kids always want to come up to
destroy my organised chaos, and rediscover
toys they binned years ago and forgot about.

3. The cupboard of doom – I have one cupboard that is out of the reach of small hands, located just above the cereal boxes. This was a land-grab I made back on the day we moved in, and despite consistent pressure to give up my rights and remove my belongings, much like a Native American in the face of aggressive settlers, I've dug in my heels and resisted. This cupboard is full of essential items like nails, screws, small household power tools,

instruction manuals for things we don't own any more, light bulbs and random tools that were once part of a set, but have since decided to go it alone. If Clemmie doesn't know what something is, she'll usually put it in here.

4. My bedside drawer – this drawer acts as an overflow for my wallet. It contains receipts from meals I can't recall, old loyalty cards, foreign change that's only useful for giving to the girls to make them think they're rich and yet more tools, this time mainly Allen keys from the multitude of IKEA items I've constructed over the years. This is also the place where I hide confiscated sweets and screens.

5. The bin – this doesn't happen that often, but there has been the odd occasion when my belongings are so knackered that no one in their right mind would look at them and think they were worth keeping, apart from me. Case in point: I have a lot of oily rags. These are important to me as they enable me to tinker with my bike without getting oily hands (if that happens, I get an immediate ban from entering the house on account of being incapable of not getting finger-marks all over the worktops). Clemmie sees these and just assumes they're rubbish, which they are obviously not. The same goes for offcuts of wood. You never know when you might need a piece of 18-mm ply that you've procured from a skip down the road, yet my wife doesn't see the intrinsic value in these things and as a result they are tossed in the outside bin. She would have hated being married to my dad as he carted around a piece of teak wood from house to house for over thirty years, before finally making it into a worktop.

This shift has gathered pace in recent years. With each new mouth to feed, the ratio of females to males has increased as well as the number of children to adults, neither of which is great news for me. As the only male presence in a house that is now completely female-orientated, I'm pretty convinced that I've started to experience a transformation. I've yet to talk to a doctor about this, but I can feel my balls retracting back up into my body as my ovaries start to develop. I blame this partly on having been surrounded by women every day of my life for the last ten years, and partly on all the oestrogen in London's water, thanks to all the contraceptive pills that teenage – now probably pregnant – girls have discarded down the loo. No wonder my nips tingle when I hear a crying baby. I'm sure it won't be long before my transformation is complete and all the signs of my masculinity will drift away.

So with the scene set, let's begin the walk-through . . .

We'll start by the front door – however, unlike on MTV, the space outside my house isn't filled with flash sports cars with 20-inch rims, sound systems that induce Niagara Falls-like torrents of blood spilling from your earholes and paint jobs that require two pairs of sunglasses worn at the same time in order to look directly at them. All you'll see is the family car and a part-folded buggy. The double buggy doesn't fit through the door and honestly, when you're heading to bed at 11 p.m. and you suddenly remember it's still out there in the dark, who can be bothered to go out and fold the bloody thing up? It must wonder what it did to deserve such a rough life, relegated to the indignity of having to spend the bitterly cold winter nights outside along with the foxes that regularly ransack our bins under cover of darkness and then fornicate in the flowerbed. It's a miracle that it's never been stolen, but since our buggy is covered in crayon scrawls, half-eaten rice cakes that are now breeding colonies for bacteria, and mud that's so ingrained even Cillit Bang won't shift it, I imagine it wouldn't command much price-wise when sold in a back alley.

The first thing you'll notice when you enter the house is that the heating will probably be on, despite me having turned it off several times during the course of the day. I'm not sure if the women in my family are cold-blooded reptiles or just have terrible circulation, but I'm constantly engaged in a silent battle over the position of the thermostat.

I was brought up in a house where if you were cold before mid-November, you put another jumper on and ran around a bit. However, my girls like to live in an oasis at a constant 25 degrees, a temperature that would allow us to start a tropical plant business from our living room.

The hallway

As you make it past the baby transportation device that cost more than my first car, you're immediately greeted by a shoe rack that looks like a small Foot Locker outlet. The rickety thing that looks like a woodwork project I gave up on at school has been with us since university. As I mentioned, I'm allowed one pair of shoes on here. The rest of the space is taken up with girls' footwear that's scuffed to the point that you'd consider throwing it out, even though it was only bought two weeks before. It seems that walking without dragging your feet across the tarmac just isn't cool these days. (Oh my God, I just realised I sounded like my mum. That was unexpected!)

As you continue in, there are two coat racks, both of which I made. The top one is for Clemmie and me and has eight hooks on it. Quickly applying your GCSE mathematics skills, you'd be able to deduce that theoretically we'd get four hooks each. One might think that was reasonable, however, in reality I have just two hooks. The rest are taken up with the multitude of Clemmie's bags, hats, jackets and coats. And these are just for this season – there are more upstairs in the airing cupboard. And in the loft. And under the bed. This means that my hooks are no longer my own and my coats end up being the ones underneath everything and getting to them involves removing each garment that's on top of them. The lower rack is for the kids as it's just at the right height for them to hang their coats up themselves. Of course, that never happens. As soon as they come through the door, their jackets are cast aside with the expectation that the magic fairies will pick them up and hang them up for them. Well, here's some news, kids: the fairies are all dead. I know this because I killed them with a can of industrial bug spray and watched them take their last breath, so you're just going to have to learn to do it yourselves.

The downstairs bathroom

Don't be deceived. On first inspection it may look like just a toilet under the stairs, but believe me it's far more than that. This is in fact a meeting point for the twins to converse and strategise about what havoc they can cause later that day. Just think of it as a dark back room in an Italian restaurant where the mafia plan their next job, just with less card playing and smoke. Not tall enough to turn on the light, they open the door, enter into the darkness and shut the door behind them. This is closely followed by a lot of giggling and then the reappearance of Ottilie and Delilah, who then trot off to do whatever it is they have decided to do.

This is also the place you can find them occasionally sucking on the Neom reed diffuser sticks and eating toothpaste.

In the days before they could open the door, we also used the room to hide the veg rack as the twins would pull it over and gum all the onions. I guess they just liked the fizz a good red onion gives out, but it rendered them useless for actually cooking with. I should have just filled the rack with chillis, that would have taught them not to mess with its contents, but I'm not quite that heartless. In hindsight, this was a real hygiene issue and had we been running an eatery out of our house, the health inspectors would have had an absolute field day with it. Ah, the stupid things we parents do for a quiet life.

As a side note, this door doesn't have a lock on it any more. That was bust open a while back when Marnie locked herself in there having not turned the light on before entering and then promptly losing her mind when she tried to exit. Like a bomb-disposal technician giving instructions to a complete novice over the phone, with my mouth pressed up against the gap between the frame and the door, I talked Marnie through how to slide the bolt back, but it was no use. In the end I had to shoulder-barge the door and rip the lock off the frame. Since that day, this room has turned into a peep show for children who have an interest in watching adults on the loo.

The kitchen/dining room

Welcome, you've just entered the hub of the home. This is also where we spend a lot of our time, usually arguing with the children about one of the following things:

- Unloading the dishwasher.
- Not eating everything on their plates.
- Not wearing roller skates at the table (this is not an American diner).
- The fact they are only being offered fruit for dessert.

This is also where you can find me cursing as I cut carrots furiously in an effort to make one of Jamie Oliver's fifteen-minute meals in fifteen minutes. I've yet to meet anyone that's actually done it.

The first thing you'll notice is a massive fairground-style sign adorned with incandescent light bulbs. It simply reads 'GIRLS'. It's like I'm living in a scaled-down version of North Korea. This sign is the equivalent of the huge pictures of Kim Jong-un that hang on all the government buildings and is a constant reminder that although I may live here, I do so under the rule of others.

The fridge is a place I come to contemplate things. I can stand in front of an open fridge for several minutes, frozen by the chilly air coursing over my face while I think about the important challenges of the day such as what I'll eat now, what I might eat later and who put the milk back in here without the sodding lid on. It's then that I'll notice the pungent smell of something that is definitely not in any fit state to be eaten, but locating the specific item in order to get rid of it is something that no one has been bothered to actually do.

The top shelf is dominated by Petits Filous yoghurts that the twins refuse to allow us to spoon-feed them. This ends up with 30 per cent of the contents on the floor, 30 per cent on the table, 20 per cent around their mouths, 15 per cent in their mouths and 5 per cent in mine. Those percentages fluctuate depending on how hungry I am and how especially resistant the twins are that meal time to having spoons waved in front of their faces with accompanying aeroplane noises.

The next shelf down is reserved for brightly coloured plastic containers that are full of non-descript leftovers from the kids' meals. No one can be sure when these were put there, so best not to check and hope someone else deals with them.

Next to the fridge is what's known as the make-make cupboard. This contains every single pen, pencil and piece of abstract artwork that the children have produced, ranging from masterpieces of expressionism that tell tales of torment and rage, right down to random crayon scribbles that are apparently illustrations of us as a family. It's at this point I should thank my employers for the forest's worth of used printer paper that I've procured from them over the years to aid in the achievement of my girls' collective goal of ensuring that no piece of paper on the planet is ever left blank.

The play kitchen lives in the far corner and is where many an imaginary tea party has been held. The food is usually so hard that your teeth splinter and the less said about the service the better. If I were to leave a review on TripAdvisor after attending this dive, it would read as follows:

Service: Both rude – the waiting staff refused to make eye contact as they poured our dinners into our laps – and overfamiliar: a number of times I was approached by a member of the waiting staff for a kiss and ended up having to wipe their snot off my top lip.

Food: Impossible to eat as it's all made from plastic and wood.

Value for money: It was free, but cost a lot in terms of my time. Ordering took forever and cooking with the power of imagination rather than an actual cooker meant meals were prepared at a glacial pace.

Would you recommend this to a friend?: No, unless I really hated them. Michelin starred it ain't.

Opening the kitchen cupboards reveals our mismatched collection of tableware. There was a time when we had a set of pristine white crockery that we were given as a wedding present. As the years have passed and the number of children hanging off us has increased, these have been chipped and broken and slowly replaced with an extensive collection of multi-coloured plastic plates, bowls and cutlery sets. When you open the dishwasher, you're confronted with what looks like the leftovers from a Gay Pride march that a unicorn has vomited a rainbow on.

The washing machine and dryer are in another cupboard. With a family of six that includes children who wear an item of clothing for less than half a day and then favour stuffing their only slightly worn clothes into the dirty clothes basket over making the effort to fold them back up and placing them in their drawers, it's no wonder these two domestic workhorses toil away for as many hours as there are in the day. The washing machine also doubles up as a congregation point for the twins, who like to place their heads against the concave glass door and watch the washing swirl around them. A minute or so later, after being mesmerised by the vortex that's engulfed them, they'll stand up, completely disorientated and stumbling around like that guy you see outside the shopping centre who's smashed off a bottle of Archers and couldn't give a shit about what anyone thinks of him.

This multi-purpose room is also regularly used as a running circuit, a concert hall, a dance studio, a workshop, a fashion catwalk, a debating practice centre and a boxing ring. Occasionally we'll eat a meal or two here as well.

The living room

This is the setting for the never-ending battle of the cushions. We put them on the sofas, and the girls take them off again. This war has been raging for about nine years so far and there's no sign of it reaching a conclusion any time soon.

This is also the location for den-building. I personally pride myself on my den-making capabilities. After years of practice I can now build something for the girls that has the structural integrity to withstand a 6.5 shock wave on the Richter scale. It's an intricate design that comprises many chambers, much like a badger's sett.

Black-framed pictures that depict our lives with our girls hang on the largest wall. When we first moved in, I spent two nights planning the arrangement and measuring out the precise gaps between each frame so that the ordered jumble of snapshots looked organised and chaotic in equal measure. Now the bottom row of pictures has disappeared as a result of Marnie knocking them off with her feet as she performs gymnastic moves on the sofa. In their place there are now ghostly outlines of where the frames once hung. These marks won't come off, no matter how much elbow grease you throw at them.

The TV sits opposite the sofa that is now stained with black marks from the time Ottie managed to get her hands on a Sharpie pen, and the remnants of food and drink that have been eaten on it despite express instructions that the living room is a no-food zone (apart from on wet and miserable film days).

The TV is now an integral part of family life, as the digital nanny is a key tool in getting the kids into a single place so we can get shit done. Being a bit of a tech boffin, I've also worked out a way to use this black hole of child attention to my advantage, and can now live-stream my face from my phone onto the TV screen from anywhere in the house. There is literally no escape from me now.

In the corner is my grandmother's wing-backed chair that we have re-covered in a dark green velvet fabric. In hindsight this was a terrible idea as any dirt stands out like a shire horse that has been entered into Crufts. In the end, we surrounded the chair with a playpen so that no one could use it. It remains clean to this day, but probably doesn't have much job satisfaction as no one actually uses it for the purpose it was designed.

Hanging above the doorway is a pull-down projector screen. This has been used twice in the year that's it been there. My sales pitch to the family was that it could be used for film days so we could all hunker down and stuff ourselves with popcorn, but the honest truth is that I wanted to link up the projector to the speakers using the mountains of cables I've acquired over the years and watch sports on it. Nice idea, but there was a flaw in my plan that I hadn't anticipated. Clemmie wouldn't allow the projector out on display as it wasn't 'in keeping with the style of the room'. Now, the projector is shut in a cupboard and is such a faff to untangle from the wires and set up, that it lies dormant, unused and unloved with the CDs that we never play and the wires to electronics that don't work any more. Sorry, projector – I had such high hopes for our relationship, but it was just never meant to be.

This room has also doubled up as my bedroom on more than one occasion. The reasons for this happening are listed below:

- Clemmie had a big day the following day and therefore thought it might be best if I slept on the sofa.
- I fell asleep on the sofa writing this book and couldn't be arsed to go to bed when I woke fully clothed at 3.48 a.m.
- Anya or Marnie had a bad dream and came into our room to sleep with us. After being kicked in the nuts several times and having a child snoring millimetres from my face, I opted to go downstairs.
- I came home after a night out and didn't want to anger the bear in my bed by stumbling around in the room it was sleeping in,

so instead I put a pizza in the oven, watched live roulette on TV for eight minutes and fell asleep bolt upright. Four hours later, I was jumped on by a child who I struggled to see through the low-lying fog that hung in the room resulting from the now charcoal-like Italian cuisine I'd left in the oven to magically transform into a black rock.

Let's go upstairs

First, a quick note on the stairs themselves. As with all staircases, these were originally developed to allow the inhabitants to move between the different levels of the house without having to scale the outside of the building and crawl through open windows. They are very practical things and learning how to deal with them is a vital part of growing up. Imagine if we never learnt how to use them – the secretive world of 'upstairs' would have to remain an undiscovered land of wonder, bungalow builders would be billion-aires and Daleks would have wiped us all out! The bottom three steps are a different shade to the others thanks to the kids not taking their shoes off as they disappear to their rooms before being reminded that footwear needs to stay downstairs. The rest of the stairs have little brown stains on them from the multiple times I've brought tea up to Clemmie in bed, only to be barged out of the way by a small girl-shaped freight train coming in the opposite direction.

These stairs have also demonstrated several other uses since we've had children:

- As the site of frequent in-house fly tipping: My girls and I have one major thing in common that drives Clemmie to consider finding out what an entire pint of bleach tastes like. We don't see mess. No, correction: we see the mess, we just don't care about the mess and see very little need to do anything about it.

  Clemmie will – pointlessly in my view – clear up during the day, and anything that needs to go upstairs ends up piled neatly on the steps. The girls and I just walk past this annoying clutter without a single consideration as to why it's there or what we should do with it. Only when Clemmie starts shouting do we acknowledge the clothing, shoes, board games, electronics, books and miscellaneous items.

- Baby racing: I regularly find the twins halfway up the stairs, smiling/squeaking, on their way up to the promised land of the big girls' bedrooms – the allure of small unguarded objects that fit conveniently in the mouth is too much to resist. So what do you do when you have too many stairs, not enough stair gates and twins that love climbing? Welcome to the dark and murky underworld of baby staircase racing. The rules are simple: take two genetically identical babies in prime physical condition (i.e. no overloaded nappies) and let them battle it out. No encouraging with food, no blocking, no pulling hair. Delilah has the edge at the moment and is filling the older girls' piggy banks with winnings while I'm down £7. Ottie is killing me – I should've known better than to back old stubby legs. Note: safety professionals are on hand at all times and are trained to give out quiet encouragement and hugs. It's a nice sport really.

Our bedroom

If this were *MTV Cribs*, I'd be saying something corny like, 'And this is where the magic happens!', but it's not, so I won't. The only magic that happens in here is the disappearance of the loose change I keep on the bedside table.

Our bedroom looks like the room of a woman in her early thirties. There are prints of lipsticks and perfumes in gold-rimmed frames, a dusty-pink tub chair covered in women's clothes, and a mid-60s dressing table in the corner. The only sign that I share this room with Clemmie is the crumpled heap of my clothes on the floor on my side of the bed, which have fallen in such a way that you'd think I'd been shot with a liquefaction gun, leaving nothing but my empty clothes behind.

The room is dominated by a king-size bed that is covered in cushions. (As I've mentioned before, I don't think I'll ever understand why women love cushions so much. The only answer I can come up with as to why more and more of these feather-filled space-takers make their way into our house is that Clemmie is the ringleader in a black-market cushion breeding programme, as I'm certainly not the one bringing them in. No doubt we'll need to move to a bigger place soon. She'll say it's because the girls need more space, but I know it's so she can fill it with yet more dusky-rose velvet chair squares.) We used to have a double bed but as the number of people in our family grew and the need to not touch each other while we slept became a necessity for fear of creating yet more offspring, we had to upgrade.

This leads me to a question: is it only me, or do all men learn to sleep on an 8-inch strip at the edge of the bed? Irrespective of the size of the bed, or how many people are in it, I always find myself relegated to the 'man zone'. I've become so used to sleeping on this limited area of bed real estate that I'm confident I could sleep on top of a wall and not fall off. On the other side of the bed (the promised land), Clemmie sleeps like a starfish all night long.

Along the wall run five IKEA Pax wardrobes. As basic KS1 maths tells you, five wardrobes divided between two people doesn't go, so I ended up with two and Clemmie with three. Over the years, it's got to the point where Clemmie has actually suggested she needs more space. My joking response was that perhaps I should hang my clothes outside the window in a large black bin liner so she could have my space. I immediately retracted my comment as I could see she was actually considering it.

The ensuite bathroom

The little room with all the plumbing in it that adjoins our bedroom also has very limited indications that a man uses it. My bottles and razors aren't deemed pretty enough to earn coveted shelf space next to the sink, so they are instead tucked away in a cupboard, while girl products of all shapes and sizes proudly stand to attention, waiting to be used. I'm not sure if these potions and creams are radiating some kind of toddler-only frequency, but the twins are drawn to them like moths to a flame. With a quick hop, skip and jump they climb onto the toilet and can regularly be found sucking the toothpaste and giving each other facials with Clemmie's eight-hour cream. Dry skin is not something that we have to worry about with the twins in the future, apparently.

They also use the bathroom bin like a lucky dip. If the bin had a guest book and the twins had the dexterity and the manners to write in it, their message would read as follows: 'Top day out here. Access was initially difficult but after some persistence and good old teamwork we gained entry. The food available throughout our brief stay, which included toothpaste and moisturiser, was second to none. We especially enjoyed the remnants of mint shower gel that made us foam at the mouth – we assumed it was a palate cleanser. The collection of tampon applicators and different types of hair was also most entertaining. The only negative was that our stay was cut short abruptly by any angry bearded giant. We will be returning.' No you won't, girls – I Sellotaped the bin shut.

The twins' room

This room is next to ours and basically consists of flat-pack modular furniture. Two cots butt up against the walls, each inhabited by an excessive number of soft toys, who have obviously taken up squatters' rights and become permanent residents. I constructed these cots with my own bare hands and an Allen key selected from my sizeable collection.

On principle, I refuse to look at the instructions when building these things. I don't know why; perhaps it's because my dad never did, perhaps it's because I feel that I'm smarter than the box of flat-pack furniture in front of me and don't need someone else's illustrated instructions to master it. Or, more likely, perhaps it's because I've made so much of the stuff over the years that it's basically all the same and I can do it in my sleep. However, with the cots, it was only after twenty minutes that I realised not only had I managed to build them around me so they were penning me in like a miniature Alcatraz, but I was also left with a multitude of screws that seemed to have no home. I opened the languageless picture book of simple-to-follow instructions to find that I needed to go back twelve steps to fit two vital screws into holes that were now inaccessible.

In the corner is a changing table that is bursting at the seams with nappies and wipes, as running out is simply not an option that bears thinking about.

A chest of drawers that we got on Freecycle eight years ago and gave a makeover to sits between the two cots. I'm almost two years in and I still get it in the neck for putting clothes back in the wrong drawers. How am I supposed to know each and every item's home address? All I know is that children's clothes have way too many poppers for my liking. Why hasn't Velcro been adopted as the worldwide standard yet?

A blackout blind whose suckers have the suction power of a thirty-year-old vacuum cleaner whose heart really isn't in it any more and just wants to retire adorns the windows. As a result, the blind is constantly falling down during the night, which means the twins wake up earlier as they become aware it's daylight sooner.

Finally there's the nappy bin. Emptying this out has to be my least favourite of the very many parenting jobs. The cheap flimsy bags I bought that were 25p less than our usual brand regularly prove their worth and rip under the sheer weight of human waste, releasing an odour into the room that a really pungent old cheese with athlete's foot and chronic halitosis would be proud of. It's my fault really. I open that bin, slide in the offending articles quicker than David Blaine's sleight of hand and leave the room hoping that someone else will deal with it when it's too full. However, I find that I'm not the only one to play this particular game and that Clemmie has done the same thing so, unable to wedge anything more into the bin, I have to step up. As I pull the bag out, my gag reflex kicks in with full force while the twins look gleefully on at a grown man having to carry 2.7 kg of nappies filled with 'gifts' out of the room, dry heaving like a cat with a hairball.

This room has also been the backdrop to a scene that I've discovered is commonplace across the globe. It's likely that somewhere in your child's room is a tube of Sudocrem. If you don't know what this is, it's an antiseptic cream whose primary function is to soothe and heal nappy rash on your little one's bum. However, it also doubles as a magnet for toddlers who then use it to decorate themselves and all their surroundings in a thick white paste.

I wasn't there when it happened, but I'm pretty sure that when they first brought it out, the product design meeting went a little something like this:

'OK, guys, I think we can all agree, we can be pretty proud – we have a great product here that all parents will use to protect their kids' cherub-like arses. We don't want to make their lives too easy though, as we all know they already have way too much time on their hands. So let's brainstorm some ideas to make this product more of a hassle than it should be. Doug, got something to say?'

'Yes, John, I've got an idea. How about we stick a red label on it so children gravitate towards it?'

'Great! I like your blue-sky thinking. Anyone else?'

'Yes, let's make the lid easy for toddlers to open – forget screw caps, just a good pull should do the job.'

'Excellent stuff. But we need more. Anne, your go.'

'OK, how about making the tub opening just the right size for kids to put their entire hand in?'

'Genius. Now we're cooking on gas. Any more?'

'We should make it absolutely impossible to get off clothes, carpets and fabrics in general.'

'Bob, you've hit the jackpot! Take the rest of the day off and go hit the spa.'

My ten-year-old's room

Now I won't go into detail here as a girl needs her privacy, but I will tell you that at this point in time Anya's room is essentially a mixture of clothes, slime and USB cables. The amount of time I spend in here has dwindled in recent years because as Anya has grown she uses it as a space to retreat into when it all gets too much. She'll spend literally hours in here playing with slime that she's made by using all of our cleaning products and glue, or making videos on her phone. There are more clothes on the floor than there are in the wardrobe and the number of posters of bands and pop stars is slowly but steadily increasing as I lose her to her tween years, but the pile of soft toys at the end of her bed tells me that I haven't totally lost her yet.

My seven-year-old's room

As above, I'll respect Marnie's right to privacy and won't go into detail, however what I can say about Marnie's room is that it can best be described as the dwelling of a kleptomaniac who has a fetish for art supplies and ponies. Under the far corner of her bed is a not-so-secret sweet collection that we know she keeps stocked by storing up her Friday sweets and by thieving from the snack cupboard in the kitchen. She still thinks we're oblivious to this mini confectionery treasure trove.

The kids' bathroom

The kids' bathroom has become a dumping ground for discarded clothing that didn't quite make it into the dirty clothes bin or the girls' bedrooms. The obligatory jeans complete with inside-out knickers lie on the floor alongside vests and T-shirts with several days' worth of dinner splattered across them, kicked to one side to make a path that links the three main points of interest in the room: the toilet, the sink and the bath.

Much like the flat field that surrounds a mighty river, the floor in the bathroom also acts as a flood plain that is regularly waterlogged, especially when Ottie and Delilah are in the process of being bathed. Girls, I'm with you – yes, it's more fun to pour water out of the bath and onto the floor, watching it slowly seep into the grouting and dislodge the expensive encaustic cement tiles, but it's an absolute pain in the arse to clear up and will no doubt get me in trouble for a) not stopping you, b) encouraging you by laughing, and c) mopping up with one of the fancy towels that's for show and not for actual use (everyone has one of these, right?).

The toothbrushes adorned with cartoon characters on the side by the sink have bristles that have splayed out to create a mushroom effect and should probably be used for scrubbing particularly stubborn dog poo off a shoe rather than brushing teeth. We really should change them a bit more regularly.

Oh, and let's not forget the bath toys . . . Bath time is slowly becoming a game of 'spot the twins among the metric tonne of foam letters and plastic squeezy animals'. I swear that these rubber creatures are procreating on their own as I'm definitely not buying this stuff!

So with that we've reached the end of the tour and now you have an intimate knowledge of our house and its accompanying stories. When we were just a foursome, there was still enough room to swing several cats at the same time, but from the moment the twins started walking, the house began to feel like a matchbox and I'm finding my head is regularly filled with anxiety dreams about the walls closing in on me. There are little people everywhere and they all come with more baggage than the Rolling Stones doing one more final world tour, which means every inch of the house is taken up with stuff. Empty space is a distant memory that I look back on with fondness. When we move, and that can't be far off, I really should have pamphlets produced to hand out to our new neighbours to warn them. I think they'll be entitled 'The Hoopers Are Coming to Town: We Bring the Noise'. Oh Lord, they're going to hate us . . .

9

Is human cloning possible yet?

I like being popular, but dividing my time between all five women in my life leaves me feeling more thinly spread than the last scrapings at the bottom of a jam jar. If I could be everywhere at once, then I would.

Is human cloning possible yet?

We all start out life in this world with a tendency to be selfish. Babies are by their very nature self-centred – they can't do anything for themselves, let alone other people, and rely on others for their every need. As parents, we wait on them hand and foot and they gleefully take it all. If we're lucky we get a smile in return, but there's a 50 per cent chance that that's wind. As children, our focus is only ever on ourselves and we only care about what we want, which is perfectly natural as the concept of sharing or giving attention to others only develops over time. Growing up, I was the oldest sibling so I got to do everything first and the focus was on me. As I developed into a young man, I was pretty selfish and as a result my past girlfriends probably thought I was a complete shit because frankly all I really wanted to do was hang out with my friends and try to buy beer from off-licences with photo IDs we'd ordered from the back of *Loaded* magazine. The idea of actually spending my time with my girlfriends made watching plants grow in a dark room seem appealing.

Fast-forward to 2005 and I met Clemmie. I'd grown up a little and my outlook had changed, along with my hair, which now had blond spiked highlights (a particularly poor choice even back in those days). This was about the time guys started to use straighteners on their hair and I'd fallen into the trap of using my female friends' straighteners at university to emulate what was seen as the style of the time. Thank God that's not happening too much these days. Anyway, I digress. When I met Clemmie, all I wanted to do was spend my time with her and do things to make her happy. She was and continues to be my everything. I'm not saying that I became a monk and dedicated my life to others, the selfish streak was still there, but it had just receded a little and been forced into the bottom drawer of my brain.

With the arrival of Anya, my ability to spend any of my time on things I wanted to do dropped even more sharply and dramatically than the stock market when the sub-prime mortgage scandal broke. I didn't fight it; in fact I welcomed it as I truly wanted to spend my time with my little family unit as much as I could. The idea of going out and getting smashed, only to fall asleep on the train and wake up in a small dark station at the arse end of nowhere, 20 miles in the wrong direction from where I lived, had suddenly lost its appeal. I was happy to split my time between the three of us. It was manageable and felt like a good balance.

As the number of children we created increased and I became more and more outnumbered by females, I found myself wishing for a cloning machine to be invented so that I could share myself six ways without completely losing time for myself. The task is almost impossible and the parental guilt I feel on a daily basis is only rein-forced when one of my girls says that 'you never spend any time with me any more!' This is a sure-fire way to make me feel terrible, worse even than the time I forgot to pick one of them up from nurs-ery and had to be called by a staff member to come and get her. But this is where my life is right now and it's hard work to get it right. The plate-spinning analogy is the best way I can think of to describe the situation, but as well as being many in number, my plates are different sizes and shapes and made from particularly brittle mate-rial. I started out as an amateur in the plate-spinning business, but over the last decade, I've moved up to semi-professional – I still get to the point where a wobble occurs but I've learnt how to correct it and divide my time efficiently so that none of them actually make it to the floor. So what's the magic trick to keeping it all going? To keeping everyone happy while also retaining a sense of who I am and what I'm about?

Well, here's how I manage to dedicate some one-to-one time to each of the women I love, keep the punters happy and keep this particular one-man show on the road, 24/7.

Me and my wife

First and foremost is Clemmie. She was the first of the five women in my life, the one I started this journey with and my one true love. (Vomit-inducing, isn't it? I'll give you a moment to grab the bucket and get past that dry heaving stage that I know displays of affection can bring out in some people.)

She's my team mate in all of this, but with each daughter that's come into the world, our time – the time we used to spend going out, dancing, getting pissed, talking crap, seeing friends and doing nothing in particular – has slowly been eroded until we've got to the point where we are today.

The time we now get on our own consists of the following:

- The two hours in the evening between getting the girls to bed and our own bedtimes – this will be spent arguing about whose turn it is to cook, what to cook, who should clear up, whose turn it is to do the dishwasher, and lounging on the sofa either discussing the kids or regaling each other with a synopsis of what's happened in our respective days. We'll both be half listening while watching a documentary about a drug lord in South America who has been on the run for forty years.

- The time we're in bed awake – we rarely go to bed at the same time but there are a few rare occasions when we're in bed together and able to fight the urge to close our eyes. We'll discuss the family calendar, which she'll have orchestrated down to the finest detail, and I'll promptly forget key pieces of information, like who's picking up the kids after school or whether I need to work from home at some point that week to cover something she's booked in, so I'll ask her again what we're doing when we wake up in the morning, which drives her absolutely insane. If I had £1 for every time she's said the words 'Were you not listening at all?' or 'I'm not telling you again, go and look at the calendar', I'd be so rich that I'd be able to pay for someone else to remember this stuff and follow me around all day to remind me. It's not that I'm not paying attention, I just think that my memory has now hit capacity and without an upgrade and a serious overhaul of the internal wiring, I've started to run slow and my files are becoming corrupted.

- The time when we're in bed asleep – during this time, I'll get woken to be told I'm snoring too much, or I've farted and it smells like something has died inside me, or I'm sweating too much and soaking the sheets with body juice, or that my feet are like particularly spiky icebergs that have drifted too close to the warm shores of her side of the bed. I have in the past played back recordings of Clemmie's snoring to her to prove she's not the only one that has to suffer the audio assault of lying next to someone who has nasal passages that you'd struggle to push a pin through, but that falls on deaf ears.

I'm sure all parents suffer this predicament as we give more and more of ourselves to our children who demand our attention like a garden bonfire that could spread and torch our house if it's not watched, yet my relationship with Clemmie is arguably the most important one I have in this family, and I know that sometimes I'm guilty of not giving it my all. That's why Clemmie and I try to go on a date night once a month to get away from the house, leave the rabble behind and just be us again. On those nights, we'll go for a nice meal, talk to each other loudly, speculate about whether the couple next to us are on date number two or six, and discuss the older couple in the corner who are sitting in silence – presumably because they are either bored of each other or have literally covered every topic of conversation ever in their time together and now have nothing more to say. After eating the remnants of the food on both our plates and paying the bill, I'll try to convince a tired Clemmie that we should go to the pub next door. I'll want to stay out later and get merry, but the babysitter is £10 an hour, meaning that before we've even stepped foot out the house, our evening out has cost a minimum of £50.

I tell myself that Clemmie and I will get our time together when they all leave home, but I read recently that children are staying at home longer thanks to increased rents and an inability to get a foot on the housing ladder, so who knows when that will be. I could find myself still calling them down for breakfast on their 40th birthday. I guess our slow transition into the elderly couple in the restaurant will come in due course.

Me and my eldest daughter

Anya and I have a special relationship. Not like the special relationship between the US and the UK that's referred to by politicians and means very little. I mean it's actually special. She's my firstborn and is blazing a trail for the other girls to follow.

The thirty minutes before lights out are the best moments of the day for Anya and me as we get to actually talk with no one else to interrupt us (apart from when Marnie comes rocketing into the room with an impromptu cartwheel display and the words 'Get out of my room!' are immediately bellowed in her general direction).

For fifteen minutes I'll just let her talk. It could be about anything, but it's important to let her get the day out of her system. To talk and know that someone is listening. To get things off her chest about school, friends, world events, things she's watched on YouTube and anything else that might be running through her mind at that point in time. She's growing up in the equivalent of the middle of a riot that has no police intervention, so having these quiet moments is essential. In the last year we've also tried to learn French together via an app, which has resulted in a form of the language that will have us laughed out of Paris; revised for some maths exams, which left me feeling like I needed to go back to Year 6 and brush up my long division; and talked through the importance of taking your time to think before you act.

Anya is also a regular on trips to the tip with me, where we talk about nothing in particular and spend the entire journey laughing at my terrible jokes and her bad impressions. Then we'll get chocolate bars and dispose of the wrappers before getting home to avoid getting in trouble. We're quite a team.

Me and my middle daughter

Marnie is a very easy-going, self-contained person and is equally happy being surrounded by her friends or on her own busily getting on with whatever it is that seven-year-old girls do in their rooms.

She is courteous, thoughtful and giving, and I'm not sure where she came from. In a house that operates at a constant 120 decibels and is busier than an ASDA selling massive TVs for £2.50 on Black Friday, she is the calming influence on us all and asks for very little.

There was always a worry that being the middle child, she'd be squeezed out by a domineering older sister and twins that require more attention than reality-TV celebrities. In a household where getting decent one-to-one time is rarer than a steak that's still mooing, the time we spend driving to one of the multitude of friends' houses, sports clubs or social engagements is really the only moment Marnie and I manage to connect. She may only be seven, but her social life is so full that it's intimidating – especially compared to my own pathetic excuse for one, which started to tail off back in 2007 and is now curled up in a ball in the corner whimpering in submission.

When in the car one-to-one, I put myself under extreme pressure to transform into a human-based in-car entertainment system that must perform on demand to keep Marnie thinking I'm the most awesome man on the planet. Bored of games of 'I Spy' that tend to end up either very obscure or toilet-related after five rounds, Marnie has taken to challenging me to do funny voices – transforming the car from a transportation device into an amateur mobile *Royal Variety Show* performance. I'm particularly proud of recently nailing an impression of an orange – a lesser man may have crumbled under the pressure of this particular request, but summoning all of my A-level method acting skills, I became the orange and was rewarded with the outrageous gappy smile and laugh I wanted.

I just hope that as she gets older, life doesn't grind her down and that she remains the happy-go-lucky person she is. The planet would benefit from a few more Marnies.

Me and the twins

My time with Ottie and Delilah is limited to four key slots:

- The thirty minutes in the morning when Clemmie is getting ready to face the day.
- The odd day I have to take off work as parental leave when Clemmie has to go to work to bring new life into the world and we can't find/haven't been organised enough to arrange childcare.
- The thirty minutes before bed.
- The weekends when everyone who has a social life leaves the house and leaves us to piss about and be stupid.

With the time I do have with Ottie and Delilah on my own, I've learnt that as individuals they are a handful but much like Transformers, when combined they turn into a force to be reckoned with. Although I find myself wishing I could graft another couple of arms onto my torso and have wireless CCTV implanted in my brain so I could see what they are up to all the time instead of running from room to room like a headless chicken E numbers, I try and spend as much time as I can with them one-to-one (or one-to-two, as the case may be). Going by my experience with my first two daughters, these early years disappear quickly. One moment they are small people who look to you for everything, and the next they're asking for your credit card details and PIN numbers, so I want to soak up as much of them as possible as they will probably be our last ever babies.

They are genuinely funny individuals and I love being around them as I think we're of a similar mental age. They're also young enough at the moment not to find me embarrassing or 'cringey' as my older girls have started to call me. So as long as armpit farts, stupid faces and ridiculous noises are still keeping the crowd happy, I'll continue to maximise my time with them to keep my ego inflated and maintain the delusion that I'm a genuinely funny person.

So that's everyone else sorted. Now what about me?

So with everyone else getting their slice of the Daddy pie, I'm left with a thin crust of very dry time-pastry to call my own. It's around 3 per cent of my day and it's barely worth hanging on to, but for the sake of my own sanity, that crust is mine and I'm clinging to it for dear life.

Like any person, I need my own time and space, just so I don't lose sight of who I am and what I enjoy doing, and to get a release from the daily pressures of parenting the future replacement band to the Spice Girls. Time on my own or at least without the kids is very limited these days. I always seem to have one clinging to my foot demanding some sort of ride, or a snack, or a pony, so it's important to maximise the opportunities I have to just switch off.

Over the years I have developed a number of ways to do this, and I've discovered that, being relatively unimaginative simple folk, dads all over the globe have been using the same excuses and gathering in very similar places since time began. These fall largely into two categories:

1. An activity that is disguised as doing something for the family when in reality it's actually an excuse to have some me time.

2. An activity that makes no excuses for itself. This is pure 100 per cent dad time.

As I roll through the ways in which I've crafted out me time from seemingly good deeds, don't be surprised to see some that you may recognise.

The DIY store

I've always been into DIY. I blame my own father squarely for this as I grew up in a household where there was always a project on. Growing up, I distinctly remember that for almost six months we didn't have a flushing toilet and were forced to shower at the local sports centre because the bathroom remodelling hadn't quite gone according to plan. OK, so I'm not as brave as my dad in terms of taking on huge projects that push marriages to the brink of divorce, but I do like making things with my hands and I love being able to solve problems for my girls as I'm a firm believer that you can teach yourself to do anything as long as you have the patience and time to do it properly. Need me to fix the broken bed? No problem. Need me to rewire a room and put in a new mains point? Sure. Need me to replace the hot-water tank without paying for an expensive plumber who'll just charge you for staring and shaking his head while silently farting in your kitchen? Absolutely. OK, the downside of being handy is that there's an expectation that I will sort all the problems, but there are upsides too. It means I get to go to the DIY store. The only thing is, the girls love going there too. They see it as a huge play space, just instead of being covered in soft foam that cushions their falls, it's covered, floor to ceiling, in potentially life-shortening sharp tools and heavy objects that are just waiting to damage children. Previous trips with the girls in tow have involved me perusing the different types of tiles on offer and considering buying yet more WD-40, while they pulled each other around in the carts and dashed between the aisles as the sixty-seven-year-old security guard who'd taken on a weekend job to fill his time and cover the shortfall in his pension looked on before shaking his head and returning to his main task of the morning: picking his nose and gazing out of the sliding doors onto the world outside. Thus when I go I desperately want to go on my own, but Clemmie is usually equally desperate to get the girls out of the house, so I find myself locked in a conversation that goes something like this:

CLEMMIE: 'You should take the girls, you know they love it.'

GIRLS: 'Please, Daddy, we want to come!'

ME: 'I don't think so – I know exactly what I need to get and I'll really only be in and out, so there's not much point. You girls should stay here and help Mummy with the twins as she needs you more than I do.'

CLEMMIE: 'Thanks. Thanks a lot. Just don't be forever.'

ME: [No response as I'm already pulling away in the car.]

As you enter these places, the smell of postcrete, solvents, testosterone and cheap coffee is unmistakable. You've probably never given it a second thought, but next time you're in one of these places, take note of how many single guys there are. A lot, right? 10 per cent of these men are 'in the trade', stocking up on bulk-buy white emulsion, drywall and screws. The other 90 per cent are dads who are hiding from their families.

They came in about thirty minutes ago for a bag of nails they didn't really need and are now holding expensive power tools and pretending to sales assistants that they may actually buy them. Before they got to the hardware section, they strolled nonchalantly down each aisle, irrespective of its contents, and considered buying items that they knew full well would never get used, and would instead be left to adorn the shelves of the shed and/or garage until they could dream up a project that might require their use. By the time this happened, they'd have forgotten they owned them in the first place and would be back in the DIY store to buy yet more unneeded goods. It's a vicious circle that we never break free from. While wandering the aisles, dads may well pick up a lock that they need to attach to the bathroom door, in an effort to fortify yet another dad bolt-hole (more on this subject later).

I can and have stretched out a DIY store visit for ninety minutes, which is pushing the boundaries well beyond the realms of acceptability. I was genuinely there to get stuff to remodel the garden, but in all honesty that could have been done in thirty minutes tops. Instead I bought a circular saw, looked at and touched every carpet sample for no particular reason at all, picked up a 2.5-litre pot of paint that I didn't need, carried it around the store with me, and then placed it on another shelf when I realised I'd forgotten the reason why I'd picked it up in the first place. I bought more nails and screws, knowing full well I had a multitude of these at home already. Then I bought a coffee from the van that was situated in the car park (they know their market well) and sat in the car just staring at the side of the building and watching other dads do exactly the same.

So next time your partner eagerly jumps at the chance to fetch the necessary goods to fix something or redo a room, just know that for at least 60 per cent of the time he's gone, he'll be doing absolutely nothing.

The weekly shop

I don't know why but I'm against doing the weekly food shop online. Perhaps it's all the substitutes you have no control over that bug me, or maybe it's the fact that they insist on only putting three or four items in each carrier bag (I mean, come on, the structural integrity of the bag isn't going to be compromised if you put a few more items in and save the planet by using less plastic, is it?). But I think I'm mainly against it as this is yet another opportunity to get out of the house and be seen doing something that is thinly disguised as a selfless act, but is actually an opportunity to have alone time. Of course, now we have four children, the chances of me being allowed to go on my own are so slim, you'd need an electron microscope to see them.

Back in the days when we weren't outnumbered and had a vaguely manageable quantity of children (two), I could get away with doing the shop on my own. I could take my time to be picky about the soft fruits and stare at price labels for elongated periods of time in order to figure out if the deal being offered was in fact mathematically better value.

When the twins came along, Clemmie cottoned on to why I so readily volunteered to complete this job and I felt the leash tighten. Now if I do the shop, I'm accompanied by at least one child, who will no doubt stuff random items into the trolley in the hope that I don't notice. It's always fun to get home and watch them rifle through the bags for the sweets they thought they had snuck in under the radar, knowing full well that I removed the offending article and dumped it somewhere on the cereal aisle. Is this mean? Perhaps, but it's how I get my kicks these days.

The loft

Since the first loft space was invented back in 38BC, when people found that instead of getting rid of their old things, they could chuck them into the space between the roof and the ceiling, men have been telling everyone that they are really the only ones who should be going up there. I know that I'm guilty of having deliber-ately painted a vivid picture of almost certain death should anyone enter the loft without my express consent and supervision, but that's what dads do. This has put me in the position where I'm the sole person who ventures north of the ceiling when something is outgrown and sent to live out the rest of its days with all the items from my pre-child life that I've carted around from house to house for no reason at all.

Having the twins has really been a great excuse to hang out up there and I now have a system in place to maximise my time among the rafters. A trip to the loft is now a much-anticipated mini break, so in order to milk it for all it's worth, I have taken to saving up the requests for items that I know reside up there like hand-me-down clothes, toys, shoes and travel cots, until their retrieval warrants an extended stay in this time warp of my personal history.

The dump

Clemmie doesn't know where the dump is. Even if she did, she wouldn't go there, because, well, it's a dump.

I spent what seems like my entire childhood at the local dump with my dad and now, thirty years on, I'm doing exactly the same thing with my girls. In this land of discarded toilets, twisted bike frames and shorted electronics, you're actively encouraged to chuck previously valued household objects into a massive metal container that makes an extremely satisfying CLANG when the broken items hit their target – no wonder they think it's as exciting as a trip to the cinema.

I have been known to return from the dump with items that I didn't go there with. I did actually find a pair of carbon bike wheels there once and had to physically wrestle them off the guy who worked there. No way did he know how much they were worth and I wasn't going to miss out on an opportunity to be able to tell this story to anyone and everyone that I came into contact with who was vaguely interested in cycling.

Recently, however, I've discovered that large signs have been erected that state 'All children must remain in the vehicle' – the nanny state is doing a great job of killing childhood memory having opportunities. Come on people – let the kids climb wobbly steps and chuck sharp metal objects into skips – it's good for them.

The bathroom

This has to be one of the longest-standing dad hideouts. The secret of the extended bathroom trip has passed from father to son, much like the family silver that everyone is too scared to use unless it's for Christmas. For any trip to the bathroom, there are a few simple rules that all men know:

If you don't announce where you're going, no one sees you go in and you stay quiet, you really only have to respond when someone tries the door handle, meaning that the potential for up to twenty minutes of alone time is possible.

This is where you can get things done that really matter, like finishing that particularly difficult level on Candy Crush.

Unfortunately, with the dawn of social media and the rise of honest parents sharing their lives, I've come to realise that the fairer sex are just as guilty of taking advantage of this child-free time, they just seem to be even more sneaky than we men think we are. It's been going on for years right under our noses and we've only just cottoned on.

Recreational sports – in my case, cycling

In my experience, men are more inclined to have a hobby that's sports-related. I've noticed this throughout my life, starting at school right up to the present day and I'm not sure why. Perhaps girls aren't encouraged enough to take up sport, or given the encouragement they need when they do participate. Whatever the reason, it seems that guys like me think we still have the athleticism of a twenty-year-old and are clinging on to the vain hope that one day a talent scout might see us, think 'That fellow has what it takes' and make us professional sportsmen at thirty-five years old. OK, it's unlikely, but we also do it for the social side and as an excuse to leave the house. Personally my vice is cycling and thus I have become what is commonly known as a MAMIL. For those of you that aren't aware of this acronym, it stands for 'Middle-Aged Man In Lycra'. However, it's not as simple as putting on some tights and whizzing off on your two-wheeled steed; there are a couple of prerequisites that you need in order to qualify for membership of this exclusive club:

- Reach thirty and no longer care what you look like in Lycra.
- Have at least one child.
- Have a dwindling social life.
- Become aware that if you don't do something about your fitness, you'll end up being airlifted to hospital covered in pie crusts, chips and chocolate wrappers for emergency life-saving surgery.

You will have seen flocks of MAMILs out on a Sunday morning, streaming past on their expensive carbon-alloy speed machines, all dressed in head-to-toe Lycra, helmets and glasses with a look of determination painted across their faces. For me, it's a form of escapism that allows me to clear my head and focus on two simple things: the road ahead of me and my breathing. That's it. There's no whining kids, no nagging to do jobs that will need doing again in three hours' time, no babies that need changing. It's me and the wind in my face for an hour or so and it's total bliss.

It's become an addiction for me and I actually start to have withdrawal symptoms if I'm not on my bike at least three times a week. But like any habit, it can be expensive to maintain. There are always new parts to buy and that leaves me with the age-old conundrum: do I buy the £1,000 carbon wheels I've wanted for the last year or do I put food on the table for my family? It's a real rock-and-a-hard-place kind of situation, as you can see. Usually the kids not starving wins out, but this doesn't stop me from making secret purchases from online bike shops through an offshore account in the Cayman Islands. Nobody else realises, but Daddy's new disc brakes are the reason everyone has been eating beans on toast for the last two weeks.

The car

A sure-fire way of ensuring that I get alone time is to ask those in my family with ovaries to help me do a job involving the car. Like rats on a ship who've lived in total darkness for the duration of their voyage only to have a 1,000-watt light suddenly burn out their corneas, everyone scatters as soon as the words 'Can one of you help with the car?' slip past my lips.

Girls just don't seem to care about the car in the same way as I do. I'm not saying that it's like the son I never had, but I do like to give it my attention when it needs it.

Perhaps it's a hereditary condition passed down from father to son, but when it comes to household mess, I have a convenient blind spot. However, the complete opposite is true when it comes to the car. I take an unhealthy amount of pride in its appearance, yet my girls see it as a limbo state where rules of common decency need not apply. They treat it like a landfill site on wheels. Clemmie would happily take it to a valet service who would charge her £20 for the pleasure of removing dried-out pens on trial separations from their lids, fossilised cream cheese that has been welded to upholstery, dummies that have slipped between the cracks in the seats, minuscule pieces of paper shredded by small humans, decayed vegetation left to decompose under the seats and important school letters that never made it into the house. I, on the other hand, would much rather do it myself. One day maybe they'll care, but until that day comes, my role of valet is secure.

I'm also solely responsible for making sure the car gets serviced. This is a great opportunity to affect the sort of accent that shows I'm one of the lads. In my head this gives me a strong footing to haggle over the price, only to find that those are the fixed prices and that my efforts to build a relationship and bond over things like the football game I've pretended to have watched are going to get me precisely nowhere.

Father's Day

OK, this isn't necessarily a place and I'm going off on a bit of a tangent, but it is dedicated to celebrating all things 'dad' and is supposed to be a day for me to do what I want, so it's worth including.

When Father's Day starts creeping up the calendar, Clemmie and the kids start scrambling to pull together ideas on what to get me, the man in their lives. I'm sure that finding something to give me is a difficult proposition. I can't speak for all men but I know that I'm not that easy to buy presents for – I'm not deliberately awkward, I'm just not materialistic and I have most of the things I want or need already. The things that I do want, I'm very specific about – I'll research them, read reviews, work out how much I need to save, etc. I'm a strong believer in buying the best quality you can afford and not settling for cheap knock-offs; as my mother says, 'Buy cheap, buy twice.'

This all leads to frustration and last-minute present buying, just so they have something to give me on the day.

Of course, there are the last-minute/easy-option presents that most dads have received at some point in their parenting career – I'm sure I gave some of these to my own father when growing up. Coincidentally, these are also the standard-issue gifts that stink of desperate present buying and only show that you haven't really put any effort in for the man who spends most of his waking minutes putting his family first. With that in mind, here are the top presents to avoid giving if at all possible:

The comedy mug – this is something that I'll grin at for the kids' benefit and use for the next two days, until it swiftly works its way to the back of the mug cupboard. The next time I'll see it is when I've forgotten to turn on the dishwasher and I'm forced to rootle around in the dark recesses for something to drink out of. I'm not a mug, so please don't give me one.

Cuff-links – I only have two shirts that don't have buttons on the cuffs but I have around twenty pairs of cuff-links. You do the maths and tell me if I need any more.

Grooming sets – you know, the ones with medium-size skin-care products and some kind of abrasive pad in them. I think dads get given these by mums indirectly through their kids as a hint that they should wash more and that they've let themselves go a little. I have sets of these in my wardrobe that went off in 2011 and they're still in their packaging.

Flowers – one of my 'dad friends' was bought peonies for Father's Day. I almost wet myself with laughter when I heard this. Never has such an obvious present for oneself been dressed up so badly as a present for someone else. Unless Dad is a horticultural wizard, don't buy him flowers.

A cheaper version of something you know I really wanted – if I've expressed a desire to buy a specific thing, it's for a reason. Take this random example – a power drill. To you, a drill is a drill, but to me a drill has impact and hammer actions, fifteen speed settings, two gearing ratios, an LED work light, lithium batteries and an ergonomic handle. Please, please, please don't buy me something that isn't the exact item I was planning on purchasing or I'll quietly cry a little inside every time I use the inferior version I've been bought. I'll know full well that you meant well, but now

I'm stuck with something that isn't quite what I wanted and is impossible to trade in without hurting little people's feelings. (This makes me sound awful but you all know exactly what I mean!)

Of course, we'll greet any present with smiles, hugs and outward appreciation on an Oscar-winning level but inside we might just be a little put out that that's all you think we're worth.

So, now I've advised you what's better not to give as a gift, let's move on to what I actually like to receive – and probably most other dads too. These things are simple in nature and can be easily achieved with very little outlay – they just take a bit of thought:

Anything made by the kids – I know my wife hates this stuff and it quickly ends up (accidentally on purpose) in the bin, but for me, if my children have taken the time and effort to make me something then it means the world to me. It could be anything from a card to a picture, a cake or something else completely. These are the kinds of things that in the future I'll look back on and smile about. The best one of these creations I received was a bird box that had been decorated by Marnie aged three. It was covered in the devil's own dandruff, otherwise known as glitter – the herpes of the craft supplies world that you're never able to get rid of, but it still sits in the box of memories next to my bedside table as it's special.

Breakfast – most days of the week I'm in charge of the morning routine, making breakfast for the children while forcing my eyes to open properly, getting hair brushed, finding missing shoes, feeding babies, changing nappies, etc. I never get time for breakfast myself and by the time I drink my tea it's lukewarm at best. What I really want is a breakfast (not in bed – I've never understood why people eat in bed, that just seems gross to me) where I do nothing. One where my kids tidy up afterwards and with tea that is hot. Perhaps even with the papers to read, but I don't want to push my luck.

A day without arguments – this might be wishful thinking but it would be lovely to have a day when I'm not prying the children apart with my fingers or breaking up petty arguments about whose doll's head is whose, or who flushed the lip gloss down the toilet. The phrase 'that's not fair' would also be banned.

Time to do what I want – I know Father's Day is a celebration of being a father, but perversely the reward should be not being a father for a day and doing what I want. An hour (or several) off from parenting to go in the shed and finish off a project, ride a bike, do some shopping or whatever else I might fancy, is important and of enormous value.

To watch something on TV that I actually want to see – with the advent of Netflix, the TV is now something that I occasionally see during the day, but can't actually watch as it's usually blaring out some god-awful American programme full of am-dram kids who wouldn't know acting if it punched them in the gut. I would like two hours to myself to watch sport/documentaries without interruption from a child saying they're bored or it's 'their turn'.

A four-pack of my favourite beer/cider – I'm not saying that I'll be drinking all day, but for someone to present me with a beer that I like would be fantastic.

Though I can't speak for all men, this should at least give you some ideas to think about. In the end we're relatively simple creatures and as you get older, wiser and more creaky around the joints, you realise that the old proverb actually rings true – the best things in life really are free.

So even after everyone's had a piece of the Daddy pie, I still manage to do things for myself with the crumbs of time that remain. Now, some of you who have paid attention may well have noticed that going out and seeing my friends didn't feature in my list. I'm not saying that my social life is 6 feet under just yet, as every month or so I'll go out and have some beers with the guys, but to be honest, the people I want to spend time with the most are all at home. Also, it's a well-known fact that although whisky and Coke mixes well, looking after young children and having a hangover doesn't, so I try to minimise these occurrences as frankly it's not worth it. I get overexcited in the company of other adults and develop a surprising lack of control when in close proximity to alcohol. It's not about the amount I consume, it's more that I still haven't acknowledged that I'm no longer twenty-one, and am now classified as a lightweight who gets drunk on three pints. My friends are mainly people I went to school or university with, and within five minutes of sitting down I'm immediately transported back to the heady days of drinking with my chums without consequence, forgetting that I need to get the last train home and that successfully negotiating a lie-in is less likely than convincing the National Lottery you've won the jackpot by showing them a piece of paper you've drawn some numbers on in felt tip.

Having revealed the secret escape mini holidays that dads commonly take, I'm now off to hide from Fathers Inc., who will no doubt have put a price on my head for breaking the code of silence. If you need me I'll be in the loft, dressed in Lycra, playing with all the excess DIY stuff I've bought over the years but never actually got round to using, while simultaneously sorting out what I'm going to be taking on my next trip to the dump.

10

Dad jobs

One of the many pleasurable jobs I have as a
father is fishing items out of the toilet. I'm sure
I'm destined to die on a cold, wet bathroom
floor with my hand trapped round a U-bend as a
result of trying to retrieve a shit-covered toy.

Dad jobs

When you become a parent, you unwittingly also start down a road that will lead you to become jack of all trades and, with a bit of patience and determination, master of a few. Within five years, your parenting CV will boast so much experience and so many new skills that you could apply for any job out there. As long as you dress it up properly, you'll stand a good chance of gaining employment. So let's take a look at my CV to see how I square up against the competition . . .

PARENTING CURRICULUM VITAE
SIMON HOOPER

SKILLS

- **Excellent written and verbal communication skills used to lead a team**
  I have successfully coordinated a team of five for the last two years, which has developed my managerial skills in conflict resolution and negotiation. My interpersonal skills allow me to effectively communicate with people of all ages.

What I actually mean: I'm a dad in a houseful of five women and my brain hasn't turned into the contents of an ice-cream tub that's been left in the sun just yet, so I must be doing something right. I'm constantly breaking up arguments over TV remotes, who actually owns the roller skates that keep tripping people up in the hallway (despite having told the girls that they need to go back in the shed or they will be making the ten-minute car journey to the dump on my next run) and who ate the last of the cereal and put the empty box back in the cupboard. If things really go pear-shaped, I'm great at sending people to their rooms to cool off. I hardly ever raise my voice as all that does is make everyone else raise theirs and trust me, that many women can get *loud*.

- **Strong financial acumen and ability to prepare extensive annual budget(s)**
  I have extensive experience in budget preparation and the formatting of financial reports, which have been

successfully put through a formal auditing process on an annual basis.

What I actually mean: I run the family finances, use online banking and can download a list of everything that has been spent without my knowledge. Despite setting up a fancy spreadsheet that is so sophisticated it's on the verge of being classified as marketable software, we're basically always two pay cheques away from being homeless. I blame this – fairly, I think, or unfairly if you ask them – squarely on the girls in my life. I don't know if there is a secret slush fund somewhere that I'm not aware of but all of them swan around in new clothes all the time, while I wear the same tops I had at university. I'm constantly saying to Clemmie, 'Oh, that's a nice top, don't think I've seen that one before. Is it new?' Clemmie's standard response of, 'This thing? Nah, I've had it for ages,' as she subtly kicks the H&M bags under the bed.

- **Expertise in operations to ensure efficient use of space**
  I have extensive experience in this area having successfully managed the coordination of layout and design within confined spaces to enable optimal operating efficiency.

What I actually mean: I can pack a car with six people and all their belongings for a week without breaking a sweat. I also live in a 1300-square-foot house with five girls. Do you know how much stuff girls have? It's a lot, and I've managed to build storage and cram things in wardrobes so that we can walk around the house and not trip over. Just don't try and open any of the cupboards or you'll get hit by a tsunami of clothing, toys and God knows what else.

- **Able to initiate, coordinate and enforce optimal operational policies and procedures**

  As a manager I am responsible for the implementation of governance structures that underpin the working dynamics of my team. Rules are enforced at ground level of operations and dramatically increase the operational efficiency of the team's performance.

What I actually mean: We've tried every star chart, money jar and bribe going to get the girls to adhere to the rules, with mixed results. These things usually work for a week and then either I forget about it, or the girls simply don't care that they won't get pocket money any more so they stop playing by the rules. They'd rather live in a lawless state where anything goes and constantly test me to see where the boundaries of acceptability are located – usually way off in the distance behind them. They actually seem to enjoy being sent to sit on the naughty step as it gives them some silence – something that is a rare commodity in our house.

- **Highly proficient in maintaining standards of health and safety, hygiene and security**

  Practising industry-standard health and safety is core to optimal operations in my current role. I am also solely responsible for all security aspects of our operations and take great pride in initiating controls to ensure the security not only of the premises but also of those that I work with.

What I actually mean: I'm militant about the girls washing their hands. Especially when they have been handling the stockpiled slime that is building up in their bedrooms. As for security, I lock the front door every night as I'm always the last one up to bed. I also installed a window lock in the kids' bathroom but it broke and I can't find the key. It's the thought that counts though, right?

- **Efficient management of stock control and reconciliation with data storage system**
  I successfully implemented a 'just in time' management system that ensures stock levels meet the needs of the business.

What I actually mean: My life is a constant battle to keep the cupboards stocked, a steady supply of milk coming into the house and enough toilet roll to cover the land mass of the United States of America. No matter how hard I try, how many online shops I do or how many trips to the supermarket for 'a few essentials' I undertake, we will always be out of milk and loo roll.

- **Adaptable and available to work long hours**
  I have worked both day and night shifts for over ten years and can confidently say that I am able to switch between the two with minimal adjustment, enabling me to adapt to the needs of the business.

What I actually mean: I'm a parent of four. I don't sleep much.

So now that we've glanced over my extensive CV, let's run through just a small number of the jobs that I, and no doubt many other parents have found themselves doing, many of which I don't actually remember applying for.

Chauffeur

When I was a kid I never really gave any thought to the sheer amount of mileage my parents put in for me to simply go about my childhood. I'm sure that by the age of fifteen I'd already contributed a good proportion of my lifetime's carbon footprint. (Combine that with the number of CFCs that were knocking about in the 1980s and my personal contribution to the greenhouse effect is probably sizeable.) I was forever being ferried around from place to place, enduring my dad's cringeworthy jokes that, like a poorly stored vintage wine, got worse over time, and listening to endless tapes of Genesis, Dire Straits, The Traveling Wilburys, Yazz, Tina Turner, Phil Collins and Eric Clapton. I'm sure by the age of four I didn't know my alphabet, but I knew all the words to 'Tears in Heaven' and 'Malted Milk'.

Having now taken on the role of unpaid taxi of dad myself, with a schedule of work that's completely dictated by the women around me, I truly have a new appreciation of the level of mileage that my parents put in. Long-distance drivers have nothing on parents – the cargo is immeasurably more valuable, the travelling companions are difficult and no journey is straightforward.

I seem to dedicate an increasing amount of time to transporting my offspring to sports clubs at the weekend. I'm not complaining as

I'm pleased they've found something that they enjoy, but why do these clubs always have to start at 8.30 a.m. on a Saturday?! When I used to take Anya swimming, all the parents would do the same thing: slip on the especially unflattering blue plastic shoe covers, sip their overpriced cups of coffee, play a game of musical chairs – without musical accompaniment – to find a seat and spend the next hour looking at their phones, occasionally looking up to catch a glimpse of their child, half-heartedly wave and return to scrolling through pictures on Facebook and Instagram of plates of food and holidays that were taken by someone they went to school with fifteen years earlier and hadn't spoken to since but are 'friends' with on social media. You could tell the ones who were hungover as they were wearing sunglasses and although they had an open paper on their lap, their loud, rhythmic breathing indicated that they were, in fact, asleep.

After it was all over, we would make our way back to the car, avoiding the luminous-coloured drinks on offer in the café for fear of turning the E-number-intoxicated children into caged animals in the back of an already cramped vehicle.

Two or three days of the week, the taxi of dad does the school run too. The journey is always the same: there are two minutes of complaining about being frog-marched out of the house, followed by three minutes of arguing about the radio station, some occasional moany comments about how we're always the last ones through the school gates and then a flurry of hairbands being pinged around the car like elasticated pinballs as a tornado of hair gets swooshed around at gale force 9 to be pulled into high ponies and pigtails.

During this time, I quietly observe the storm of crazy from the comfort of the driver's seat and wait for it to blow itself out. As the girls disembark, the gale turns into a gentle breeze that dissipates into nothingness, leaving me and the twins to drive home while conversing like three people from different corners of the globe – with broken English, mispronunciation and lots of nodding without any understanding of what's being said.

Plumber

From what I recall, baldness doesn't run in my family, and yet my girls seem to shed hair quicker than any canine I know. If I could be bothered to measure the total amount of hair possessed by the females in the family, I'm sure I would find you could wrap it around the earth multiple times and still have enough to use as a stunt wig in an amateur dramatics production of *Rapunzel*. It's a lot of hair, so when combined with the fact that they seem to have follicles with the grip of someone whose hands are covered in butter, it results in one thing – blocked shower drains.

When the shower tray starts to fill and the water level passes my ankles, it means it's time to get on my hands and knees and clear the congealed hair that's taken up residence beneath the chrome-effect drain cover. This has to be one of my least favourite jobs, as it involves reaching into the pipe and retrieving what could be mistaken for a bedraggled Cousin Itt from *The Addams Family* – a hairball that's bonded together with shampoo, conditioner and mould.

As I hold the offending article aloft, the girls usually proclaim, 'Oh, Daddy, that's so gross!' Yes, girls, it is. And it has precisely nothing to do with me – yet here I am, the only one clearing it up.

My plumbing skills aren't limited just to hairball removal, however. I have no idea why, but all children under the age of two seem to have a fascination with the toilet. Ottie and Delilah are no different. Perhaps it's the noise of the water or the fact that it's the perfect height to use as an aid to stand or maybe it's as simple as the fact that they see people going in there all the time and want to know what all the fuss is about. Whatever it is, they love a good porcelain bowl. They love to play with the lid, to put their hands in the water and to post objects into the toilet to test our patience.

I've lost count of the number of times I've had my arm wedged round the U-bend of a blocked toilet after a child has flushed everything they could get their hands on. Once or twice I've actually had to disconnect the toilet and take the pipework apart to dislodge the offending object. The last time I did this, I found a poo-covered fluffy unicorn had wedged itself into the waste pipe. That means a child must have flushed the unicorn and then, not satisfied they had done enough, sat down and took a shit directly after. That's a different kind of dark. Rather unsurprisingly, after a thorough and complete investigation to identify the culprit, it was deduced that Mr Nobody was to blame again. He has a lot to answer for in this house.

Now running the bath isn't strictly plumbing but it involves taps so I'm going to go with it. After dinner, while the kids are racing around and wiping their spaghetti-Bolognese-covered fingers all over the place I'll make an announcement:

'I'll go and run their bath.'

To the casual observer I look like I'm helping, but as I mentioned earlier – and as any parent knows – this is simply a way of snatching five glorious, peaceful minutes for myself.

Food critic/chef

Dads get a bad rep in the kitchen so I'll do my best to dispel this myth – after all, the culinary world is full of men, so we can't all be that bad, can we?

I'm the baker of the household. I blame my mum squarely for this as she made it so much fun when we were kids and she got me hooked. There's something about the process of baking that I love – the accuracy of the measurements, the precision of the decoration and the flavours involved all appeal to me. The problem is that I'm a perfectionist, especially when it comes to birthday cakes. As every birthday approaches I'm thrust into competition with myself to outdo my previous year's efforts. I really am my own worst enemy sometimes, but to see their faces when they blow out the candles makes it all worth the effort.

I also attempt to get my girls involved whenever I can. It's an important life skill and will serve them well when they have kids of their own and are forced to work well into the early hours to make cupcakes for a school bake sale that their own offspring have notified them of the day before the sale is due to happen.

The only thing is that baking with kids is both messy and slow. Have you ever seen a child try and stir a bowl of cake mixture as they summon all their strength from their bone-thin arms? I could pop out to the pub, sink a few pints and watch an entire rugby match and on my return they'd still be struggling to complete the first circuit of the bowl. And I haven't been able to do much about the mess as frankly I'm usually the one who uses every single utensil in our kitchen to make twelve cupcakes and then leaves the dishes out covered in butter and flour, but I did manage to do something about increasing the speed of the process. Lacking in electric mixing tools, I jammed a normal whisk into a power drill and then let the kids go for it. Baking with power tools is fun, but it comes at a price as due to the speed of the drill, at least 30 per cent of the mixture was flung off in all directions, coating the kitchen units in a thin but very tasty veneer of uncooked cake goop. We ended up with seven cupcakes of varying sizes, but they were hands down the most fun cupcakes I've ever made in my life.

The other thing I struggle with is portion control. My girls are generally good eaters, but I find myself handing out adult-sized plates of food and then arguing with them when they don't finish it. I forget that they are less than half my size, so expecting them to eat the same amount as I do is perhaps a little unfair. As a result, I find myself eating a lot of leftovers. This is common practice for many parents, but with four of them leaving food on their plates, I find myself eating what is essentially a full meal at 5.45 p.m. and then having a second dinner with Clemmie later on. No wonder I've been dubbed the human dustbin. I just hope my daughters contribute towards my medical bills when I'm wearing 60-inch elasticated-waist trousers and am physically incapable of getting out of my chair.

Hairdresser

I'm not sure how this came about, but I am now the only person that is allowed the honour of washing, drying and brushing the girls' hair. Apparently 'Mummy is too rough and tells us to stop complaining', whereas I am deemed acceptable. I'm pretty sure Clemmie has done this deliberately so that she can have a break on hair-washing nights, but I've yet to confront her on that one. Long hair is an absolute shitter to brush, especially if you have wavy hair like all my girls do. Having been in the Scouts, I'm usually good with knots and I know my sheet bend from my clove hitch, but the girls' hair produces knots you won't find in any manual. Imagine a sheep with dreadlocks. Then imagine a pile of string that someone just bundled up and stuffed into a drawer. The knots found in my daughters' hair are their love children. We even have a name for these now – they're called 'seriously hard impossible to sort hairy octopus-like weaves', or SHITSHOWs for short.

As for hair-drying, in theory this should be an easy process. Sit down, dry the girls' hair with a hairdryer while brushing it, finish it off with a hairband and *voilà*, you're done. The reality is somewhat different though. When I'm drying the twins' hair, all they want to do is turn around, open their mouth and turn their gullet into a mobile wind tunnel. They also like to shout at the hairdryer and constantly try to grab the tip of it, which is hotter than the sun. I like to spice up what can be a mundane task by blow-drying and backcombing their hair into some kind of 80s disco bouffant and laugh at the results (if only they had tiny little 80s power suits with

I also do hair modelling. You'll never know real
pain until you've had a hair clip driven into
your scalp by a child who then laughs as blood
rolls down your temple. It's fun. Sort of.

shoulder pads, the look would be complete). The words I usually hear from Clemmie are 'Why have you ruined my babies?!', to which I reply, 'Because it's funny.' My response is met with a face that snipers could use to kill people with from 1,000 feet.

Nail technician

All children seem to have nails as sharp as very small but very real box-cutters. Need to open an Amazon box but can't find the scissors? Use your kid's nails. Want to cut off that annoying label in your top that keeps scratching you? Use your kid's nails. But as well as being useful, they can also cause grievous bodily harm. That's why keeping the talons filed down is essential. However, since 'The

Gusher' incident of 2010, Clemmie has been afraid of cutting the girls' nails. When they were small their nails were softer and we could bite them off, although that involved putting a baby's fingers in your mouth and that's not pleasant as you have literally no idea where they've been. They could have been playing with the next-door neighbour's cat's bum-hole for all I knew. Clemmie and I could take that no more so we upgraded to clippers and within the first two days of use, Clemmie managed to snip a bit of finger off. Not that she was the only one: when Anya was little, Clemmie was away so I took it upon myself to perform my first baby mani. Within just ten seconds, I'd also managed to cut a bit of her finger off, producing a worryingly large and seemingly unstoppable flow of the red stuff. Enough, it seemed to me, to put all blood banks in a 100-mile radius on standby. Who knew you needed the dexterity of a keyhole surgeon combined with the skills of an experienced alligator wrestler to perform what seems from the outside to be such a simple task.

I am also surprisingly proficient at painting nails. I never saw this job in my future as a twenty-one-year-old man, but fast-forward fourteen years and I am the go-to guy if you want your nails painted. Anya and Marnie seem to acquire nail varnish in the same way others collect shells or rubbers. What started as a small collection to have for fun has turned into the biggest stockpile of nail-related products the world has ever known. If for some reason production of all nail products ceased today, we would still have enough to see us – and everyone else – through to the next century.

The girls love painting their nails, but haven't quite got to grips with the technique yet, so the overpowering stench of nail-polish remover rolling down the stairs like a dense sea fog is a not uncommon phenomenon in our house. This is then quickly followed by a child entering the room with half of their fingers covered in neon orange OPI. In an effort to avoid this I started painting their nails, and much to my surprise discovered that I'm actually quite adept at it.

Performing arts critic

Like many parents I find myself constantly bombarded with requests to 'come and see the latest show' that's being hosted in the kids' bedrooms. I take the same position for each performance – wedged in the corner of the room sitting on a bean-bag. I'm issued with a ticket with the name of the play and time of the performance crudely scribbled in felt tip, and a drink of water that's served to me in the cup we usually use to hold the toothbrushes. It tastes rank. After a lot of whispering and nudging between the actors, all the lights are turned off, except for the desk lamp that shines like a spotlight on the stage. As anticipation builds, a hush ripples through the audience (of me and twenty stuffed toys) and the performance begins.

I think I must have been to at least 200 'shows' throughout my parenting career, all of which have the same themes running through them.

- There will be a princess shoehorned into the story.
- Anya will be the main character and will perform a long meandering monologue that I'll get lost in.

- Anya will perform a dance.
- Marnie will play the role of either a sister or a servant.
- Marnie will have one line, which she will need prompting to say and then be told was wrong by Anya.
- Marnie will stand motionless while Anya performs yet another dance.
- Someone will die or get hurt in the play. This is usually Marnie.
- The show will end abruptly mid-story as rehearsals had only got that far.

It's at this point I'll be asked for my honest opinion. I then duly provide my 'honest' opinion that it was brilliant and that I especially liked X, Y and Z and I felt like I was really there. In reality, the storyline was so butchered that I lost all sense of time and space and my brain shut down all non-essential functions apart from my eyes, which were locked on the stage to give the illusion of paying attention. But I'd never tell them that.

One day I'm sure I'll get to the end of one of these performances and find out how the story is resolved, but it hasn't happened yet.

Biology teacher

Clemmie and I have always been open to talking about our bodies with the girls. After all, as children grow up, they are naturally inquisitive about their own bodies and those of the opposite sex, so instead of going red in the face and hoping they will either give up asking or learn from school, we answer any questions they have.

Both of us can confidently address the most obscure lines of investigation, but when it comes to the male body I'm the only one that's equipped to provide the answers.

As the only man in the house, the girls find my body hilarious. There's nothing quite like getting out of the shower to find yourself surrounded by five women aged between one and thirty-two, all laughing and pointing at your manhood, to ensure your self-confidence is so low that it would definitely win any limbo competition going. As they don't have a willy, they see it as a curiosity – something you might queue up to see at the freak show (although if you're queuing up to see a willy, then you have some serious questions to ask yourself). Their fascination with my appendage can make life very difficult though. Going for a wee standing up, like a normal adult man, is a stressful experience, as I'm never quite sure if a twin is going to suddenly pop up and try and thrust their hand into the stream of urine – or worse, try and grab the hose. It usually ends up with me doing the toilet dance – small shuffling steps around the loo while using my knees to block the inquisitive child, all while trying to maintain a consistent flow rate and trajectory. I have now taken to sitting down to pee, it's safer.

Here are some questions about my anatomy that I've had to deal with from my girls, along with my accompanying answers:

What's it like to have a willy?

I don't know any different as I've always had one. I like having one though, as there's hardly ever a queue in the men's toilets.

Doesn't it get in the way?

Sometimes – that's why boys always have their hands down their pants. We have to constantly rearrange the luggage to make sure it's packed properly. Girls will never understand this.

Have you ever caught your willy in your trouser zip?

Yes, once, but let's not talk about it as that was a dark time in my life.

Why are you so hairy?

I wasn't always hairy, but as men hit puberty, they get hair in places they didn't have it before. I shaved my chest when I first met Mummy. She laughed at me so much that she almost wet herself and said I looked like a chicken before it was cooked, so I grew it back and vowed I would never do it again.

Why has your hair started to go grey?

Because of you, sweetheart.

Why do men have nipples? Isn't that pointless?

I totally agree – it is pointless, but think how odd we'd look without them.

Why are willies so ugly?

Because if they were pretty you'd always have them out and no one wants to see that.

I'm not convinced my teaching style would go down particularly well in any school I know of.

Negotiation specialist

Breaking up fights between warring siblings is something that most parents have the pleasure of doing several times a day. The reasons for these spats vary hugely but I've compiled a quick list of the most common ones in our house:

Between Anya and Marnie

- She keeps looking at me.
- She's had longer on the computer than me and it's not fair.
- She's too close to me and is taking my space (usually said in a room that is 95 per cent empty).
- She won't get out of my room.
- She ate the last of the cereal.
- She said she would give me [insert the name of an object that you really couldn't care less about as a parent] if I gave her [insert the name of another object you care even less about] but now she won't swap.

Between the twins

- Like a midday mugging in full view of the public, one twin will simply take food directly out of the other's hands and eat it without a single word being uttered.

- Hair-pulling.
- Stealing of a prized toy.
- Shoes – more specifically, who has the right to wear which pair.

All of this means that I'm forced to strap on my UN-style parenting peacekeeping jacket and insert myself into the line of fire, taking care to avoid the swinging arms, razor-like nails and flying insult shrapnel, as verbal hand grenades explode all around. Once in the war zone, it's important to find a middle ground and bring the two parties to the table to resolve their differences. Depending on the circumstances, I will adopt one of the following personas before resorting to dropping a nuke on them all:

- The 'understanding' dad – a quiet approach that aims to get everyone talking rather than yelling. Take it in turns to find out from each party what the problem is, forcing each person to listen to the other's perspective. They should then shake hands and separate. Note: expect the argument to resume, just in a different room, within five minutes.
- The 'physical separation' dad – take one child out of the room, leading them by the hand. Talk to them separately and ask one to go upstairs and one to stay downstairs. Then park yourself on the stairs, mid-flight, with a cup of tea and a newspaper to become a physical barrier for at least five minutes. Expect children to poke heads round doors to see if you're still there or not.
- The 'this isn't my problem' dad – ignore the argument completely and pretend it's not happening. Distract yourself by

doing something else that is away from the noise. The risk of using this tactic is that if your other half comes in and you're standing there making absolutely zero effort to resolve things, you will get a death stare.

The 'strike fear in their hearts' dad – this is a fun tactic but it can't be used regularly or it loses its impact. Similar to a SWAT team using a flash-bang grenade when storming a building to render the occupants disorientated and immobile, you enter a room at speed while employing a loud booming voice that brings on heart palpitations in the young offenders (I very rarely raise my voice so when I do, they know I mean business – this is a technique my dad used on me when I was growing up and it still scares the crap out of me now). Get close to their faces and use passive-aggressive tones to hammer it home that this behaviour will not be tolerated and then turn and leave the room as quickly as you entered, letting the girls process what's just happened. Hopefully the speed and noise level will have completely disorientated them into forgetting what they were fighting about.

Mother and Daughter Peacekeeping

This one is a little more complicated. I don't know if this is the case for all mother-and-daughter relationships, but through my observations over the last ten years, I've come to a conclusion. If there was a spectrum for the relationship between a mother and a daughter, it would have two extremes: at one end would be love – this is when they can't get enough of each other, the sun always shines, flowers are blooming and they are basically BFFs. At the other is end hate – if divorce was possible, the paperwork would have been filed a long time ago and someone would have moved out already.

The void between these two extremes is a no-man's-land that lies completely untouched. What makes it harder for me to understand is that the relationship can oscillate between the two opposite ends of the scale several times a day without any prior warning.

When the relationship is firmly in the 'hate' camp, I am unwillingly cast in the role of middle-man. With both parties as stubborn as each other, unwilling to pull up the guy ropes and move their tents to a common ground to avoid the rising stress levels, they look to me to come in and sort things out. To be clear, in the vast majority of cases, I haven't been around when these disputes have started. I have nothing to do with them at all, yet as soon as I'm in the door and am hit with the shock wave of noise, I'm put into facilitator mode and have to solve a problem which I know literally nothing about. Clemmie gets pissed off if I don't support her, but how can I support her in an argument I only have secondhand, biased information about? It's like only getting my information from the North Korean government – I'm only going to be seeing one perspective. Then of course the child in question will hate me for not listening to her side of the story and get defensive.

Between the two differing versions of events, the truth lies somewhere – probably curled up in a ball, shaking like a rescue dog that's just been pulled out of a squat. The problem is that finding it is about as likely as me getting out of the situation unscathed, i.e. zero.

In the end, both sides usually find common ground as they part company and go to cool off, but things haven't been resolved in a way that global peacekeeping forces would classify as successful. The thing that brought them together was a newly found, deep and concentrated mutual loathing for me! Fantastic. I wasn't there when it all erupted, I didn't want to get involved, and yet I was still dragged into it against my will. I did all the right things, let everyone talk in turn, tried to understand the issues and develop a solution, yet somehow I came out of it being the guy everyone hates. No wonder men hide in the toilet so much.

There are many other jobs I could add to this list but I need to try and keep this book under 1,000 pages long so I'll summarise by saying that parenting is a learning curve that you never quite get to the top of. There is always a new skill to master and a new string to add to your bow. I for one certainly don't want to get to the end of my parenting career to be met at the pearly gates with a report card that reads 'Could have tried harder', so although I may not have signed up to being a lifelong student, I will embrace it and learn all I can while I have the opportunity. After all, looking back ten years to when I started, I'm pretty proud of my accomplishments so far.

11

Oh, the places you'll go

Going places can sometimes leave you wondering why you bothered as you cram everyone into the car, wipe their tears and pray the heavily filled nappy's structural integrity doesn't give way like a biscuit that's been dunked one too many times.

Oh, the places you'll go

So you've managed to get everyone dressed, and despite multiple arguments over the missing shoe that's holding everyone up and why it's necessary for anyone to bring more soft toys than they have hands for, you've finally closed the door on your home. (You can deal with the fact that the house resembles a cross between a Primark closing-down sale and an explosion in a ready-meal factory later.) Now you're ready to go, but as parents of miniature adults in development, where do you go?

In my pre-child-rearing days, the world was my oyster. Of course I didn't really realise that so I spent much of my time watching reality TV and bad documentaries on Channel 5. Had I known that when I became a parent my free time was going to be reduced so dramatically, in hindsight I would have perhaps chosen to spend it more wisely, filling it with cultural experiences that would stay with me for the rest of my life and help shape the person I was to become.

Now I'm not saying that those windows aren't still open to me, but when you have a child hanging off your limbs while rubbing snot on your jeans and crying because their sister ate the last of the emergency chocolate biscuits that were supposed to be for every-one, your energy for pursuing those opportunities isn't quite what it used to be.

I've found that the number of places we visit as a family has become rather limited in recent years. This isn't because we don't want to go and see the latest art installation at the Tate, take a day trip to a town we've read about in the travel section of the paper that's famous for making the world's biggest cup of tea, or watch the film that everyone's raving about and insisting we must see. It's just that getting all six of us from A to B is a logistical nightmare that will involve a tantrum, the loss of at least one crucial item and us arriving at our destination thirty minutes before it shuts, just in time for us to question why we ever left the house in the first place when it's nearly time for us to turn around again to make the long journey home.

To make life easier for all of us, we usually use the following criteria to decide whether we can go somewhere or not:

- Is it less than an hour, or two at the most, away from our own front door? If the answer is no, then this is not a day trip, this is classified as a holiday.
- Is it child friendly – i.e. can they charge about like little drug-fuelled maniacs and not be told to leave by a massive man in a security uniform?
- Can we get a buggy in and out easily? [Side note: unless the place you're going to has an aircraft-hangar-sized door, you're pretty much screwed everywhere with a double buggy.]

- Will we have to remortgage our home to pay for the family entry price? (FYI we can't buy a family ticket anymore as we have too many children. Oh, joy).

This leaves us with several options of places we can frequent, which I'm sure will be familiar to you if you're already a parent:

The park

The local patch of open land containing coloured metal climbing apparatus has to be the number-one go-to location for families who need to get out of the house, but can't face going too far just in case everything falls apart while they're out.

These places are gathering points for local parents to congregate and watch their children from a distance while checking their phones and drinking rapidly cooling coffee bought from the 20-year-old entrepreneur who set up a pop-up coffee shack literally metres from the entrance and is making a killing from frazzled parents. If you stay long enough, you'll probably see him leave in the evening in a Ferrari.

This is also where parents lose sight of the fact they are in their thirties and mentally become the same age as their kids, queuing politely to go on the slide, hanging on the monkey bars, bouncing on the spring-loaded little horse and jumping from the swings at the highest point, all while looking for validation that they are awesome from both their kids and partner. A validation they rarely receive.

The playground is also a great place to rack up the injuries. My favourite thing to do is to see how long it takes for a parent to come to their child's aid when they hurt themselves. The older the child, the longer the gap tends to be.

When a scream is heard across the playground and a parent slowly realises it's in fact their child who's fallen off the slide or been booted in the face by a 15-year-old on a swing who really should be in school, they do that funny half-run, half-walk across the asphalt.

It is almost a legal requirement that upon entering a playground, all dads must immediately revert to being five and prove they still have the upper body strength to do the monkey bars while their partner looks on and rolls their eyes from a distance.

They immediately put on the most caring voice in the world to prove that they are a good person to the gathering crowd of other parents who got there first. The fact that they're literally the last one to arrive at the scene multiplies the shame and guilt. It's usually at that point that they decide it's time to go home, collect everything as quickly as humanly possible and leave, knowing eyes are still burning a hole in the back of their head.

Baby classes/pop-up events

When I first started out on our parenting adventure, the choice of classes was relatively limited. You could go to mums' groups, music classes or baby sensory, but over the last couple of years, things have changed as people started to notice that although the babies were enjoying themselves, the parents were bored senseless. I'd do my level best to appear interested and amazed at the wonder of my daughter vaguely reacting to music or bubbles being blown in her face, but frankly it was exhausting. The fact of the matter is, those classes are dull as ditch-water for most adults, and as babies become toddlers, even their interest dips.

Still, when Anya was young we took her to these types of classes as it was what you were supposed to do. To be clear, when I say 'we' took her, I actually mean Clemmie took her and I'd hear about it at length later on in the day after I got back from work.

In theory, these classes were a way for Clemmie to get out of the house and provided an opportunity to hold a conversation with other people who could stand up under their own power and had the ability to talk, while their babies crawled around and generally dribbled on a mat.

In practice, they turned out to be a whole lot of stress that she didn't need.

Anya hated the classes with a passion and spent the whole time crying. She wanted nothing more than to be in the comfort of her own home and to be held by her mum. Clemmie would end up sitting on a bench in the corner of the room breastfeeding and having made a block payment, she was now locked in to attending another five sessions.

After the second session, Clemmie and Anya both decided they'd had enough. Now you could throw the old adage of 'if at first you don't succeed, try, try again' at the situation, but who was this really benefiting? Not Clemmie, as she spent the whole time feeling like a failure while developing a headache that an industrial shipment of paracetamol couldn't shift. Not Anya as she spent the entire time screaming and turned the same colour as an undercooked sirloin. And not me, as I could see that both my girls were unhappy. I think the only one that benefited was the class organiser, who no doubt went home each night and took a bath in the cash new parents threw at her (OK, that's not fair, I'm sure they don't do that at all, but that's the mental image I conjured up).

Clemmie vowed not to put herself or our child through that particularly hellish experience again. Yet eight years later, the lessons we'd learnt had gone the same way as my credit card PIN numbers – forgotten, and when the twins came along, Clemmie was at these classes again.

Clemmie would take the twins to these groups and come back looking broken. The moment they entered the room, Ottie and Delilah would give a passing glance to the activity happening in the middle of it and promptly take the executive decision to splinter off in opposite directions and do something completely different. Within seconds, one would be smashing a window with the palm of their sticky paw and the other would be making an arrow-straight charge towards the table of biscuits. Clemmie would then spend the next thirty minutes rounding the twins up – a process akin to herding cats – while other mothers looked on and thanked their lucky stars that their eggs hadn't split in two at the point of conception.

Baby groups have moved on these days, too. The old-style music groups and playgroups still exist, of course, but the current generation of new parents want more.

In an effort to re-engage parents, a whole host of 'alternative' parent-and-baby events have started to pop up. Baby disco, baby yoga, all sponsored by some children's clothing brand you've never heard of and a drinks company who have sent along two seventeen-year-old kids to hand out close-to-sell-by-date products to parents. One-off events are hosted in abandoned warehouses, churches and trendy pubs somewhere in east London.

The last one I can remember attending was Baby Rave. This had no doubt been set up by people who were once club kids, and after abusing their bodies for years, had decided to give up the drink, take up yoga, embrace veganism and settle down with 2.4 children, yet they still wanted to retain some of the spice from their past lives. What better way to do this than by setting up a daytime rave for children? It's just like the Berghain, only instead of half-naked men dancing furiously to deep house, questionable things happening in dark corners and coming back out into daylight having lost all sense of time and space, you find parents with babies strapped to their chests, kids running around like it's a wedding where Uncle Joe has been slyly topping them up with wine and an arts and crafts table next to a girl selling glow sticks for £2 a pop.

It's at these kinds of events that I find myself in a game of hide-and-seek I don't remember agreeing to play – trying to find kids in a nightclub setting. Finding your friends is hard enough, but these people are waist height and move like shadows. You finally grab one to realise their eyes are as big as saucers and they are talking at the speed of light. No, they haven't popped an E, they just found an unguarded stash of sweets and without supervision, deemed it a good idea to bosh off a whole year's supply of flying saucers in under five minutes. Visions of having to strap them to their bed while they withdraw from their self-induced sugar high flash before my eyes, and I decide it's time to leave. It's 1.34 p.m.

Soft play

If you have never experienced soft play then a) count yourself lucky, and b) you're probably not a parent. Let me paint the scene for you to help you visualise this place of wonder. Close your eyes and imagine a gigantic hamster cage, one of those fancy ones that have multiple levels and lots of toys for the hamster to play on.

Now imagine this cage is in a large room with a thermostat that's stuck on Sahara Desert mode and has the same amount of ventilation as a vacuum chamber. Now imagine what seems like 1,000 feral children ranging in ages from one to twelve all thrown into that cage, hydrated only by fizzy drinks, who know that they are free from parental supervision for the next forty-five minutes to an hour. Finally add in the stale smell of crap. Congratulations, you are now at soft play!

There are two types of parent that come to these places: the ones who are dropping their kids off at a party – you can tell who these are a mile off as they're legging it to their cars with a huge smile on their faces and a bounce in their step. I've only been privileged enough to be this type of parent twice and it was fabulous. Then there are the ones who are staying for the duration – they will have brought snacks, a book and headphones.

Clemmie and I usually go as a team to these places but when we're there we have set roles. I'll escort the older kids over to the shoe racks and lay down the rules (look after your sister, don't push people, please come when I call you, etc) while Clemmie tries to grab a table (these are like gold dust, so when parents find one, they spread their shit everywhere, placing bags on multiple chairs and coats over tables to ensure that they mark their territory. It would be easier just to piss all over the place, but that might be going a bit too far, even for soft play).

Once they're in the foam-padded maze, we get to sit and wait until the time's up or someone needs help – a pastime that parents become professionals at.

Here's a quick list of things that are likely to happen in the hour your kids are belting around without a care in the world:

- Your child will come out crying because a big kid knocked them over. This has happened to me on multiple occasions. I'll get them to point out the kid so I can think about all the horrible things I'd say to them should I ever have the pleasure of meeting them in a dark alley.

- You'll have to retrieve a child who has got to a point where they're scared as they are too high, trapped in a set of rollers or frozen at the top of the massive 'accident waiting to happen' slide that they thought they could go down but bottled after reaching the top and looking over the edge, resulting in a queue of twelve-year-olds building up behind them, each considering whether they should push your little one off the edge.

- You'll see a parent lose their shit. It might be done quietly, but you know that inside, they are fuming. This usually occurs at going-home time.

I have been that parent on more than one occasion. During one of these delightful outings, having decided we all – OK, Clemmie and I – had had enough, I went to round up the big girls. Despite having made fleeting eye contact with Anya and deploying the international sign of over-exaggerated watch-tapping to indicate that we were leaving, she disappeared into the labyrinth of plastic-covered poles.

I then followed the path that many parents had trodden before me around the periphery of the cage to see if I could spot her. I started to call her name in the way that people do when they're trying to look like they aren't beginning to unravel, but after several minutes, my frustration had built to the point where I was yelling her name for all to hear. The cloak of decorum and restraint I usually wear snugly around my shoulders had fallen to the floor and been trampled to death, and I could sense all eyes burning into the back of my head as other parents looked up from their phones and made themselves comfortable for the fireworks display that was about to unfold in front of them. I'm sure that some were judging me, but I know the majority were thinking that in just fifteen minutes they'd be doing exactly the same thing when they tried to extract their own little bundle of joy from the maze of noise and moving bodies. It was at that moment Anya came to the edge, looked down at me, poked her tongue out, smiled and ran away again.

As I walked back to our table muttering to myself about how I was going to happily murder my firstborn, I caught a glimpse of Clemmie in the ball-pond with the twins. All I could see was the tops of their heads floating around like buoys in the ocean. Clemmie's eyes were saying, 'Help me.'

Having recovered my composure, I formed a plan and mentally mapped the layout of the foam-covered battlefield. There were only two exits and if I moved quickly and quietly, I could surprise Anya, forcing her towards the one place I wanted her to go to more than anything – the way out.

She was trapped up in the darkest reaches of the cage and like a convict on the run who'd been cornered by the cops, she was only going to come out of there in one of two ways: in a blaze of glory resulting in her being put in a body bag, or dragged out kicking and screaming. With a heavy exhalation I rose from my solid plastic chair and after the pins and needles had worn off and I was able to walk without limping, I entered the madness to retrieve her.

Of course, Anya saw this as a big game of cat and mouse and was shrieking with laughter as I rounded each corner, waddling like a duck as I hunched over to fit through the tunnels and tubes.

Having finally rounded all the kids up, it was time to leave, but it turned out soft play wasn't done with me yet. Inevitably some-one was missing a shoe. It had been in the rack forty-five minutes earlier, but some little arsehole who had the same shoes as my daughter had taken it, which meant instead of getting out of this warehouse of farts, and breathing clean air again before I went into respiratory failure, I was forced to walk around looking, while pretending not to look, at all the other kids' feet to see if I could spot a shoe that looked like the one missing from my child's foot. It was at that point I realised that to everyone else I was just a sweaty-looking adult staring at kids' bare feet, and could easily be mistaken for a sex offender. Five minutes later, having defensively explained to the other worried parents that I was in fact the parent of a child in the building (which probably got their suspicions up even more), I slowly returned to base camp demoralised and empty-handed to find Clemmie and the girls in their coats, heading for the door.

Turns out she found the shoe and chose not to tell me.

Splash sessions at the pool

I have to admit that I do love going swimming with all my girls. I mean, who doesn't have fun in a pool that's full of floats and inflatables – you're never too old for that, are you? But before you can enjoy dunking your toddlers under the water and seeing if they can hold their breath, or throwing them to such a height that other parents start to hate you as their kids now want them to do the same, you have to deal with the family changing rooms.

Family changing rooms have been designed to cater for normal-sized families. Usually the 2.5-metre-square box is just enough space to get everyone in without feeling like a brood of battery hens. However, when you're a family of six, the walls seem to close in. At some point all six of us will be naked and despite my best efforts to get changed into my swimming shorts so quickly that you could class it as a magic trick with the potential to get through to the final round of *Britain's Got Talent*, the girls in my life still find the time to point out the main piece of my anatomy that differentiates me from all the other occupants of this temporary prison – my penis. This is followed by stifled giggling that then gives way to live comedy show-type laughter that everyone in the other changing rooms can definitely hear. With my male pride bruised, I take comfort in overhearing other dads in neighbouring cubicles dealing with similar situations with their children. As comments like 'Don't touch that, that's private', 'Stop looking, just turn around', 'Leave me alone' and 'Budge up or you'll get a bum in the face' drift over the top of the 12-mm-ply wooden boxes of naked families, a smile spreads across my face – I'm not alone.

Dining out

Going out for a meal used to be a treat and it still is, but only when we've got a babysitter booked and have left the kids at home. There are, however, still those times when we're either tired of eating the same meals among our own belongings, or when we're out for the day and opt to venture into a restaurant in order to eat food that someone else has prepared and try and function as normal members of society.

First things first: if you're a family with young kids, your time slots for wolfing down food are limited, usually to lunch or early dinner, before childless adults wanting a civilised dining experience turn up. Lunch is acceptable and on the rare occasions we're out around 5 p.m. we can just about squeeze in an early tea, but past that time, you start to get into the realm of adult-only eating.

Here's a summary of every meal out we've had with all four girls ever.

Request 1: Hi, can we have a table for six, please? We'll need two high chairs if possible.

This request will usually be met with a smile and a long walk through the restaurant to a corner table away from other diners, usually next to the toilet or the kitchen. The double buggy will be left by the entrance with all the others for potential diners to negotiate their way around.

Request 2: (literally thirty seconds after sitting down) Do you have any colouring-in for the kids to do, and some bread?

Restaurants are now basically stationery stores that serve food from time to time. The only problem is that the boxes of pencils provided are of such low quality that to achieve even a half-hearted weeping of colour you have to press down so hard that the tip snaps, transforming the pencil into a cylindrical piece of coloured wood that people will slip on after it falls, discarded, onto the floor.

Within two minutes of bread being brought to the table, it will have been devoured, giving us parents a maximum of one hundred and twenty seconds of quiet time to try and glance at the menu. The amount of bread we give the girls will come back to bite us in the arse as they won't eat all their food later on, but the silence is worth it.

Request 3: Do you happen to have any high chairs with working straps?

I don't know why, but 95 per cent of all high chairs in restaurants seem to either be broken or have been designed by a person who either has no children or has children that aren't contortionists like my twins. Within ten seconds of the bread being finished, they will be standing in their high chairs, irrespective of how tight I've yanked the straps, about to embark on a stroll across the table to either Clemmie or myself.

Request 4: Do you have a cloth? My daughter spilt her drink [said through gritted teeth].

Despite telling the girls, 'Don't drink your drink all in one go as that's the only one you're having. Make it last!', one will be guzzled pretty much immediately, while another will almost certainly end up on the floor.

As the millennia have passed and bodies have evolved, children's elbows have developed to do one job perfectly – knock over exorbitantly priced carbonated drinks literally within seconds of them being delivered to the table, resulting in all napkins in the vicinity being immediately pooled to soak up the lake of brown liquid that is creeping its way to the edge of the table, destined to end up in someone's lap.

Request 5: Can we order, please?

I've learnt that as a guy with a biggish family, I now no longer need to order food when we're out. Despite our best efforts to persuade the big girls to select their food from the children's menu, which promises three courses for £6.99, they now want to choose from the adult menu.

OK, I tell them, you can have something from there, on the condition that you finish it. If you don't then you're not getting dessert. Understood?

This ends up the same way every single time. Ten minutes into the meal, Anya will be dislocating her jaw to take on the burger that's a size not dissimilar to her own head, while Marnie pushes her pasta, whose sauce she's finding too rich and creamy, around the plate. It's at this point I know I'm about three minutes away from being offered their unfinished food, and this is now my standard meal out – leftovers from four different lunches. Some chewed, some not. I genuinely don't care what anyone thinks about me eating this, as I refuse to pay for a meal when I know I'll be getting a 'free' one.

Request 6: Can I have the bill, please?

Upon leaving, we'll look back at the destruction in our wake. Like birds that fly south for the winter, 90 per cent of what was on the table when we were first seated will have migrated to the floor underneath our feet. You too can play a fun game of under-the-table bingo towards the end of your next meal out. Below is a checklist; award yourself one point for each item you find down there:

- Napkins (some will be wet, others dry).
- Colouring pencils (the yellow one always seems to be the first to hit the floor).
- A discarded colouring mat.
- At least two pieces of cutlery.
- Some non-descript liquid.
- A crust.
- Some pasta.
- Peas (you may not have even ordered anything with peas, but they'll be there all the same).

Honestly, every time we go out for food as a family in a place that involves sitting down with other humans in a space where sound carries, we walk away saying to ourselves, 'Why do we put ourselves through that? We're down £80 and we're leaving embarrassed and more stressed than when we arrived.'

The answer of course is because we have to keep trying to go and do normal things. One of these days we'll walk away and be able to say, 'That was genuinely a pleasurable experience. What lovely, well-mannered, polite children we've brought up and what a varied palate they have. We must be really good parents.' We're not there yet, but we will be one day. Probably.

The local museum

The idea of going to the museum is lovely. A walk through history that helps to educate our children while they have fun at the same time. And to top it all, it's free.

Free, that is, apart from the £55 I spent in the café for a lunch that I assume was made three weeks previously at a local primary school as part of a food tech project.

When we've all had enough and decide it's time to leave, everyone is guided like cattle to the exit, which is always through the gift shop. Immediately upon setting foot in this place, I'm shaken down by my girls for money to buy items they will look at in the car on the way home, break, cry about for ten minutes and then forget about for the rest of their lives, all before we even get home. The only items that will survive the transit will be bouncy balls and rubbers. The bouncy balls will go over the garden fence within two days, and the rubbers will get put in a pencil case, no doubt to be rediscovered when they leave home for university in ten years' time.

A cultural experience – the art gallery

I'm not a culture vulture but I do like walking around Tate Modern and taking the whole place in. Last time we went, it was supposed to be just Clemmie and me – a rare adult-only afternoon to stare at artwork, nod like we know what it's all about, sip a nice coffee, people-watch and even splash out on a late lunch overlooking the Thames. However, like all great plans, my vision of a child-free afternoon of art, small talk and just being us fell apart when we couldn't find anyone to look after the girls for the afternoon. We tried to pull in every favour we could think of, but no one wants to look after four kids at once, especially if they aren't theirs. I'm sure people see our numbers pop up on their phones and turn them off as they know we're after free childcare.

The visit was topped off when I took Marnie into a dark room in a corner of Tate Modern I'd not been to before. I pulled back the curtain covering the door to reveal a room filled with silhouettes of people who were all staring at the walls. It was at that point I realised that I'd walked into a video-projection room that was showing the photographic work of a Brazilian street-worker who had taken graphic pictures of rent boys in varying states of undress. I quickly turned on my heel and made a hasty retreat to the light outside but it was too late. The images had been burnt into the retina of my then five-year-old daughter and she had questions.

Why was that man's willy all big and long?

I don't know, sweetheart. I'm not sure I understood that.

Some of them looked like they were fighting with each other.

Yes [knowing that it wasn't 'fighting'].

Can we go back in?

No [raising my phone to my ear to take a fake call], Mum's calling me so we'd better go.

I'm sure she's forgotten this experience by now, but it will haunt me forever.

A trip to the shopping centre

This is one place that I would not class as a fun day out. I hate shopping for a number of reasons, but here's my top three:

1. There are too many people – children get lost in a sea of emotionless window shoppers resulting in the tannoy announcement that every parent dreads hearing: 'Could the adult responsible for Marnie Hooper please come to the information centre.' Roughly translated this means: 'We found your feral kid running around as you obviously couldn't be bothered to keep an eye on her. You are the worst kind of parent and I'm using this public service announcement to let everyone in the shopping centre know it.'
2. I hate spending money.
3. I don't try clothes on and I hate waiting for hours while the girls do it – I think this is because I hate being in shops so much that I would rather buy essential items that I absolutely have to replace and live with something that doesn't quite fit me, rather than waste precious time squeezing into items that immediately remind me I'm not twenty-five any more and definitely can't pull

off this look in public. The girls, meanwhile, are all too happy to turn me into a personal assistant who loiters outside the changing rooms rocking a buggy back and forth while they try on an endless succession of outfits.

To be honest, the only reason we're ever in a shopping centre is because, despite the bricks I place on their heads and my insistence that they stop, the girls keep growing out of their clothes. As a result, my shopping experience is centred around prolonged periods of time in the man chair. You can find these outside all women's fitting rooms and they're filled with dads just like me – staring blankly into space, surrounded by bags and waiting for one or more family members to come out and do a twirl.

[Side note: the more I write, the more I realise that I have become my father. Not a bad thing at all, but it's scary how it creeps up on you.]

There's a never-ending list of other hangouts that parents drag their children to and vice versa, but in my experience we've covered the most common ones. So next time you're in one of these places and see a fellow parent's hairline receding in front of your eyes as their kids run them ragged, don't just walk on by and roll your eyes, especially if they're flying solo. Ask if you can do anything to help – the following week, it may well be you in that situation.

Now I know I've painted a picture of every single trip out having some kind of nightmare woven into its fabric, but in reality, days out are good for everyone as life doesn't stop when you have children. If anything, having the girls expands the number of things we do at the weekends and although it's an effort to get everyone pointed in the same direction and out the door, we all come out the other side tired but relatively happy – after all, that's the aim of these trips, isn't it? To give the little people in our lives new experiences that broaden their horizons while simultaneously draining their internal batteries so that we have a fighting chance of an evening without having to race up and down stairs multiple times to tend to children that won't settle. If that fails, at least we'll have tales to tell them later on in life, probably in front of future boyfriends, to make them cringe.

12

Family logistics

Going anywhere requires more patience than waiting in A&E on a Friday night. It's also a little-known fact that travelling with children can lead to you either strongly considering disowning your own offspring or just never going anywhere ever again. I now understand why parents say they need a holiday to get over a holiday.

Family logistics

I could quite happily spend all the hours of my life locked up in the confines of my own home. It's where I feel safe, and being at home enables us to contain the levels of crazy generated by four sugar-enriched children. However, unfortunately it's deemed socially unacceptable to not see people ever, so we're forced to leave the nest and break out into the big wide world on a daily basis. Sometimes we even manage to go . . . wait for it . . . *on holiday*. So, having covered some of the places we visit on a regular basis, let's take a look at how we actually get to them . . .

There was a time in my life when, if I wanted to leave the house, I'd put my shoes on, do the old 'Wallet, keys, phone' pat-down dance that everyone does to check all of life's essentials are on your person, then simply open the door and leave. If I was feeling particularly adventurous I might put on a jacket, but other than that, the process of deciding to leave and actually leaving would be completed in under thirty seconds. It was a task so simple that I barely needed to bother my dozing grey matter: it could be completed on autopilot.

But when you add four children to the equation, the complexity escalates dramatically to the point that you need to employ the services of a supercomputer to work out all the variables that will impact on your actual departure time.

Me making the snap decision to go out is usually met with groaning and the quick establishment of child rebellion. Anya will stomp around like an elephant in lead boots, claiming that it's unfair and questioning why she has to be involved at all, and Marnie will simply ignore the fact that we're going to leave the house and instead stay in a trance-like state in front of the television. She may not have even heard us, to be honest, as I'm starting to think that she may only be able to use one sense at a time. If she's using her sight, it means that her senses of smell, hearing, touch and taste are all closed off. This could go some way to explaining why she's taken to eating with her eyes closed. Who knows. The twins, on the other hand, become excited to the point that they basically resemble small dogs that have been told it's time for walkies. Their arms shoot up like miniature rockets and squawks of delight rush out of their tiny mouths – *finally, we can get out of this house and away from our moody sisters*, they think. They are the first ones to toddle off to the rickety IKEA rack next to the front door that's bowed under the weight of our collective footwear.

So here's a walk-through of what it takes to get this particular collection of people who live together on the road:

Getting dressed might seem like an obvious place to start and you might think no one could argue with that. Common decency requires that when going out where other people can see you it's polite not to be in your birthday suit. Trust me, I know this from experience. The time I went to a pharmacy in the buff to pick up yet another bottle of Calpol was not a good day. OK, that never happened, but it could have and it wouldn't have been good for anyone. Also, clothing is designed not only to look nice but to actually protect you from the elements so, all in all, it's generally a good idea.

However, persuading the girls to actually get dressed in appropriate clothing is a complex task and requires time, encouragement and bribery. With four girls of different ages, each presents us with a slightly different challenge and therefore the approach has to shift as I walk purposefully from room to room.

Anya is ten but already thinks that the world is totally unfair and that she should be able to make independent decisions about what she can and can't do with her life. To some extent she's right: the world is unfair, especially if you're a child, as all you see is adults seemingly doing whatever the hell they feel like. Yet in a non-life-changing moment like going out to get a food shop done, although she has already made it crystal clear she doesn't want to go anywhere with us, I have the ranking authority. Nonetheless, she'll make a stand. Her heels will be dug in so far you could put branches and leaves on her and call her a tree. A hurricane wouldn't shift her, or at least that's the outward impression she gives us. Who knows why leaving the house is such a big issue for her these days, but it is. I like to think that it's because we've made such a nice home environment, she simply can't stand the idea of not being here. In reality, my hunch is that it's because she's fretting she won't be in range of any Wi-Fi and will therefore have to break free from the ongoing Minecraft marathon that she's been locked into for the past two hours.

The gently-gently approach is my initial go-to strategy.

'Sweetheart, we're all going out as a family so please can you get out of the dressing gown you've been wearing all morning and put on something a bit more appropriate?'

This is usually met with a shrug of the shoulders, or a sentence that women have secretly handed down from mother to daughter through the generations; a sentence that is specifically designed to infuriate men everywhere:

'But I have literally nothing to wear!'

This is usually said in front of an open wardrobe that is so full, it's spewing its contents onto the floor as if it was suffering from an allergic reaction to cotton and nylon. The chest of drawers is pulled open to reveal yet more clothes. These were once lovingly folded by her parents, but in the subsequent days were pulled out and scattered all over the floor until we instructed her to clean her room. Her response was to squash down all of her clothes so hard into the drawers that the density of the contents is now such that you can't get anything back out again.

'You've got literally all the clothes. You could wear a different outfit every day for a year and you still wouldn't get through everything you own. Please, please just get dressed.'

'Fine.'

We now move onto strategy two – the 'you're old enough to sort this out on your own' technique.

As I leave the room, I make it clear that there's a time limit to this task. Five minutes max. For me, getting dressed takes about a minute as the process is as simple as completing a Rubik's cube with sides that are all the same colour. I peer into the wardrobe, consider wearing something that I haven't for a while, quickly change my mind and put on the traditional dad uniform of jeans and a white T-shirt, which is lying crumpled on the floor next to my bed. I then mentally question why I was even considering wearing anything else when I knew full well I'd end up wearing the same thing as I did the day before and the day before that.

But over the years, I've come to learn that the whole dressing process is very different for girls. They genuinely care about making sure things go together and that they are fashionable in the eyes of others. I personally think girls have it hard. There's simply too much choice. It's like going to a fancy restaurant that has a menu so long you could class it as a novel. By the time you get to the end of it you're considerably older than when you arrived and you can't remember what any of the options were. This is the point where you opt for the last thing you read, then immediately regret it. It's the same with my girls and clothes – too many options make them indecisive, turning a relatively simple task into a long, drawn-out process that involves multiple outfits, long stints in front of the mirror while turning from side to side and swishing clothes, wearing two different shoes at the same time and lifting each one like a flamingo to see which one works best with the bottom half of the outfit, WhatsApp messages to friends with photos of outfits to get their opinion and, finally, the opinion of a man – me, in this case – to cast judgement over whether the outfit works.

This is a crap position for anyone to be put in, but it's one that guys find themselves in more regularly than they might want. It's like walking on a tightrope with a bed of recently sharpened razor blades on either side, ready to slice you to ribbons should you lose concentration, say the wrong thing and fall. Clemmie does this to me all the time and I'm starting to see it develop in Anya. If we're going out, I'll sit downstairs like an uninterested judge on *Britain's Next Top Model* waiting in the green room before the show's filming. I'll have been ready for a while by this point and will no doubt be making small talk with the babysitter, while trying to convince the taxi driver that 'she'll only be a couple of minutes' so that he doesn't drive off. At this point Clemmie won't even have tried any of the accessories that are needed to finish off the outfit, nor had the fourteen necessary frantic shoe changes. It'll be another thirty minutes at least before my opinion is finally solicited.

'Si, can you come here a moment? I need your help.'

My palms immediately begin to sweat and I start to get that feeling in the pit of my stomach not dissimilar to the one you get when you know you've done something wrong and suddenly feel incredibly guilty.

'What do you think of this outfit?'

I try to stop my eyes wandering to the bed that's covered in clothes and the wardrobe that looks like it's been ransacked and concentrate on the task in hand.

'Yeah, that looks great, really nice. Not sure about the shoes, are they supposed to look like that?'

This is the point where I quietly punch myself in the forehead and immediately regret not having the ability to filter what I'm saying before the words come out of my mouth. Why, oh why, did I have to add the last bit? I was almost home and dry. Always just say yes, give a compliment and return to whatever important job you were doing before being summoned to the bedroom to pass judgement.

'Oh great, so I have to change everything now, thanks. Thanks a lot. I don't know why I bother to ask you sometimes.'

The response I want to give is 'I don't know either, but you do', but fortunately that stays locked away with all the other witty retorts that have been piling up over the years, silently whispered a thousand times internally, destined to be consigned to the mental mind-dump.

Anya must have seen this play out hundreds of times by now, and it's obviously rubbing off on her as she is becoming equally picky about what she wears.

The five minutes is up, and she now has clothes all over the floor, but is still wearing the sodding dressing gown.

Right, strategy two bombed, so on to strategy three – the 'I'm serious now' technique.

With my frustration levels rising to the point that I can sense my voice is becoming squeaky, I become more forceful in tone and make it known that this is simply not acceptable and the show is now not only not on the road, but the stage has been empty for so long that the paying public are demanding their money back.

'Anya, get your clothes on now. It's not a fashion show; we're going to the shop to buy food, batteries and toilet roll. No one you know is going to see you and if they do, so what? I want you downstairs in two minutes, and I'll take you in whatever you're wearing or not wearing – I've had enough of this.'

As I turn to leave, her iPhone makes a noise in her pocket. It's like I'm a criminal investigator and I've found the crucial piece of evidence that makes everything else fit. Instead of dressing, she went on her phone as soon as the door was shut and pissed around, completely ignoring my polite request to not be naked. Busted. I go over to give her a hug to make her feel better and remove the phone from her pocket at the same time without her noticing. I would be a really good petty criminal. Ten seconds after leaving the room, as I'm running downstairs, I can hear the victim of my crime stomp around as realisation dawns that she's just been mugged by her own father.

Two minutes later, a very angry, but dressed, Anya comes downstairs in the same way a person wearing an old deep-sea-diving outfit might. Slowly and very loudly. I choose not to point out that the socks don't go with the outfit and the T-shirt has a stain on it, because, well, we'd be back to square one.

Fifteen minutes has passed. One down, four to go.

Marnie is the next target, but she is a lot more responsive to being asked to do something. Because she loves gymnastics so much, she basically lives in leggings and leotards, so really the only thing she needs to do is get some socks and shoes on, which on the face of it seems like child's play. The main problem with her is getting her attention in the first place and stopping her doing never-ending cartwheels and splits all over the house like someone in training for the Cirque du Soleil. I know my daughter all too well, and the promise of a chocolate bar upon finishing the shop is enough to get her up from the completely unnatural position known as the spider that she's been honing for a while now. It basically looks like she has bones made of gelatine and that she has secretly removed some vertebrae to enable her to get her legs to bend backwards over her own head and back onto the floor. She ends up looking like the result of a terrible accident that a 'no win, no fee' lawyer wouldn't touch with a barge pole.

With the thought of confectionery now dominating the small section of her brain that isn't reserved for memorising lyrics to pop songs and learning YouTuber names, she's off up the stairs to get socks. This is going well.

Five minutes later, I find Clemmie and the twins sitting on the kitchen floor playing with potatoes. I have no idea why out of all the toys they have available to them, they chose to go to the vegetable rack for their entertainment, but then again, who am I to question what makes babies tick? Anya is on the sofa in a huff and only producing one-word answers, which is fine by me. Marnie still hasn't reappeared, so I yell up the stairs to hurry the whole process along. No response. I yell again, this time repeating her name over and over again until a small voice comes back down and acknowledges my existence.

'I'll just be five minutes.'

'No, Marnie. No, you won't.' Begrudgingly I climb the stairs for what feels like the twentieth time in the last thirty minutes to find Marnie colouring in a picture of a princess who seems to be strangling a cat – and she still doesn't have her freaking socks on. The only option now is for me to physically put her socks on her. Perhaps this was her plan all along and I'm just the mug who's been played like a fiddle by a seven-year-old and didn't even realise it. I can't believe I'm actually putting her socks on her feet for her – royalty don't get this kind of service!

With a swift downing of pens and a fireman's lift to the rest of the waiting family, the last task is to get her shoes on.

Finally, we're all by the door and dangerously close to leaving the confines of our own home. By this point I've forgotten why we were going out in the first place and am questioning our life choices when it comes to the number of children we have. Is it still daytime? Have we missed the day through procrastination and our inability to herd the cats we have for offspring? No, it's OK – we've missed lunch but the shops are still open and if we hurry we can make it back in time for the twins' nap (missing this would be a disaster as it throws everything off and means that by 5 p.m. Ottie and Delilah give up on being nice little humans and turn into back-arching screaming machines that stop at nothing to make everyone else feel as rotten as they do).

The last task is coats, which both the big girls flatly refuse to wear.

'I wear that one to school and it's all itchy. I'm not wearing it.'

'Fine, we'll put it under the buggy and you can get it when you need it.'

'But I won't need it because you said we're going in the car.' (She has a point here, but I've already made a stink about her wearing it and I don't want to be the one to back down.)

'Fine, I'll carry it.'

I can't help but feel like I've lost this one, but the coats are coming with us so in a very roundabout way, if you squint and tilt your head, you can kind of see it as a win.

The key turns in the lock and we're off. It's taken a little under an hour from the announcement that we were intending to leave the house to actually completing the task. I've been involved in house moves that have completed quicker than this and my beard is definitely a lighter shade of grey than it was when we started, but the family unit is on the move.

Now we just need a mode of transport.

Going anywhere with almost a whole netball team can be testing, but each mode of transport we might choose to take brings its own challenges in getting us all from A to B without killing each other.

Let's start simply . . .

On foot

You may be thinking that travelling on foot implies travelling light, but you'd be wrong. Getting all twelve feet to point in the same direction and keep them moving requires the same amount of equipment as a battalion deployed to the Middle East. Through a quirk of evolution that happened rapidly about ten years ago and, oddly, coincided with the invention of the scooter, children over the age of five can no longer walk further than a few hundred metres without complaining. Now if we walk anywhere, we are accompanied by two girls who fly off into the distance on brightly coloured scooters that glide across pavements like ducks on a frozen lake. This leaves us lagging behind, stuck behind a double buggy that's so wide, people coming towards us are forced to stand to one side for fear of being mown down. Many opt to simply cross the street.

Don't get me wrong, scooters are great as the girls can coast along and it brings the whinging down to acceptable levels. However, there really should be the equivalent of a driving test that children have to pass before they're allowed out on the pavements. There is no etiquette or consideration when a child is on one of these things. They hare towards little old ladies at a speed that warps space and time, locked in a game of chicken that their target knows nothing about. At the last minute, the girls will swerve out of the way, leaving the OAP in question short of breath and with a full colostomy bag.

It's then down to us to chase after them, breaking into a sweat and trying not to look like absolute lunatics as we shout their names.

The girls also seem to have way too much trust in the braking mechanism of these things. It's not a particularly complex system – just a small piece of plastic that hangs over the back wheel, which when you stand on it, creates enough friction between the wheel and the plastic to bring the potentially lethal ride to an end. They have no awareness that these components break all the time, and as a result race towards junctions, leaving us to shout out, 'STOP RIGHT NOW!', expecting a car to round the corner at any moment and for our children to end up as flattened 2D versions of themselves as the car runs them over. Of course, they slam their feet down just in time, come to a halt and look back at us as if we've completely lost the plot. This is usually then followed by a comment like, 'Of course we were going to stop, we're not stupid, God, you're so embarrassing', as we kneel down next to them and give them yet another mini lecture on why they need to slow down.

The wobble that scooters do when they're hurtling downhill at speed has to be one of the worst things a parent can watch. I know because I've experienced it several times and it takes you way past the point of feeling like your heart is in your mouth. It's more like your heart has fallen out of your mouth, been picked up and savaged by a passing dog and then discarded in the road where the number 68 bus runs it over, then backs up to pick up some passengers and runs it over again.

I recall being in the park with Marnie at the top of a relatively steep hill. The moment she set off and began travelling faster than I could run, I knew it was going to end with a child in a crumpled heap on the ground, a large amount of skin on the tarmac and a whole lot of blood. It was like it happened in slow motion, handlebars wobbling from side to side and cries of terror as she realised she was no longer in control and had become just a passenger that needed to hold on for dear life. Then, finally, the moment when she was airborne before bouncing and ending her journey on the grass, screaming. I was completely powerless to do anything other than watch the horror unfold in front of my wincing eyes and be prepared to scoop up the remains after it was all over.

The twins have it made. Their feet quite literally don't touch the ground. They get into the buggy, are strapped in and then chauffeured everywhere. The only problem they have is when they express an interest in walking and need us to bend down and extend a finger for them to grab on to. I love that. It makes me feel needed. Knowing that they want to explore the world but that they still need the security and reassurance of holding on to me is wonderful. The only downside to this is that they aren't quite tall enough yet for us to hold hands while I'm standing up straight, so I'm forced to adopt a hunched position that I have to stay in for a prolonged period of time. If I was twenty-five again, this wouldn't be a problem, but being thirty-five my back ain't what it used to be and it means I develop shooting pains that feel like being struck by a tiny lightning bolt many times from my arse down to my ankles. While the twins amble along, giggling at flowers, grins painted across their faces, I grimace and clutch my lower back, trying not to let on that a spinal cord replacement has suddenly shot right to the top of my Christmas list this year.

Being low to the ground and out of the buggy, the twins have access to a whole host of interesting objects that people have discarded, which they readily pick up, manhandle for a while and either put in their pockets, place back down where they found them, or if they're feeling adventurous, pop into their mouths. Back in the days when we had one child, it was easy to stay on top of the delights Anya picked up but with the twins, who knows what they have in their hands at any given time.

Walking with the twins also means that any original ETA we may have had in mind is led into a secluded field and shot in the head.

There's absolutely no chance we'll stick to it as their speed is but a tiny fraction of our own. They are also incapable of walking in one consistent direction. Have you ever seen that video online of a spider that's been given LSD? It knows it has to make a web, but it can't think straight and ends up meandering all over the place, making something that's reminiscent of a half-finished dream-catcher. It's the same with the twins. We could head for a target that's 100 metres away as the crow flies, but by the time we get there, Ottie and Delilah will have covered over a kilometre deviating this way and that.

Public transport

The occasions when we take public transport, be it trains or buses, are few and far between for us. Not because there's anything wrong with it – on the contrary, it's cheap and efficient. The problem for us is that if we get the bus, we end up taking up approximately 50 per cent of the lower deck and that's if we manage to get on in the first place. If the buggy spaces are taken up, then there's no other option but to watch the bus close its doors and drive away, leaving us to wait for the next one to round the corner.

Trains are more preferable. They're wide and spacious and the ones on the line near where we live have built-in monkey bars, otherwise known as handles for those standing. OK, so trains don't always run on schedule but as far as public transport goes, they're the best option of the bunch. The issue I have with being on trains is not the trains themselves, but the fact they're a relatively quiet mode of transport which, when combined with my girls' inability to modulate their voices or filter what they're saying, makes for some uncomfortable moments.

'Daddy, why does that person have their hair shaved like that?'

'I don't know, but can you just lower your voice a little bit, sweetheart?'

'But she looks like a cat after it's had surgery at the vet's.'

It's at this point that the lady in question, who has the side of her head shaved, looks up and makes eye contact with me and I mouth the word 'sorry'.

Cars

Cars are by far and away my top choice of transport. I love them. I come from a family that has Castrol oil coursing through its veins. My dad was always in the garage, conducting open-heart surgery on an engine block or some rusted-out chassis that he was looking to bring back from the dead. Cars are personal as you invest your money in them and they're a place where everyone comes together and where memories are made. In fact, now I think about it, they probably come second in the list of places you spend the most time together as a family. Hell, they even get given names, start to take on their own personalities, and end up in family photos.

That's why I like to take pride in my car. I'll be the first to admit that when we're at home, I have selective sight. I don't class myself as a particularly untidy person, it's just that Clemmie and I have differing views as to what constitutes an acceptable level of disorganisation. Her view is that everything must be put away, all surfaces wiped clean and nothing should be out of place; mine is that as long as I can walk from A to B without stepping on food, then it's OK. However, when it comes to the car, I like to keep it in the state I took it on – so clean I could happily eat my dinner off the dashboard.

The problem is when you place four children in the car, you can guarantee that within a couple of days it will resemble a rubbish tip. The crevices between the seats act as collection points for all manner of discarded child paraphernalia and food. Recently I was on my hands and knees in the back of the car trying to scrub off the remains of a salmon and cream cheese sandwich that had welded itself to a head-rest. I honestly couldn't recall when we'd even last had salmon and cream cheese – had it been there for days, a month? Short of rustling up a DIY carbon-dating kit and putting the specimen through rigorous testing, I have to resign myself to putting that question into the bucket with all the other ones I don't know the answers to, like who ate the last slice of birthday cake that I'd been saving and where *do* all the hairbands go?

Here's a very quick game we can play to demonstrate just how good children are at spreading their junk around the car. I put my hands down the back of the seats while cleaning the car and pulled out eight items. Cover up the bullet points below and have a guess at what they were. You get one parent point for each one you get right, which are worth precisely nothing and can't be traded for anything of any value:

- A very old piece of fruit.
- A colouring pen with no lid on.
- A hairclip.
- A hairband.
- A sweet wrapper.
- A screwed-up school letter about a trip that's already happened.
- A dummy.
- Crumbs. Lots of crumbs.

Much like at the dinner table, everyone has a set position in the car and a role to play. I'm pretty sure Anya gets the short straw these days. While we silently consume banned confectionery and generally swan about up front in first class, back in cattle class, it falls to poor big sister Anya to hold down the fort in the middle row while sandwiched between the type of travelling companions you would pay good money to move away from: the twins in all their fully immersive, surround-sound screaming glory. With each increase in decibel level, the pressure in the car builds until something has to give – usually either Clemmie or me. Anya has been thrust into a parent role she neither wanted nor asked for, with little thanks or gratitude from us – forget middle-child syndrome, this is middle-seat syndrome and by all accounts, it sucks. So thank you, Anya: without you, a two-hour journey would take days – you're a great big sister and we don't tell you that enough.

Being confined in the car with your loved ones generates a lot of chaos, and it's also a place where tempers can become frayed quicker than you can say, 'Are we there yet?'. You're locked in position next to the person that's pushing your buttons and there's nowhere to escape to, unless you fancy flinging yourself out of a metal box on wheels that's hurtling along at high speed. The main sources of frustration that seem to come up inside the pressure cooker we call our car are as follows:

- Adults being allowed to eat, but not children.
- Infrequent toilet breaks.
- Not being allowed to get out at the petrol station when I'm filling the tank.
- All the USB points being used.
- Indecisive radio station selections.
- Out-of-tune singing.
- Running out of snacks/drinks.
- One or both of the twins filling their nappies.
- A seat belt that refuses to cooperate.

On the other hand, there are also those moments when the decibel levels decrease and we actually just get to talk, something that's almost impossible at home as there is always something else to do or another room to go into to get a piece of the most precious commodity you can have in a large family: privacy. I've been reflecting on this recently and I can truthfully say that some of the most open and honest conversations I've ever had with my girls have happened in the car. We could just be going to the shops or dropping them off at a friend's house, but in that fifteen minutes, we can discuss anything and everything and feel connected again. OK, it's not exactly confession and I'm definitely not a priest, but being able to let the words just flow out without having to look someone in the eyes is somehow easier. Before you know it, we've covered space, pop stars, what they want to be in the future, how a squirrel can balance on fences and the best formula to make slime (which is now banned in our house after more unsuccessful attempts than I could count using both my fingers and toes). If you're ever having a hard time with your kids, you should try it – take one child out with you in the car and just talk. It's amazing what some one-to-one time can do.

Planes

Imagine yourself in a small room with your family where you have to sit almost on top of each other while strapped down. Now add two crying babies that you can't console. Now imagine strangers are piled into the room with you and tell you using only the look in their eyes that they want nothing more in the world than for your babies to stop crying.

There's no way of painting this any differently. Travelling by plane with all four children is hard work, but the world's a big place and we want the girls to experience it all, so getting on these flying tubes is a necessity.

In the days before we had the girls in our lives, going to the airport and catching a plane to some far-flung sun-drenched destination in order to escape the monochrome rat race we called our daily grind was exciting. Being at the airport signified that we were leaving all responsibility behind us along with the shirts and ties. Packing consisted of dedicating thirty minutes of time to standing in front of a wardrobe and throwing things into a waiting open case on the bed. Like other adults, we'd get a taxi to the airport and we could afford to travel at a time of day when the sun has already been hanging in the sky for several hours. During the flight we'd hold hands and sip drinks while smiles radiated from our faces. On arrival we'd carry our luggage out to the taxi rank and would be next to the pool with an unpronounceable fancy foreign cocktail within an hour of the plane wheels hitting the tarmac.

However, as the number of children has increased over time, a shift has occurred. Going on holiday has started to feel like putting in a lot more effort simply to essentially do the same things we do at home, just in a slightly hotter place with a pool and a time difference thrown into the mix, resulting in sleep routines being screwed up for the first couple of days.

Packing bags for the family has become a full-time job that spans the length of time of your average festival. We can lose two or three days to packing, which is sometimes longer than the actual amount of time we are going away for.

Each child has a bag, apart from the twins who now use the suitcase that Clemmie and I used to share. I'm not allowed to pack this case as previous experience has taught us that I'll either pack completely inappropriate clothing for the destination, or I'll forget essential item like the monitor, muslins and bottles. My services are only called on when Clemmie is crumpled in a heap, sitting in the crater of a fabric volcano partly hidden by the pile of clothes that surrounds her. Selecting garments and ensuring they have everything they could possibly need is Clemmie's strength. Getting it all into the luggage without the zip going through a crisis of confidence and separating permanently is mine.

Once the bags are finally packed, I do a tour of the house, picking up the luggage from each room like an unpaid porter and transporting it down the stairs one bump at a time. It's usually at about this stage that two things happen:

1. I realise that, despite having built up a respectable upper-body strength from lugging twins around, my best efforts to move the bags are having little to no effect. They each weigh the equivalent of a hippo. A hippo that has really let itself go and is struggling with its weight after a particularly nasty break-up. It's usually Clemmie's bag that weighs the most and it doesn't take a set of electronic scales to know that this is destined to be one of those bags that is immediately slapped with the obligatory 'CAUTION: HEAVY' label as the airport conveyer belt buckles under its vast weight. The excess baggage fees that I was desperately trying to avoid are mentally added to the total of the holiday spend. I don't know why I ever think it's going to weigh anything under 23 kg. It never has in the last ten years, but I live in the vain hope that one day Clemmie's packing will become more efficient and she'll decide eight pairs of shoes and ten dresses for a week-long holiday just doesn't make sense.

2. I'm reminded not to scratch the paint on the walls as I negotiate my way past the toys on the floor and the random items of clothing and electronics that have unhelpfully piled up at the foot of the stairs.

With the kids now in their bedrooms, but too excited to sleep, it's my job to fit seemingly everything we own into a standard-sized family car. I'll come back to this topic in a bit, but let's just say I have never been beaten when it comes to packing. With enough time and planning, I'm pretty sure I could lever an elephant into an eggcup.

Flying as a family of six means that your choice of flights is limited, unless you fancy forking out over a month's salary before you even get to your destination. That leaves us with only one option: the first flight of the day, otherwise known as the zombie-travellers flight. In order to catch it, we have to set three or four alarms to go off at one-minute intervals only two hours after we made it to bed. When they do, my head feels like it's made of wool that's been left to soak in porridge overnight, but I have to shake it off. I don't know why, but as the man of the house I feel it's my role to take charge of holidays, so I put on my clothes, which are placed next to my bed like a fireman ready to jump into action, and do what any self-respecting British person would do – go and make some tea. By the time it's made, Clemmie is up and we both venture upstairs to wake the older girls from their slumber.

With four out of six of us convened downstairs, talking in hushed tones, we make a final check of all the travel documents in the plastic wallet that people only ever use for going on holiday and move towards the car. When everyone has managed to wedge themselves in among the bags, the final piece of the puzzle is to get the twins, who are still curled up and dreaming about whatever it is babies dream about. Performing the transfer from bed to car seat is similar to the way I'd imagine carrying a uranium fuel rod, slowly and with caution – should you manhandle it, the next forty minutes in the car could be like a nuclear winter. It's 3.35 a.m. and it's time to leave.

Having made it to the airport after a thankfully uneventful thirty-minute blast down the motorway, the next task is to park the car. Having been told several weeks ago to book the car park closest to the airport, preferably with valet parking, I reviewed the prices online and immediately opted for the cheapest. A decision I always live to regret, but find myself making every single time. My eyes took one look at the prices and my brain interjected: 'If you go for the cheaper one, you'll have £30 more to spend on holiday – that's a meal and a couple of drinks!' I wish I could put my grey matter on mute sometimes, but before I knew it, my card details had been entered and it was booked. I didn't opt for the payment protection plan or the ability to cancel and get a refund as that was another £2.50, which is basically daylight robbery. However, now that we were going through with having to park the car miles away from the terminal and wait for the airport shuttle to arrive, I was seriously questioning my choices.

Airport car parks are strange places. They're full of families dressed for 30-degree heat at 4.15 in the morning. It's still dark, yet the guy next to me has a sun hat on and shades. His children couldn't look more embarrassed and both have their faces planted firmly in their hands as their father strolls up and down, waiting for the bus. I'll be that guy in a couple of years, and secretly I'm really looking forward to it.

After waiting for twelve minutes, we finally round up all our luggage and tow it towards the bus. Anya is pushing one buggy and dragging along some carry-on luggage, Marnie is pulling a suitcase that's the same size as her, Clemmie has a buggy and a bag, and finally there's me bringing up the rear, the amateur Sherpa, struggling with three cumbersome pieces of luggage that keep smashing into my legs. It would have been easier to drag three dead horses across a ploughed field.

There is no greater feeling than that of getting rid of those bulky bags at check-in. Finally we can all manoeuvre freely and we're safe in the knowledge that although we cut it fine, we're going to get the flight. The next ninety minutes are spent milling around, intermittently changing nappies, nipping to the loo and making trips to the shop to get plug adapters (which I'll find I've already brought four of when we unpack). It's still only 5.30 a.m. when Anya, who has been sent to look at the board to see what's happening with our flight, comes rushing over.

'It says final call next to the flight!'

Bugger. This results in all of us doing the 'we're running, but trying not to look like we're running' run through the departure lounges as we file into a line in height order like a scene from *Home Alone*.

Fortunately the plane doesn't leave without us, and once we're on board, a quick glance around confirms that the composition of passengers follows the usual formula for these super-early flights, namely:

- 35 per cent overexcited children who haven't had enough sleep.
- 35 per cent tired parents who are stressing about how low the battery is on the iPad and how their kids are going to react when it gives up the ghost.

- 10 per cent elderly people who will sleep the entire journey.
- 10 per cent twentysomethings getting away for some cheap sun and the possibility of an STD.
- 10 per cent others.

Of course, once everyone's settled in their seats, it doesn't mean it's all plain sailing from now on. Far from it. We will spend the next three hours grappling with the following things that all children do on planes and that drive their parents crazy:

- Reach through the seats in front of them and touch other people.
- Stand on laps and grab strangers' hair.
- Argue over the coveted window seat.
- Get parents to buy overpriced drinks, only to spill them on the floor after two sips.
- Ask 'How long to go now?' at least four times.
- Ask to go to the toilet so much you suspect a urinary tract infection or potential intravenous drug use.
- Drop items that then roll under the seats in front, so you have to retrieve them, arse in the air.

Still, there are ways to make flying with children easier, and I have acquired precious knowledge in this area over the course of the past decade. First and foremost, bring their favourite toys – on one flight to Greece, we sat in front of a lovely family of six. The dad (who was obviously more prepared than I) had emptied the entire toy box into a carry-on bag and he kept pulling things out to entertain both his own kids and ours. Without this superdad, we would have been screwed. (FYI, superdad – I'm pretty sure Delilah's light fingers squirrelled away one of your tractors, so on the off chance you're reading this, I owe you a piece of farmyard machinery.)

You should also make sure that any tablets, phones, etc are fully charged and that you download enough programmes to avoid arguments. Then there's snacks – bring snacks with you. Lots of snacks. The stuff they sell on budget airlines is a) so expensive you'll feel like you've been a victim of a very polite, but very real mugging, and b) tastes exactly the same irrespective of what you choose.

When flying with very little ones, there are a few key things that it's really worthwhile remembering. Firstly, do not ever forget to bring milk with you if you're formula feeding. When Clemmie and I took the girls to Morocco for some winter sun, we got on the plane only to realise we hadn't brought bottles with us and as a result Ottie and Delilah screamed so much, they stopped making noise and instead entered that silent stage where they just turn red and look like they're about to combust. The only way we were able to rectify the situation was by taking thirty individual self-serve UHT milk sachets and pouring them into a cup, which promptly ended up in my lap.

Also, always try and change little ones before you get on the plane – when Marnie was small, I carried her onto a plane with a full nappy. The odour in the air did not go unnoticed by the other passengers, who looked directly at me. Hang on, guys, I haven't shat myself, it's her! Thankfully a kind flight attendant let me do a lightning-quick change before the plane took off, leaving the next poor sod to use the bathroom to get a noseful of my daughter's waste products.

Finally, don't be afraid to walk around the cabin with your little ones. They need to exercise.

My absolute top tip, though, is this: if at all possible, try and avoid travelling with children in the first place.

So what have I learnt when it comes to preparing to leave the house and transporting my harem of blonde-haired beauties around? Well . . .

- Travelling with an adult to child ratio that is 1:1 or better is preferable. I look back on those days when we had one or two girls and think about how easy it was in comparison to the poorly executed military operation it has turned into now.
- You can pack as much travel entertainment as you can physically carry and it will never be enough as children have the attention spans of particularly forgetful goldfish.
- Make sure that all electronic items are charged and that you have the right USB cables stashed in an easy-to-access location. A dead iPad is worse than death itself.
- Any kind of strap, be it in a buggy, car or plane will be seen as a challenge to escape from by any child under the age of three. They will contort, scream and wriggle until they are free of their restraints, at which point you'll look down and be totally flummoxed by how they did it.

- For every child you have, expect to leave fifteen minutes later than you planned. This simple formula seems to stand up to testing. Prior to the twins, we'd leave roughly half an hour after we planned to. Now with four in tow, being an hour late is standard.
- Irrespective of the volume of luggage my girls throw at me, I am more than capable of getting it into the car.

As anyone who's packed a car for a long journey knows, getting a roof box is just cheating. It's not a proper family road trip until every inch of free space is taken and children have to put their legs over their own shoulders to fit in.

- I do not need or want a roof box (also known as a wanker box) as the 3D-Tetris packing skills that I inherited from my dad enable me to get twenty cubic metres of stuff into ten cubic metres of space. Yes, Clemmie will have no leg-room, the kids will have to keep pushing items back into place and I wouldn't know if an articulated lorry was about to crash into us from behind as I can't see anything in the rear-view mirror, but I can smile as we got everything in and as the driver, I have absolutely nothing crammed in beside me. Fact-based evidence has been waved under my nose that getting a roof box would make my life easier, but I'm pig-headed and determined, so if I give in now, I'll be a disappointment to myself. And my dad.

- Babies cry on planes. It happens and you have to get used to it, along with the burning sensation you get around your ears when you know that everyone is staring at you thinking you're the worst parent ever. Being a parent doesn't mean you have to be confined to the borders of your own country – you're entitled to a holiday too, so don't feel bad about it. Just remember to pack the milk!

13

Fatherly failings:
acknowledging that perfection doesn't exist

When I dress the twins, they always end up looking like hungover hipsters who rummaged through a bag of secondhand clothes, then got dressed in the dark. Baby fashion has never been one of my strong points.

Fatherly failings

I spend my days trying to be the perfect father; however perfection itself is like a mythical creature that people talk about but never actually see. It's the pot of gold at the end of the parenting rainbow that's always just out of reach. My inability to achieve perfection leads to heavy doses of parenting guilt, something that anyone who is responsible for a small version of themselves knows about all too well. So with the never-ending journey towards perfect parenting still under-way, I feel it's important to acknowledge my failings so that I can move past them, safe in the knowledge that I do excel in other areas, such as:

- Cobbling together passable costumes for school events that I'm notified of at 7.30 p.m. the day before the event takes place. (I work well under pressure so knocking up a scientist's outfit for science week, a Jacqueline Wilson character for World Book Day or a dead bride for Halloween out of garden wire, dust sheets and extensive use of Clemmie's expensive make-up is all in a day's work for me.)

- Making up games to play with the kids using anything within a two-metre radius.
- Assisting children who have the ability to destroy a room just by looking at it, to make it even more of a mess.
- Creating the perfect voices for characters when reading aloud (if you ever read *The BFG* to your children, make sure you do the giant's voice in a West Country accent or you're simply doing it wrong).

However, while I might shine in these areas, I also have plenty of failings . . .

My inability to control more than one child at a time

From the age of anywhere between five months and a year old, babies stop being just little balls of squishy flesh that shit themselves and that you constantly have to walk around with to stop them crying. A magical transformation happens, and it happens quickly. Before you know it, they develop characters and the ability to move independently.

While I'm always happy when they have fully functioning motor skills, it also poses a problem. I used to be able to put a baby down somewhere, leave it for a bit to do something, and be 99 per cent sure that when I came back, the baby would still be there. I say 99 per cent sure as once, I left one of my daughters on the floor to go to the bathroom and Clemmie moved her to another room deliberately, then ran away to make me think she'd learnt to crawl in the time I'd been in the toilet. Oh, how we laughed. Well, she did. Me? Not so much.

Now I've got four walking, talking people to control and without employing G20-style kettling or taking them to the vet to get micro-chipped it's almost impossible to know where they all are all the time. Some of this is down to me not paying attention and some of it is because they think every minute of every day is some kind of unofficial attempt at the world's longest game of hide-and-seek.

If the twins are going to insist on spending a large proportion of their time under tables and sideboards, then I really should start considering attaching cleaning implements to them like cloths and floor mops in order to get them to start pulling their weight. I'm sure in Victorian times they would have been operating a huge industrial weaving machine by now, or at least sweeping chimneys, so what's a little floor cleaning?

In our previous life without children, we could leave things on the floor. We could display our lovely ornaments and exotically scented candles on low side tables and have cables tucked away, knowing that they'd stay there. We could also put things in low cupboards and expect them to be there next time we came back looking for them. Not any more.

My ineptitude at climbing control

Have you ever seen Sly Stallone in *Cliffhanger*? No, neither have I as I heard it was a terrible film, but I'm assuming that he's a good climber as it's a film about climbing. Well, he hasn't got a patch on what small children can climb and once they start to learn that they now have vertical options as well as horizontal ones, they really go to town. When Anya and Marnie were at this stage, there was always an adult that could supervise; after all, we had a good ratio going. One parent to one child – it was simple and easy to manage. When the twins came along, the ratio was thrown completely out of kilter – 2:1 meant that there would always be two of our children who were allowed to do as they pleased.

The twins are a force of nature and have obviously devised a tag-team system whose rules we don't really understand. You'll find one climbing the chairs in the kitchen, only to turn around and catch a glimpse of the other one on top of the sofa, sending Morse code signals to the neighbours by opening and closing the shutters.

They're just at that stage now where they're almost out of their cots, and when they finally manage to escape from that particular baby prison, we are officially screwed. At the moment we're able to use the cots to separate them if they're fighting, to put one in if we're changing the other and generally to ensure we know where at least one of them is at any given time. As soon as they're able to scale the bars and do a Pablo Escobar (and by that I mean escape from confinement, not become one of the biggest drug kingpins in the history of the world) it's going to make baby management a lot more difficult. Combine this with the fact that they are now at a height where they can reach door handles and know how to use them, and we'll be getting night-time visits from these little unwelcome visitors any day now. One of my friends sent me a video of a set of twins that had got to this stage with a subject heading that simply read: 'You're fucked.' He doesn't have a particularly elegant way with words, but the fact is he was right.

My piss-poor attempts at multitasking

It's a commonly held belief that men can't multitask. I would love to be able to reel off a number of stories that would completely blow this cliché out of the water, but if anything, the stories I have only serve to prove it even more strongly. The only thing I've ever really done well that you could class as multitasking is tandem feeding the twins, but in reality that's only one job. I have the ability to do one thing well at a time or I end up personifying the delightfully derogatory term that my mum has coined for my dad: 'Half-Job Hooper'. My wife, on the other hand, with the phone tucked between her ear and her shoulder, can carry twins while closing drawers with her knees, reading letters from school about headlice, signing admin forms and cooking dinner for four people. I get tired just watching her sometimes.

My continual avoidance of doing jobs I hate

I know of no parent that claps their hands and shouts, 'Yippee, they've done a poo. My turn to change them. My turn!!' It just doesn't happen because changing nappies is at best unpleasant and at worst a back-hunching, gag-reflex-inducing experience which leaves you looking like a cat struggling with a particularly huge hairball after a marathon self-cleaning session. That's why we have all, at some point, tried to either ignore the smell until someone else does something about it, or made ourselves busy doing something – anything – else to avoid staring at our children's nappy offal.

On this subject, and I don't know when this first started, but Clemmie and I are locked in a never-ending game of nappy poker. You probably play it as well, just without knowing it. All you need is a child who's still in nappies, and two parents.

Here's how you play: one parent will change a nappy. They can use that as an excuse not to change the next one, and if it was a poo they get a green card to skip several nappy changes. It's worth even more if it's an up-the-backer, otherwise known as a poonami, or one of those ones that leak so that the child's clothes have actually changed colour. Add in the additional bonus associated with changing a shitty nappy at night, and your partner could be looking at needing to change one pooey nappy during the day and at least three wet ones to get back to level pegging.

Here's a real-life example of this game in action:

I woke up first and got the twins up. As I pulled them from their beds, I could see that their nappies resembled two bags of wet cement. One of them was so heavy, it had fallen halfway down their legs. I immediately changed them.

Later on that morning, it was obvious that unless someone had delivered a package of shit through the letterbox, one of the twins had pooed.

CLEMMIE: Well, it's your turn to change Delilah.

ME: How is it my turn? I changed them both this morning.

CLEMMIE: Because I did two really bad ones the other day. Remember when I came running downstairs gagging? It's definitely your turn.

ME: OK, I guess.

CLEMMIE: Hold on, you might as well change Ottie at the same time because she hasn't been changed since this morning.

ME: Hold on, how does that equal out? I'm now doing four nappies to your two.

CLEMMIE: Yes, but I had to change Ottie in the night the other day while you were asleep. [Obviously there is no way I can confirm this; I'm pretty sure it's what's known in the industry as faking the change, but you can't call someone out on it unless you have proof.]

ME: OK, but we're even after that.

CLEMMIE: We'll see.

Despite years of practice, I seem to always be down on nappy poker. I have a feeling that Clemmie is just better at keeping count. She'd make a killing in Vegas on the blackjack tables. I wouldn't be surprised to find that she's actually got a page in the back of her diary documenting exactly how many nappies she's changed and what sort, versus what I've done myself – she's always got an ace up the sleeve.

My inability to tell the twins apart

I've got a 50 per cent chance of correctly identifying which twin is which, yet somehow I get it wrong 90 per cent of the time. We've tried all the tricks like painting a nail red, tying the hair differently and even buying tops that have ginormous O and D letters on them, yet I'm still getting it wrong more than I get it right. It's got so bad recently that I have resorted to avoiding saying their names

I have literally no clue who's who. None. To me,
they'll always be 'this one' and 'that one' at least
until they can say their own names. Even then
I won't be 100 per cent sure I've got it right.

altogether, instead using generic terms like 'this one', 'that one' and 'the twins' to sidestep the shame of being known as the man who doesn't know who his own kids are. When I've posted a picture online with a comment about what Delilah was doing in the photo, I've been publicly shamed by my wife on several occasions with a simple yet effective 'That's not Delilah, that's Ottie'.

Clemmie says that it's laziness on my part and that I should make more of an effort to get to know them, which frustrates me no end. Why on earth would I deliberately avoid being able to tell my children apart? I genuinely do make every effort to see the differences in them, but I think I must suffer from a rare form of face blindness as I just can't see it. There have been times when I've spent the whole afternoon with one of the twins, thinking it was one child when it was the other. Poor Delilah, I gave her the wrong blanket, I fed her food she didn't like, made her sleep in the wrong cot and even tried to force a dummy on her. Clemmie can tell the difference between them; so can their sisters and grandparents. I guess I'll just have to wait until they can tell me who's who, but even then that's not a 100 per cent guarantee as twins are renowned for stealing each other's identities when it suits them.

What has reassured me is that I've discovered I'm not the only one who struggles with this. There are people out there who are still getting it wrong even though their kids are now teenagers, so there's hope for me yet. Should we get to the twins' sixteenth birthday and I'm still muddling them up, we'll be heading down the local tattoo parlour to get their names permanently inked onto their foreheads. If that's not an incentive for them to help me learn who's who before that point, then I don't know what is.

My inability to dress children nicely

For a guy, this whole area is a potential minefield anyway, but even more so if you're dressing girls. I can colour match with the best of them and I know the difference between a dress, a shirt, a halter-neck and a romper, but when it comes to dressing children, it seems this is an area I can never get right.

I was left to get all four of my girls ready one day as Clemmie was busy doing something that involved looking into the mirror on her own for over twenty minutes, so I set to work and put them in what I thought were perfectly reasonable outfits for the day.

It was only when Clemmie finally came in that I realised my views on what's fashionable for one-year-olds might be very different to other people's.

Colours were clashing to the point that they were actually quite jarring to look at. Soft, small, open-toed shoes were fastened to their feet with no socks on underneath, even though it was January and raining outside.

They had no vests on. Just T-shirts and tops. The trousers I'd chosen were in fact pyjama bottoms – I mean, how the hell was I supposed to know that? They all have animals on them and are relatively skin-tight!

We've now resorted to Clemmie laying out the clothes on the floor that she wants the girls to wear so that there is absolutely no way I can mess it up. I find it all rather patronising, but to be honest this isn't a battle that I particularly fancy fighting. After all, it's now less work for me than it was before so I really shouldn't be complaining.

However, deciding on what they should wear is only one part of the job. The other part is actually getting them in the bloody stuff and persuading them to keep it on.

My girls fidget and contort when I'm dressing them, which makes the process of getting their legs into their trousers not all that dissimilar to trying to thread a needle, if the thread were made of jelly and the needle was a frankfurter sausage with a hole in. I've had to resort to using my legs as a vice to pin the girls into position as I dress them.

Anything with buttons or those tiny little poppers is a pain in the arse. I find myself trying to push a button through a buttonhole that is almost impossible to locate, and when I do finally find the bugger, my sausage-like man fingers don't have the dexterity to actually complete the keyhole surgery required, as both the button and the hole are completely obscured by my meaty digits. And as if this whole process wasn't complex enough, for some reason, in the dim and distant past, someone decided that women's buttons should be sewn on the opposite side to men's buttons. I'm told that is because in the olden days ladies were dressed by their ladies-in-waiting, therefore shirts and dresses were made this way so that it was easier for the person assisting to complete their work. Men never had this luxury as we were deemed capable of dressing ourselves (though the judges are still out on this one, I think), so from the day I learnt to dress myself the buttons have always been on the other side. Now I've had to completely relearn how to do up a series of buttons and I'm telling you, it's a complete faff.

Poppers are even worse. If you have baby-sized hands they're perfect, but I have normal adult-sized hands so trying to squeeze these together in the right order first time is impossible. I regularly give myself a mental high five after completing the run of poppers between the girls' legs, only to find that I've miscounted and that there's one popper left over. I then have to undo the whole thing and start from scratch so that the girls aren't lopsided – another minute wasted on baby clothing admin that could have been spent doing something much more productive, like staring out of the window or pretending to be asleep on the kids' bedroom floor.

My lack of patience with baby-led weaning and my reluctance to clean up afterwards

Weaning can be a pain in the arse, but it's an important part of introducing your children to the multitude of colours and flavours that the culinary world has to offer. Plus, when we decided to wean the twins, I was ready for them to transition away from non-descript blended mush because I was getting a bit bored of snacking on it and wanted more substantial leftovers to nibble.

The problem was we'd opted to do baby-led weaning. This is when you give your child a bowl of real food and let them chow down themselves. This in itself wasn't the issue as they'd happily sit restrained in their high chairs, picking about in the food for morsels they were prepared to try. The issue was that a) mealtimes now took what felt like the entire lifespan of the universe to complete, and b) baby-led weaning is messier than when the foxes get in your rubbish.

Usually I'm a patient man, but watching two babies spend an hour rifling through a bowl of semi-chewed food, only to then tip the contents of said bowl onto the floor, the chair and themselves, made inserting the entire length of a knitting needle into my ears seem attractive. Ninety per cent of the food would end up within a 2-metre perimeter of their high chairs, so that from above it looked like a Venn diagram of food groups children won't eat. Becoming increasingly frustrated by the glacial pace at which the twins were grasping the concept of feeding themselves, I decided to demonstrate how to eat by taking things from their plates and providing step-by-step audible instructions. This was of course accompanied by the obligatory aeroplane noises as I piled one thing after another into my mouth to illustrate how they were supposed to complete the challenging task. Then I'd try to fly the plane laden with nutritional goodness towards the twins. The landing strip looked clear for a good touchdown but I'd usually find the hangar doors would close at the last minute, promptly followed by a hand slapping the cargo to the floor, dispersing the wreckage across a large area and thus making recovery impossible.

Watching this would drive Clemmie insane, but it wasn't the initial mess that really got to her. It was the fact that after mealtimes, I would clean up the girls and simply walk away from the table without making any effort to clean up the debris that we'd left behind.

If my wife won the lottery, she'd probably live in a minimalist white box next door to us that had an adjoining door that only she had a key to. That way, she could come and go as she pleased and simply walk away when it all became too much. Actually, come to think of it, that's probably something most parents would quite fancy, isn't it?

Anyway, in a desperate attempt to keep everyone happy I bought a very large blue tarpaulin. I carefully measured out places for arm and head holes and placed it over the twins. It was so big that it reached from wall to wall and there was absolutely no way that any food was going to touch the floor. I was personally overjoyed at my invention. The *Dragons' Den* lot would have been all over it like flies on a dog turd, but apparently it had to go.

In the end, I discovered patience and just not caring that much about the mess was the key – it's a phase that every child moves past, after all. I just wish they moved past it a bit quicker.

My status as the worst disciplinarian in the world

Clemmie would make a great detective. She can see through a child's lie like it's a freshly installed piece of double-glazing, and can piece together the smallest scraps of evidence that what she's being told is in fact a fabrication. I, on the other hand, take the statements made by my children at face value. I want to believe them, so they make me look like a complete mug that's taken for a ride on an almost daily basis. I just hope I'm never called for jury duty as I'm not sure I'd be particularly helpful.

My girls have had me figured out from the moment they set eyes on me. I'm not sure if it's because I've been manipulated or if I'm just a soft touch, but when it comes to enforcing the rules and regulations of the house and disciplining the girls when they break them, I flex like a willow branch in spring and allow them to get away with way too much. They could be standing over a bloodied body, holding a knife and repeatedly saying the words, 'I did it and I'm not even sorry about it,' and I'd still find myself saying, 'It's OK, sweetheart, I'm sure it was an accident. Let's just clean this up and not tell your mother.'

A great example of this is when I once asked Anya to tidy her room. The initial request was made at 3.30 p.m. on a rainy Sunday when she had nothing else to do. I left the room feeling confident that I'd laid out the requirements of the job clearly. However by 7 p.m., I found that the queen of procrastination had basically done nothing. The room was a real-life spot-the-difference in which the changes were so subtle you had to spend hours staring to notice them. Then her phone made a noise from under the pillow. It turned out that she'd spent the first thirty seconds kicking a few items of clothing slightly closer to the cupboard and then used the remainder of the time to piss around on the internet. I removed her screen, then sat down and explained that this was unacceptable and that I was disappointed, fully expecting her to feel guilty and clean up as soon as my back was turned. I returned thirty minutes later to find that she had taken *all* her clothes out of the drawers.

I guess it's because I'm not a confrontational person by nature, and come from a long line of people who avoid arguments like the plague, that when the girls want something and haven't got the response they were looking for from Clemmie, they'll immediately make a beeline for me as they know I'll probably say what they wanted to hear in the first place.

I know this means the kids get conflicting messages, and that me not toeing the party line makes Clemmie's life difficult when it comes to laying down the law, but sometimes I just don't think the punishment fitted the crime. This will inevitably lead to a heated discussion about whose parenting technique is right, at which point the young offender in question will slope off while we're distracted to go and continue with the illegal activity they were engaged in before.

I must try and be better aligned with Clemmie when it comes to discipline and present a united front, but I have a feeling I'm always going to be a soft touch for my girls.

My absence from PTA meetings, parent/ teacher evenings and parent nights out

Making time to go to events at school or with other parents of kids in my girls' classes is important, yet I have failed dismally at this. It's not that I'm not interested – in fact it's the complete opposite as I want to support my girls to make the most of themselves – but finding time to be an active member of the school community would mean either having to duplicate myself so I could be in two places at once, or finding a way to elongate the day so it was fifty hours long.

My own mum was the head of the PTA and I had grand visions of following in her footsteps by organising bake sales, running the tombola at the parents' drinks evening and being in charge of splat the rat at the school fete, but in reality I barely have time to tie my own shoes. The best I managed was manning the bouncy castle for thirty minutes at the summer fair last year, which turned into a mosh pit of varying-sized children and a lot of people losing shoes. I'm sorry to say that I've even missed the last two parents' evenings as it's physically impossible for both Clemmie and me to make it there. I'm still included in the parents' email group but to be honest I'm very much a silent participant. I'll see the invite to a drinks evening in a month's time, and be included in the responses from the eager parents who are looking for an excuse to get a babysitter, but as the date comes and goes I will have remained mute.

I must get better at making time for people outside my direct family. If anything, they are a good source of free childcare and lifts to school.

To be honest, whatever you do as a parent, no matter how much effort you put in, you will still somehow end up riddled with guilt. No one can be perfect, so sometimes doing an OK job is just fine; after all, no one is handing out parenting awards so we should go easy on ourselves a bit more and stop trying to reach the insane benchmark set by what you see in the media or online, as frankly it's not worth the effort. When I'm juggling a day job, being outnumbered by my family of little women, being the best dad and husband I can be and maintaining my night job (social media and this book), all while trying to retain the essence of myself along the way, some things are bound to slip through the cracks. That's just life. Learn from the lessons and move on – the most important one being that you can't do everything at once, and that's OK.

14

Who's the daddy?

I want my girls to think of me as the best possible
version of a man. That way, when they have
boyfriends, the bar will be set so high that no one will
match up to my example. Knowing my luck, my plan
will backfire and they'll bring back the dregs of society
just to annoy me. I'm looking forward to that. Not.

Who's the daddy?

Now the title of this chapter may be a little bit misleading. I mean, you only have to look at my girls to know that my genes are strong contenders in the 'World's Strongest Genes' competition. They all have my daft face and the same blond curls that I was issued with at birth. I was also party to the conception of each and every one of them, so unless Clemmie got friendly with a postman who is my doppelgänger, I'm 100 per cent sure they're mine.

No, I want to talk about what actually makes a man a dad. Sure, getting someone pregnant is the pretty obvious first step, but it's what you do after your child has entered the big bad world and how you support them when times are rough or cheer them on when they succeed that allows you to justify calling yourself a daddy.

Over the last thirty or forty years, the role of the dad has changed dramatically and I for one am so glad about the ongoing evolution of the parenting team.

The authoritarian dad was concerned with the idea that his children should be brought up to be respectable members of society and follow the rules. The family was run like a business where fear and intimidation were the tools of choice.

The traditional dad's role was to be the breadwinner. This guy would spend most of his waking hours at work so that he could provide for his family at the cost of spending time with them. Traditional dad would leave the house as his family were still trying to clear the sleep from their bleary eyes and return just in time to read a bedtime story and kiss everyone good night. Mums were responsible for running the household and bringing up the kids while the absent dads provided the funds to do so.

Now, though, things have changed a lot and we're starting to see new types of dads.

The would-be balanced dad is someone who is constantly struggling to find the right mix of work and family life. Like most fathers these days, I find myself in this category. We're all working parents who are trying to be as present as possible and make every moment count with our children, while simultaneously doing the best we can at work too. We probably come from families that had traditional dad as a role model and we have made a silent promise to ourselves that we'll work just as hard as our father, but still make time to be the most engaged dad that we can be.

The stay-at-home dad is someone who I aspire to be. If I could afford to give up my job and not work in the traditional sense of the word, I would. I know some parents will roll their eyes at this and say, 'Yeah, you're just writing that in a book to look good' and ten years ago I'd have said the same thing as back then I didn't have a paternal bone in my body, but having children in my life has changed me and my priorities dramatically. I would much rather be at home with my girls and be responsible for helping them become the best versions of themselves than tap numbers into a spreadsheet. In the grand scheme of things, that really doesn't matter very much to me. I think over the next ten years, with flexible working being encouraged, rather than employers offering it out of legal necessity, parenting responsibility should become shouldered more equally between mum and dad.

Of course, there are many shades of dadding between these categories and we take different elements from each approach to create the version that works best for our personal circumstances. No two families are exactly the same as there are simply too many variables in life for there to be carbon copies.

My own dad is somewhere between the traditional and the balanced dad: a dad of the 80s who, had he had access to the internet and work-from-home flexibility, probably would have been at home with us more. He's amazing and I couldn't have asked for a better role model. He worked long hours in order for us to be able to go to the schools that would give us the best opportunities and take holidays that provided us with experiences and memories that we still talk about fondly to this day. He spent every weekend working on a project around the house or in the garage and would get us involved when there was an opportunity, even if it was to mix cement that he'd then remake later on under cover of darkness when we were all tucked up in bed. Now I look back on it, we were basically used as cheap child labour, paid in ham salad sandwiches. We loved it. Somehow my dad managed to make everything seem like a game, even when we were shovelling sand into the cement mixture or mowing the lawn. During the week, though, we really didn't see him much. I remember we would speak to him on the phone and send him imaginary neckties down the line, and if he was alone in the office, he would put on a poor Russian accent and become 'Boris De Spy', but I don't have many memories of him being at home in the evenings before we went to bed.

On the odd occasions he was left in charge of my brother, my sister and me alone, we could almost guarantee that we'd be feasting on one of three meals:

1. A pasty bought from the local shop that we'd all have piled into the breeze-block-shaped 80s Volvo estate – complete with sticky leather seats – to get. The pasty would be served with a sea of baked beans that would stretch to the edge of the plate.

2. A sausage and mash volcano (also surrounded by a sea of baked beans). For those of you that are uninitiated in the ways of the sausage and mash volcano, take a pile of lumpy mashed potato – lumpy so that the kids can make a point of how it hasn't been made properly – and make it into a cone shape. Then layer sausages around the outside and poke a hole down the middle, which you fill with ketchup to make the lava. To finish it off, pour baked beans around the base and *voilà*, you have a dad special that everyone loves.

3. Sausages and chips. This would invariably end up with burnt sausages and a kitchen filled with a cloud of smoke that covered the ceiling.

How do my own children see me?

I often think about how the girls see me, yet it's not a question I've ever asked them, so as a way of getting them to contribute directly to this book, I decided to give them some dad-centred homework and asked them how they would describe me to someone who doesn't know me. FYI, if you plan on doing this, be prepared to hear some home truths that might make you consider taking a long hard look in the bathroom mirror. The honesty of children is often blunt and humbling in equal measure:

- He's funny and he knows it.
- He can fix anything.
- He likes going to the DIY store on his own.
- He does amazing armpit farts and can burp the longest out of anyone I know.
- He has nice hair.
- He's really strong and can lift me up above his head.
- He's kind and doesn't shout much.
- He talks about bikes and rugby a lot.
- He has a beard that tickles when he kisses me.
- He always wants to play.
- He's on my side when Mummy is shouting.

I'll take this. I think they've boiled me down to eleven bullet points that capture me pretty accurately.

What should a dad be?

So, drawing on the different types of dads out there – including the kind of dad my father was, and the kind of dad my girls consider me to be – I've made a stab at writing down what I believe makes a man a good father.

A dad should be kind

As I said earlier, I'm a soft touch. I know this because Clemmie tells me so all the time and she's right on the money, of course. The girls know how to wrap me around their little fingers and I'm almost powerless to stop it. If and when I do ever lose my cool I boil over quickly, and I'm very apologetic about it straight afterwards.

A dad should be a shoulder to cry on, not someone to cry about

There is nothing worse than knowing you are the reason a child is crying. It's happened to me on several occasions and the guilt it brings is all-consuming, making you feel like just about the worst human to ever walk the planet. It also comes with a membership card to the exclusive 'I made my own child cry' club, which you immediately want to snip into little bits and whack into the bin.

I desperately try to make up for these moments by being the one to talk things through with my girls when they're having a shit time, and give them that ever-important bear hug that lets them know

I'm there for them and that as their human shield, I will let nothing hurt them while they're in my arms. I do my best to be there for them in times of emotional turmoil, but when it comes to the physical injuries that are part and parcel of being a child, I'm resigned to the fact that the SOS call that will go out across the playground at 120 decibels will be 'MUMMY!!!' every time. In these situations, I will always come a close second.

A dad should be a calming influence in times of conflict

I have no idea why, but it seems the mother-and-daughter relationship is an extremely complex one. It's either love or hate with a gaping chasm of nothingness in between. I think Clemmie and Anya are so similar that they know exactly how to push each other's buttons, and both of them are awful at admitting when they are in the wrong. Getting an apology of any worth out of either of them is as difficult as reeling in a blue whale using only a garden cane and twine. It ain't gonna happen. As a rule, when in these power-broking situations, I try not to shout. That only adds to the already deafening noise and if I do it too frequently, it loses its desired effect. I only resort to shouting when I really want to scare them. Then they know I mean business.

A dad should be the best representation of men he can be

As a dad, I have a duty to be a role model for my children and as the sole male in an otherwise all-female household, the pressure is on me to represent men well. I want to set the bar so high that my girls' expectations will struggle to be met by 95 per cent of future boyfriends, at which point I'll get involved in the vetting process of the 5 per cent that scrape through. I aspire to be like my own dad (a sentence I'm sure I never thought I'd say when I was a moody teen-ager), who taught me that fathers should respect you, and be respected in return.

A dad should be there when it counts

In a world where we take our emails everywhere, I can see no reason why dads can't make it to important events in children's lives. If your work is more important than watching your child perform in a play – even if they're just playing the part of a tree, or sheep number 6 – slide around a muddy field playing sport in the dead of winter or listen to them wield a trumpet (even if it does cause everyone within a 2-mile radius to bleed from their ears).

A dad should be handy

I'm not saying that you need to have a degree in structural engineer-ing or take night classes in household electrics, but at least have a few tools around and the patience to try to fix problems, as then your kids will think you're a superhero.

If you don't at least have some strong blue rope, a can of WD40 and some gaffer tape in the cupboard under the stairs, then you may be forced to hand over your dad credentials when the DEA comes knocking at your door. And when I say DEA, I'm obviously talking about the Dad Enforcement Agency, not the agency that stops drug trafficking – if they're standing on your doorstep at 4.30 a.m. putting you in handcuffs while you're shivering in your boxer shorts, you've got a whole other kind of problem to worry about.

A dad should be able to listen

Making time to let your children talk to you is massively important. More than anything else, it's enabled me to learn about my girls' lives as they become increasingly independent from us. Giving them a chance to unload to someone without interruption, judgement or without siblings to annoy them by doing nothing in particular has been a part of my daily routine ever since the older girls started school, and it brings us closer together. Invariably, I'll start to tell a story about a similar situation I was in when I was younger to reassure them that they aren't the first person on earth to go through the problem they're facing, only to realise they stopped listening thirty seconds in to my reminiscing ramble. I'm sure some of it goes in, but how long they retain my sympathetic tale is anyone's guess.

A dad should not be above acting like a child

No one wants to be remembered as the person who sat on the side, kept their hair in a tight bun, tutted a lot and was more boring than heavy-duty oil-drilling machinery.

I'm essentially an eight-year-old trapped in a thirty-five-year-old's body and can't stop myself being a berk for 95 per cent of the day. I think Clemmie just wishes I'd grow up a little bit when the kids aren't around.

So now that we've taken a look at what the role of a dad is, and what makes a good one, I think and hope that I can say I'm doing a decent job. Although I'm not perfect, I do the best I can and I think that's all anyone can ask. As long as my kids are happy, smiling and still laughing with me and not at me, I can go to sleep every night feeling like I'm managing to balance everything that's asked of me and be proud to call myself a dad. It truly is the biggest achievement of my life.

The end of the road?

So we have our brood of girls and we're doing what we can to help steer them through life and be nice people, so what's next? Everyone's always asking me, 'Are you going to go for a boy next time?' Even if we did 'go for a boy', I'm clearly genetically predisposed to making girls, so the likelihood of creating a baby with anything other than a vagina between its legs is not 50/50. It's more like 20/80. I'm not a betting man, in fact I'm generally quite risk averse, so I'm not even going to try – I think they'd call that 'throwing good money after bad'. I made my peace with the fact that I'm only ever likely to be a father of daughters a long time ago and I'm now ready to retire from the baby-making game.

That's why I probably need to take some decisive action to ensure that our family of six doesn't become a family of ten in which, given my track record, I would undoubtedly be the sole male, waving my sad little man flag in the corner as I become buried under girls' clothes I disapprove of, glossy fashion magazines, hair-related products and make-up. I'd be beyond outnumbered, I'd be out-everythinged. This has led me to ponder the following . . .

To V or not to V, that is the question . . .

The 'V' I'm referring to is a word that has many a man clutching his manhood and wincing. It is, of course, vasectomy.

Historically, we men have been great at relying on women to put things in their body to reduce the chances of surprise children. Whether it's the pill, a coil, a diaphragm, an implant or another form of contraception that I'm not aware of, women put up with it all, so if we're truly done, it's only fair that after twelve years with Clemmie, I take the plunge and do something a bit more permanent that will mean my wife can finally not have a constant flow of hormones shooting around her body, throwing off her cycles and generating force 9 mood swings.

Logically speaking I know that a vasectomy is the right thing to do, but there are some thoughts knocking around in the dark recesses of my mind that I just can't shake. Us men are often accused of thinking with what's between our legs and not with our brains. I've never really had that problem before, but this time I'm genuinely confused about who I should be listening to.

In one corner, my brain is sitting there, dressed in a smoking jacket, propped up in a comfy lounge chair next to a roaring log fire.

Putting aside the encyclopaedia and peering over his half-rimmed spectacles, he's telling me to 'just get on with it and have it done'. It's fifteen to thirty minutes max, it will mean Clemmie doesn't have to be the vessel for contraceptive devices any more and we'll get to maintain our family at the size it is right now, which is what we both want.

In the other corner, my cock and balls (in my mind's eye, they're a loudmouth pair of cockney wide boys) are yelling at me, fighting for their right to survive. They're letting me know that they think I'm a mug for even considering what my brain is telling me and that if I go through with it, they'll hate me forever and will shrivel up and disappear, but not before I've been robbed of any sense of manhood I have left in my soul.

I'm caught between these two opposing views and as a result I'm still on the fence, ticking away like a sperm-filled time bomb. These are some of the – frankly ludicrous – reasons why I shouldn't get it done, which will hopefully give you a glimpse into the weird world of my man brain:

- What if the nurses laugh at me while I'm naked and under anaesthetic? I really shouldn't care as I wouldn't know about it, but for some reason this really bothers me.
- What if I get called upon to repopulate the earth after World War III? I'd be useless and would be the sole reason that the human race died out. (We'll just skip over the small detail of why I would be the only surviving man on the planet.)

- What if it goes wrong and I plug away thinking I'm completely safe, and somehow we end up with Clemmie becoming pregnant with triplets? (Because that would be just my luck – they'd be girls of course as well, as a final kick in the nuts.)
- What if the surgery leaves me with real pain that doesn't go away? (This is a genuine worry as I've read up about this and between 5 and 10 per cent of men are left with a lasting aching pain that doesn't go away.)
- What if the surgery leaves me with nerve damage elsewhere in my body and I lose the ability to walk? This is obviously crazy talk, but my man brain is prone to taking things to extremes.
- What if I somehow become/feel like less of a man because I can no longer procreate?
- What if my sex drive packs up and fucks off as a result of the surgery?

Ironically what I really need to do is just 'grow a pair' and get the vasectomy sorted, as if I end up waiting for the male pill, there's a strong chance I'll be back in that delivery room, fetching ice and generally getting in the way. I'm not the first person to have this done and I definitely won't be the last, so I think it's time to grow up and take some responsibility.

My dad got a letter from the NHS congratulating him that he could no longer have children when he had it done, so I've got that to look forward to I guess. I can store it in my box of achievements in the loft, filed neatly next to my 2:1 degree and my sports medal.

And so, with that lovely thought, we've reached the end of our journey through my life of dadding to date. I hope you feel that I've managed to give you an honest and (hopefully) humorous glimpse into my outnumbered world as a father of four and that you've managed to take something away from this 'peek behind the family curtain'. It may be the feeling that this guy is an idiot and has really only supplied me with a series of lessons on what not to do. It could be that you managed to glean some useful tips on how to get through those early years. Hopefully you're left with a sense that you're not a terrible parent after all as everyone is messing up all the time, even if the people around you just don't talk about it. Whatever it is, I just hope you enjoyed it and that all my very late nights sitting on the sofa, nursing an ever-cooling cup of tea while my family slept soundly upstairs and I tried to interrogate my brain to recall the highs and lows of my life with kids, have been worth it.

There's still a long way to go for me, and the challenges of parenting will evolve as my children grow up. I'll need to adapt to keep up. Yes, I'll be older. Yes, my body will start making squeaking noises when I stand up that I can't explain. Yes, my beard will be more salt than pepper. Yes, my bank account will move closer and closer to constantly scraping the bottom of the overdraft and yes, my jokes will cease to be a source of humour and quickly become a source of embarrassment, but I look forward to it all.

Who knows, perhaps I'll write another book in ten years' time to cover the teenage years, which will no doubt mainly consist of stories about waiting for my daughters in a car outside a house party, but we'll cross that bridge when we come to it.

What I do know is that if the first ten years of negotiating the winding streets of bringing up small people has been anything to go by, then I can't wait to navigate the rest of this seemingly endless journey. I can't see the horizon, there's no satnav (and there's no parenting break-down service available) but with all my girls strapped in beside me, it's a road trip I'm grateful to go on.

These people are my everything. I'm proud
I can call myself a husband of one and a
father of four. I may be forever outnumbered,
but they make my life worthwhile.

Acknowledgements

Two years ago, I was just another dad who was quietly getting on with life. Then, on a dark night in March 2016, sleep deprived and with a beer in hand, I decided to post my first picture on Instagram to share my perspective of parenthood as an outnumbered father. This turned out be the first step on a long journey that's resulted in me being a published author with 800,000 social media followers, which is just insane.

I couldn't have got to this point without the support of lots of people to whom I owe a massive thank you so I'll to jump straight to it.

Living on five hours sleep a night, I was unsure I had either the time or the energy to do a book justice, but my book agent, Paul Stevens and both Grace O'Leary and Louise Bury at Independent Talent gave me the confidence to put pen to paper. You convinced me that I had a story that was worth sharing and guided me through the alien world of publishing. Thank you – without you in my corner, I'd have been lost.

I also owe a huge debt of gratitude to Charlotte Hardman and the whole Hodder team who saw something in my writing and agreed to take me on. Thank you for letting me write the book I wanted to write and for not hounding me when deadlines approached and then disappeared over the horizon. Your email inboxes must be filled with excuses as to why I was once again late submitting and for that I can only apologise. I don't want to point fingers, but I blame my tardiness purely on my family. At least the finished article looks great and that's largely down to the wonderful cover photos by Philippa James who captured my life as father of four girls perfectly.

The contents of this book would have been very thin indeed had it not been for my girls who are my inspiration, not only for my writing but in every part of my daily life. Anya, Marnie, Ottile and Delilah – you're all hard work and hilarious in equal measures. Thank you for accepting me for who I am and putting up with my stupidity. I'll try not to embarrass you too much as you grow up, but I can't promise anything. Of course, those girls wouldn't be here if it weren't for the wonder woman I started this whole journey with – Clemmie. Thank you for choosing me and lugging around my 'mini me's for a combined total of 27 months of your life. We may be knee-deep in kids, but you always come first and now I've finished this book, I promise you'll see more of me in the evening.

Not wanting to sound too much like an Oscars lifetime achieve-ment award, I'll also take this opportunity to thank my parents who have spent their lives bending over backwards to provide both me and my siblings with the best start in life. You guys set an incredibly high benchmark when it comes to parenting and I'll continue to try and live up to your example.

Finally, none of this would have happened in the first place without all my followers on social media. You are the ones that drove me to put my efforts into my writing in the first place and quite frankly, if you didn't follow my journey, I wouldn't have had this opportunity to share my experiences in a book. Thank you for commenting, sharing and generally being lovely people. I hope this book has lived up to your expectations!